VERTICAL
GARDENING

GROW UP, NOT OUT, FOR MORE VEGETABLES AND FLOWERS IN MUCH LESS SPACE

Text and Photography by Derek Fell

RODALE.

For Carolyn and our three children,
Tina, Derek Jr., and Vicki

© 2011 by Derek Fell

Direct hardcover and trade paperback published in April 2011.

Rodale books may be purchased for business or promotional use or for special sales.
For information, please write to:
Special Markets Department, Rodale Inc., 733 Third Avenue, New York, NY 10017

Printed in the United States of America
Rodale Inc. makes every effort to use acid-free ⊗, recycled paper ⊗.

Illustrations by Michael Gellatly
Photograph on page 21 courtesy of the Green Education Foundation, Walpole, Massachusetts
All other photographs courtesy of Derek Fell

Book design by Christina Gaugler

Library of Congress Cataloging-in-Publication Data

Fell, Derek.
    Vertical gardening : grow up, not out, for more vegetables and flowers in much less
space / Derek Fell.
        p.   cm.
    Includes index.
    1. Vertical gardening.   I. Title.
    ISBN 978–1–60529–082–9 hardcover
    ISBN 978–1–60529–083–6 pbk
SB463.5.F45 2011
684.1'8—dc22   2011003131

Distributed to the trade by Macmillan

2 4 6 8 10 9 7 5 3 1 hardcover
2 4 6 8 10 9 7 5 3 1 paperback

We inspire and enable people to improve their lives and the world around them.
www.rodalebooks.com

Contents

Vertical Gardening: The Sensible Way to Garden Effortlessly

Vertical gardening is the way to grow! You can make the most of your garden space by growing delicious vegetables and fruits and colorful flowers up on a trellis, on garden netting, in a tower of pots, and over garden structures, while enjoying the benefits of easier maintenance, healthier plants, effortless harvesting, and higher yields.

GROWING "UP" FROM HERE

Once you learn how easy it is to change your garden from a horizontal system to a vertical one, you'll be rewarded with a garden that involves less work and more benefits. Even people with plenty of space for a garden are finding that traditional ways of gardening (with long horizontal rows) can lead to disappointing results—the more space you try to cultivate, the more likely you are to get discouraged by aggressive weed growth, encounter problems such as pests and diseases, find that watering a large area is a never-ending commitment, and get overwhelmed when there's so much garden to care for on a weekly basis.

After years of research in my

Create a visual vertical garden by simply placing containers at different heights. Here abundantly flowering coleus and geraniums fill containers on the steps and railings of a patio.

Cedaridge Farm's large vegetable garden features raised beds with bamboo trellises, offering the opportunity to grow and test hundreds of varieties of climbing, foundation, support, and container plants. In the background, topknots of Japanese dappled willow outline the neighboring herb garden.

own gardens, I've developed and honed the art of vertical gardening, and I'm anxious to spread the word. Vertical gardening will change your old way of growing plants in rows and beds. If you're one of the millions of people who want to experience gardening for the first time, one of the millions of gardeners looking for easier and more rewarding ways to garden, or one of the millions of gardeners who have given up on gardening because of disappointing results, consider the incredible benefits of my vertical gardening experience:

- Growing plants up, not out, in beds with a small footprint

- Less soil preparation and digging from Day 1

- More plant variety in much less space

- Many opportunities to create bottom-up and top-down plantings

- Less weeding in vertical beds, spaces, and pots

- Many space-saving container and stacking options

- Fewer maintenance chores

- Improved air circulation and less risk of plant diseases and pests

- Easier tending and harvesting—all at eye level

- Less bending and less backbreaking work

- Larger yields in a compact space

- Top-performing vertical vegetables, fruits, and flowers—especially vining types

- And much, much *more fun*!

The biggest mistake gardeners make in planting a garden is starting too big. After they dig the soil in a large garden plot and plant a traditional horizontal garden in long, straight rows or large raised beds, summer days get hot and humid, encouraging a forest of weeds and creating a daily need for plant watering. Gardeners get busy with summer activities, and it's a challenge to find enough time to tend flowers or vegetables. When the harvesting, cooking, and preserving becomes time-consuming and overwhelming, gardeners give up and just let their gardens sprawl out of control—until a cold snap hits and the disappointing results are "put to bed" for another year. But it doesn't have to be this way!

Author Derek Fell displays a day's harvest from his tomato plants, including large 'Beefsteak' varieties and small, multicolored cherry tomatoes.

> "My father grew delicious beans—not the dwarf kinds, but pole varieties in manure that produce tall vines and dense foliage to give them the best flavor."
>
> —Jean Renoir, *Renoir, My Father*

Vertical gardening saves time and work, allowing you to spend less time tending and more time enjoying your garden. As you delve into each chapter of this book, you'll find my best advice and tips for creating planting beds of small spaces or strips of soil; using trellises and supports in new and attractive ways; and choosing the best plants for climbing, cascading, and growing vertically.

MY LIFE IN THE GARDEN

Some people find their passion late in life; I found mine in childhood. I planted my first vegetable garden at the age of 6, after my grandfather gave me a packet of garden peas. It was during World War II, and food was scarce. I lived with my parents in a row house in the north of England, with a small walled-in concrete yard that backed onto a narrow lane. The only patch of bare soil was a narrow sunny strip between our back wall and the lane. As my grandfather instructed, I dug up the soil and mixed in all kinds of organic ingredients he said would feed the plants—wood ashes from our fireplace, tea leaves and coffee grounds, crushed eggshells, and horse manure collected in a bucket after our milkman delivered milk each morning from a horse-drawn cart. I made a trellis from scraps of lumber, forming a frame for a network of crisscrossed string to support the pea vines.

I checked the site daily for signs of germination, and after 7 days of suspense, I saw small green shoots poke through the soil. I watered them, helped the tendrils grip the makeshift netting, picked off slugs whenever I saw signs of their chewing, and watched the vines grow up toward the sun. It was thrilling to see the plants set dozens of white flowers and then develop shiny green pea pods. As soon as the pods fattened up, I picked them, shelled some of the peas, and ate them fresh off the vine. They were

"A healthy soil means healthy plants and healthy people."

— Dr. W. E. Shewell-Cooper,
Soil, Humus and Health

sweet and delicious—a memory I will treasure forever. The rest of the harvest I proudly showed to my grandfather, who cooked up a special meal of dumplings, pork, and sauerkraut with cooked peas as a side dish. I have been growing gardens vertically ever since and never miss a year with peas!

At age 17, I wrote my first garden article for the *Shrewsbury Chronicle* newspaper group about the Shrewsbury Flower Show, interviewing contestants who had grown giant dahlias and leeks as thick as a man's arm. At 19, I began working for Europe's oldest established seed house, Hurst Seeds, as their catalog manager. After winning an award for their wholesale catalog, I was invited to move to the United States to work as a catalog manager for Burpee Seeds, the world's largest mail-order seed house, at their Fordhook Farm research facility in Doylestown, Pennsylvania. I quickly realized the value of having a test garden to evaluate plant varieties and different growing techniques. After 6 years with Burpee, I was appointed executive director of both the National Garden Bureau, an information office sponsored by the American seed industry, and All-America Selections, the national seed trials. Immediately I set a goal to own a farm for the purpose of conducting my own trials. In 1974, as head of the National Garden Bureau, I was appointed by the Ford Administration to be chairman of a committee to plant a vegetable garden at the White House; one of my vegetable garden designs had appeared in the Sunday edition of the *Washington Post* and was endorsed

Climbing morning glories and nasturtiums need only a little support to quickly clamber over a rustic gate, welcoming you to the flower garden.

by its garden columnist, the late Henry Mitchell, who called himself "Earthman."

Shortly after my White House experience, I resigned from the National Garden Bureau and All-America Selections to write garden books and create a photo library of plant portraits and gardens. I purchased historic Cedaridge Farm in Bucks County, Pennsylvania, and since 1989, its 20 acres have served as my home and test gardens. Founded in 1791 as a Mennonite dairy farm and fruit tree orchard, it

The footprint of these vegetable beds is actually quite small: Growing vertically on simple posts and netting enables pole beans, tomatoes, cucumbers, and squash to grow up, not out.

has been my outdoor studio—not only for testing plant varieties and growing techniques, but also for staging garden photography for books and magazines. It is also where I developed the famous "tomato/potato" combination plant (see page 230) and designed a series of unique garden structures.

The soil at Cedaridge Farm is mostly hard clay, but by composting and adding manure from local stables to the soil, I now have a vegetable garden and flower beds that are fluffy and fertile. I have not only tested thousands of vegetable and flower varieties, but also many organic methods of fertilization, irrigation, container gardening, and deer control, and dozens of other ways to make gardening successful. For example, when I began experimenting with ways to garden vertically, I tested freestanding and wall-mounted units and found that a wall-mounted unit (especially attached to the south-, east-, or west-facing wall of a house) promotes earlier plant maturity and heavier yields, because reflected light from the wall promotes vigorous growth, and heat from the house or building will also protect against late frosts. This testing led to my inventing the Skyscraper Garden trellis, a kit that enables a gardener to easily grow plants vertically against a wall or as a freestanding unit (see page 47).

Vertical gardening possibilities are vast, so don't think you're confined to growing traditional climbers like pole beans and morning glories. Yes, both of those plants are included in this book, but you'll be delighted to learn that there are hundreds of other plants with vertical capabilities—available as seedlings at your local garden centers, in racks of seed packets, and by mail-order and Internet sources. From among dozens of foliage and flowering plants and climbing vegetables and trainable fruits, I'll describe my top choices for vertical gardening that reach for the sky or cascade downward to create stunning displays.

At Cedaridge Farm, more than 30 vegetables grow up trellises and supports. Ivies climb up mature trees in our woodland to provide textural interest up into the tree canopy. Virginia creeper covers the sunniest side of our farmhouse to give it an old, established appearance. Trellises affixed to walls of a toolshed and barn support pink climbing roses and blue clematis; these entwine their stems and knit together so they bloom simultaneously to create an attractive color harmony. Wisteria climbs up the sides and over the top of several arbors, and a 'Madame Galen' trumpet creeper

The bountiful garden at Cedaridge Farm uses many types of bamboo supports to raise climbing vegetables in raised beds.

climbs up a brick chimney to hide the bare bricks. Even at the edge of my koi pond, I extend visual interest high into the sky with a series of 10-foot waterfalls planted alongside to add to the effect. Blackberry vines are trained along a split-rail fence bordering my fruit orchard. In my cutting garden, sweet peas climb above head height on bamboo canes that I grow on the property. Even low-growing plants like lettuce, cabbage, and parsley can be grown as foundation plants at the base of climbing vining plants, simply by planting them in a narrow raised strip of soil. Moreover, you don't

This do-it-yourself top-down planter is made from a wire cone and chicken-wire frame and yields an abundance of Roma tomatoes.

even have to have garden space to grow vines, because a vertical garden can be situated on concrete or flagstone using a container or window box planter filled with a fertile soil mix to provide a weed-free growing medium.

After 20 years spent gardening at Cedaridge Farm in Pennsylvania (located in Plant Hardiness Zone 6), I purchased a property on Sanibel Island, Florida, in order to extend my experience to a virtually frost-free Zone 10 garden. Cedaridge Farm South consists of an acre of mature plantings just a block from the famous Sanibel shelling beach. The property has 30 mature coconut palms in addition to fruiting banana trees, a small citrus orchard, mango, papaya, avocado, and other exotic plants that can be grown only indoors in other parts of the United States. Although summers can be too hot and humid even for tomatoes, winters produce a prime growing season for a wide range of both cool season and warm season vegetables. I'm eager to start new tests and trials for vertical gardening in this warmer climate. And I'll be sure to continue touting the benefits of growing up, not out, for more vegetables, fruits, and flowers in much less space.

What Is a Vertical Garden?

1

I'd like to welcome you to a garden where vegetables, flowers, and fruit all grow, climb, and twine upward to create a beautiful landscape that saves space, requires less effort, produces high yields, and reduces pest and disease problems. Whether your goal is armloads of flowers, a bountiful vegetable garden, or a productive fruit harvest, I'll show you how narrow strips of soil, bare walls, and simple trellises and arches can be transformed into grow-up or grow-down gardens with just a few inexpensive supplies or purchased planters. I've been testing gardening methods in my own 20-acre garden at Cedaridge Farm in Bucks County, Pennsylvania, for 20 years, and I want you to discover the same delights and benefits of vertical gardening that I'm enjoying.

Vertical gardening is an innovative, effortless, and highly productive growing system that uses bottom-up and top-down supports for a wide variety of plants in both small and large garden spaces. There are hundreds of varieties of vegetables, fruits, and flowers that are perfect for growing up freestanding and wall-mounted supports and in beds or containers.

Best of all, vertical gardening guarantees a better result from the day your trowel hits your soil—by shrinking the amount of garden space needed and reducing the work needed to prepare new beds. Chores like weeding, watering, fertilizing, and controlling pests and diseases are reduced considerably, while yields are increased, especially with vegetables like beans and tomatoes. A vining pole bean will outyield a bush bean tenfold. Moreover, a vining vegetable is capable of continuous yields—the more you pick, the more the plant forms new flowers and fruit to prolong the harvest. A bush variety, by contrast, will exhaust itself within 2 to 3 weeks.

With vertical gardening methods, you'll also discover that many ground-level plants pair beautifully with climbing plants, so you can combine different types of plants to create a lush curtain of flowers, foliage, and bounty. With a mix of do-it-yourself and commercially available string

A Japanese wisteria vine twines upward through the canopy of this small-scale replica of Monet's bridge. The long flower clusters offer an intimate and fragrant resting spot while viewing the water garden at Cedaridge Farm.

supports, trellises, pergolas, raised beds, Skyscraper Garden trellises, and Topsy-Turvy planters, vertical gardening saves a lot of time and work, lessens backbreaking tasks, makes harvesting easier, and is perfect for any size space, from a patio container and a 1 × 4-foot strip of soil to a landscape trellis and the entire side of a building.

LAYING THE GROUNDWORK

I first encountered a successful no-dig garden at the Good Gardeners Association in Hertfordshire, England. I visited the home of the group's founder, the late Dr. W. E. Shewell-Cooper, in 1970, when I went to interview him for an article in *Horticulture* magazine. On my return to the United States, I also discovered *The Ruth Stout No-Work Garden Book,* which was one of the first books that advocated a system of no-dig gardening through in situ (in place) composting. Stout explained how she created planting beds by putting down newspapers to suffocate existing weeds and grass; piling on layers of organic waste, such as spoiled hay and kitchen scraps, as mulch to decompose; and then planting directly into this compost. This system of gardening has appealed to many people during the past 40 years, even though its focus has been gardening horizontally.

Many no-dig plots based on Ruth Stout's book have been established in public demonstration gardens, including one maintained by the ECHO Foundation (Educational Concerns for Hunger Organization) near Fort Myers, Florida. The foundation began its first no-dig garden in 1981, which remained in continuous production for years as a vegetable garden in the middle of what had been a lawn. It was never plowed, cultivated, spaded, or hoed. Around the same time, engineer-turned-author Mel Bartholomew introduced his own concept in his book *Square Foot Gardening*, which promoted raised beds and intensively planted crops that allowed gardeners to grow more in less space. Mel has convinced millions of gardeners around the world to switch to easy no-dig raised beds. And then along came Patricia Lanza with her blockbuster book *Lasagna Gardening.* After struggling to amend the soil in her gardens, she, too, realized that layering compostable ingredients was the best way to start new garden beds, and she's been growing flowers, vegetables, and herbs for years in her "lasagna" layers.

For the past couple of decades, I've studied, tried, and implemented gardening systems that produce better results in less space with less work. Many no-dig methods were developed specifically for gardening horizontally, but I've found that these same no-dig techniques are even better suited to vertical gardening. With vertical gardening, plants require much less space than plants that grow horizontally, so those same layering techniques are even more efficient when used in conjunction with the small-footprint beds I recommend. While most no-dig systems suggest that a 6-inch depth of fertile soil is adequate, I prefer a soil depth of 6 to 12 inches in a raised planting bed, because vining plants generally have more vigorous root systems than dwarf plants or plants grown horizontally. Plants grown in 6 to 12 inches of fertile soil respond magnificently to that extra soil depth by delivering maximum yields.

THE BENEFITS OF GROWING VERTICALLY

If you've gardened in long, horizontal beds for even a single growing season, you've probably thought to yourself, "There has to be a better way." Well, you're right—there *is* a better way. Vertical gardening offers many advantages over horizontal growing.

Smaller beds to prepare and maintain. When growing plants with a vertical habit, you'll need a bed only as large as the root systems of those plants—one that's much smaller than a traditional bed. When you plant horizontally, you tend to have narrow rows of plants and wide swaths of soil between them. It's those wide swaths that drink up much of the water, send up innumerable weeds, and consume the nutrients needed by your plants. With vertical gardening, you prepare only small spots or strips of fertile soil—just enough to give plants a nutritious base from which to climb up supports. These vertical garden beds require less compost, fertilizer, and

A simple vertical garden is perfect for a paved or soil surface, 2 feet wide × 4 feet long, with room for four vining plants such as a tomato, cucumber, climbing spinach, and pole bean.

water, and only a few bucketfuls of mulch or a little black plastic to control weeds. Compost goes further when you cut back on bed space, so you won't need to buy, generate, or use as much compost in order to amend your soil each season. And whether you plan to water with a watering can or use a drip irrigation system, you'll find that watering your small plots of soil is a cinch, and your drip hose can be short.

I'm an advocate of no-dig beds, because I've seen the results others have achieved, in addition to my own successes. You can easily create a no-dig bed by spreading homemade or store-bought compost onto bare soil—or onto a layer of newspapers to kill surface weeds or turfgrass—and leveling the new bed with a rake. Spreading compostable layers on top of your newspaper weed barrier will create a fluffy, nutrient-rich planting bed (the method called in situ or sheet composting).

To compost in situ, I make sure my newspaper layer is at least 15 pages thick and that the edges overlap like the scales of a fish. This excludes light from the ground beneath, killing grass and weeds. On top of this, I generally place a 6-inch layer of grass clippings, a 6-inch layer of shredded leaves (I use a lawn mower to shred them), and then a layer of kitchen waste (often including banana peels, eggshells, fish bones, and potato skins). This stack is then topped off by a ½-inch layer of wood ashes. Other good composting ingredients include well-rotted animal manure (like cow and horse), sawdust, shredded newspapers, pine needles, and hay. Hold the sides of this in-situ compost bed in place with boards, landscape ties, or even stones or bricks.

Do-it-yourself supports and trellises. While vertical gardening depends on a variety of supports and trellises, you'll find that it's easy to make your own. I make many of my own trellises from bamboo canes that I grow myself, or from pencil-straight pussy willow stems. It's simple to take

canes or willow stakes and space them 1 foot apart to make posts, and use thinner, more pliable canes threaded through them horizontally to make strong, good-looking trellises. You'll see lots of examples of homemade trellises in the photographs in this book. Of course, ready-made trellises are available from garden centers, large hardware stores, and even big-box discount stores. Sturdy metal ones are suited for heavier vines, like melons and winter squash. In this book, you'll also discover the Skyscraper Garden trellis, a post-and-netting support I designed specifically for growing

Skyscraper structures can be assembled above a raised bed to create a freestanding unit, ready for edible vines such as pole beans and indeterminate tomatoes or flowering vines such as morning glories and climbing nasturtiums.

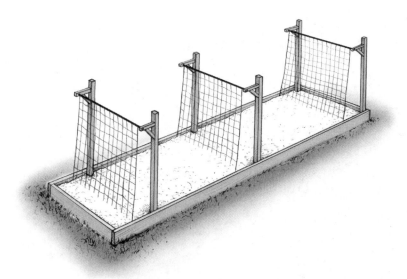

At Cedaridge Farm, I've created long raised beds and use Skyscraper Garden trellises to support vining crops above low-growing foundation vegetables and herbs.

vegetables and flowers vertically. Skyscraper Garden trellises can be freestanding or wall-mounted and can be grouped in raised beds to create an efficient, highly productive, and attractive gardening space.

Vertical pots and containers for very small spaces. If you don't have any (or much) garden space—say, just a concrete patio or a balcony—or if you can't easily amend your soil or build a raised bed, then consider using tower pots or other containers that help you grow upward in a column. Tower pots are commercial containers that stack one on top of the other and enable you to grow vertically a variety of plants that don't vine (such as lettuce, peppers, and strawberries). Plus, you can easily add trellises and supports within containers or "planted" just behind containers to create a vertical garden in a limited space. And if you need to be really creative with garden space, try mounting containers at various heights on a fence or wall to create a visual vertical garden.

New plant varieties to explore. The choices of climbing plants may surprise you. Among the vegetables, try growing climbing spinach (it's heat resistant and tastes even better than the regular cool season spinach),

On this shady fence, wooden buckets are mounted at various heights with strong metal brackets and feature lush plantings of fuchsia and impatiens for an appealing vertical flower garden.

trellis-loving snap peas with edible pods, and the fabulous climbing 'Trombone' zucchini that produces a vine 10 feet tall and loaded with fruits. All of these grow up, not out. Vining cucumbers, single-serving vining melons, and even sweet potato vines are all suitable for growing upward, instead of sprawling outward across the ground and consuming more space than you can easily care for during the season. And if you've ever grown vegetable spaghetti (also known as spaghetti squash) in a traditional garden, try growing it up a trellis instead: Allowed to grow across the ground, vegetable spaghetti is an aggressive vine that will suffocate anything in its path; but when it's grown up a trellis, it shoots skyward with tendrils that grasp latticework or garden netting, producing up to a dozen fruit on a vine.

You may even find that vertically grown vegetables taste better. Bear in mind that all that vine foliage collects more chlorophyll than a bush variety of the same vegetable, and this may help to promote better flavor. It is said that the French Impressionist painter Pierre-Auguste Renoir had such a refined taste for good food (his wife, Aline, earned a reputation as one of the finest cooks in France) that he could tell the difference between snap beans grown on poles and those grown on dwarf, bushy plants, because to him the vertically grown beans had superior flavor. Based on my own experience, I agree with him! Of course, the king of vegetables—the tomato—benefits from growing vertically, especially those varieties classified as indeterminate (with vines that can reach 20 feet or more) in seed catalogs and on plant labels. When you look at world-record harvests for tomatoes, all of the winning plants were staked to grow vertically, with some growing more than 25 feet high, producing hundreds of fruit from early summer to fall frost.

One of the bigger benefits of vertical gardening is being able to grow many different fruits against a wall or along wires or a split-rail fence. Of course, vining fruits like grapes and hardy kiwifruit are ideal, but so are berry crops with long, flexible canes like blackberries and raspberries. Even fruit trees with strong, sturdy trunks have pliable side branches that can be trained to grow flat for long distances against a wall or fence. This practice, known as espalier, significantly reduces the amount of space needed for a generous harvest of apples, peaches, pears, and other orchard trees—and reducing the growing space footprint is one of the tenets of vertical gardening. Be aware that many fruit trees are sold in standard, semi-dwarf, and dwarf

You can try many new plant varieties in your vertical garden. Using a strong trellis or a bamboo support and heavy-gauge garden netting, experiment with the edible gourd 'Cuccuzi'; long, straight fruits develop when the fruit is allowed to hang.

sizes, referring to the mature height of the tree. For espalier in a home garden, the semi-dwarf and dwarf are most suitable, producing full-size fruit
regardless of the extent of dwarfing.

Flowering vines also tend to be everblooming and provide armloads of
flowers for cutting. Sweet peas, nasturtiums, and morning glories will produce curtains of color planted in a short row to climb up garden netting
(either attached to a sunny wall or strung between posts as a freestanding
trellis). Grow all three together for an incredible kaleidoscope of color.
Then explore the dozens of other choices of upwardly mobile and cascading flowers and vines to create a garden that's filled with interesting "living
walls," dividers, and curtains of foliage. See the two chapters on flowering
ornamental vines (annual vines as well as the perennial and woody vines).

Fewer pests, diseases, and problems to handle. When you begin to
garden vertically, you'll notice a big difference in the health of your plants.
Lift flowering and fruiting vines and crops off the ground, and pests and
diseases are not as destructive. Ripening fruit and vegetables remain clean,

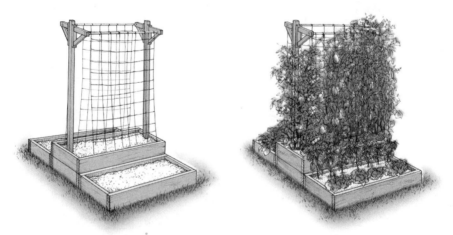

This small-space, nonstop vertical garden is created by positioning a Skyscraper
Garden trellis in a 12-inch-deep raised planter box, with a 6-inch-deep planter box
on each side. Look at how productive a vertical garden can be! Four varieties of
climbing vegetables (such as cucumbers, pole snap beans, tomatoes, and vegetable
spaghetti) are growing on both sides of the garden netting in the deep bed, and
non-vining foundation plants (such as bell peppers, herbs, and lettuces) are thriving in
the shallower beds.

show fewer deformities, are less susceptible to rot, and don't require tedious washing to remove garden soil. With plants up off the ground, you'll easily spot any potential insect infestations before they have a chance to reach plague proportions. Simply blasting the bugs off the vines with a strong jet of water and rubbing stems with a cloth to destroy dormant insect eggs are often all that's needed to avoid problems.

Increased yields in a small space. By concentrating on growing upward in columns rather than outward in rows, you're reducing the soil footprint needed to grow plants while encouraging denser growth. Most trellises and supports can accommodate plants growing on both sides. When growing edibles against a support system mounted on a wall, you need to project the trellis or garden netting away from the wall by only about 6 inches, to allow plants to produce yields in back as well as in front of the support. This also improves air circulation and discourages mildew and other fungal diseases.

A single pole snap bean variety (such as climbing 'Blue Lake') can surge to 6 feet high or higher from a mere square foot of growing space; compare that to a 2-foot-wide, 6-foot-long row of bush snap beans (totaling 12 square feet), and you'll find that the climbing pole bean produces a larger yield than the bush one. That's because 'Blue Lake' pole bean can produce a vigorous tower of beans that doesn't exhaust itself after 2 to 3 weeks like a dwarf bush bean does; the pole bean continues to bear all season long.

Less bending, fewer backbreaking chores, and easier plant care. With smaller footprint beds, there's less digging, less bending to tend soil and plants, and much easier plant care in general. And rather than feeding the soil with fertilizer, consider how much faster and more efficient foliar feeding can be: You can apply a liquid fertilizer directly to the plants' leaves. Many organic fertilizers today are formulated to be diluted with water and sprayed onto leaf surfaces. Leaf pores can take in nutrients and send them straight to feeding the flowers and fruit. Foliar feeding has proven particularly beneficial for fruiting plants like blackberries growing

This healthy planting of sugar snap peas is in full flower, growing up river-birch branches for support and easier harvesting.

on trellises and strawberries growing in tower pots. And, maybe most importantly of all in making gardening easy, vertical gardening is eminently suitable for gardeners who may have physical limitations and need to find a new and different way to engage in their favorite hobby. Think about how much easier it is to care for a single bean plant growing high up off the ground than for a long, low row of puny plants!

Easier to harvest. Harvesting is certainly much easier when flowers and fruit are within easy reach at waist and eye level, instead of low to the ground. There'll be no more kneeling and lifting vines in a horizontal bed when it's time to harvest!

PLANNING VERTICAL SETUPS AND SIZES

There are two main components in any size vertical garden—the planting bed and the plant support. The bed can consist of amended soil in situ, a raised bed, a container or tower pot, or even a growing pouch (like this year's popular Topsy Turvy bag). The supports can range from the simplest stakes, netting, and trellises to elaborate arches, arbors, and pergolas. Think of the bed as the home base for flowers, vegetables, fruits, and herbs, and the support as the launch mechanism for growing skyward.

Vertical gardens can be sited almost anywhere, so you'll need to decide where you'd like to place one. How about in the middle of your vegetable garden, in front of a fence, or next to a patio? Would you like to try a free-standing vertical garden or one that's positioned against a wall? And will you use a purchased support or make your own? No need to decide right away—just browse through the ideas and photographs in this book for inspiration and encouragement.

Sizing the Bed

When deciding the size of a vertical garden, I like to think in multiples of 4 feet since many commercially available trellises and garden netting come in 4-foot widths. And a 4-foot width is easy for one person to handle alone.

I like to create raised beds because they drain easily and give me a generous soil depth. I allow a 12-inch-wide strip across the raised bed width for each row of vines; I allow for a 24-inch-wide strip when both sides of the trellis or netting are planted. A 4-foot section of the raised bed can be devoted to all one variety (such as 'Sugar Snap' peas), or up to four varieties can be planted together. Space them 12 inches apart, shoulder to shoulder, and allow the vines to knit into each other for a solid wall of foliage and fruit.

If you decide to grow your plants in a raised bed, consider a host of materials suitable for keeping the soil in place—such as wooden boards, landscape ties, wicker edging, bricks, stones, or even straight sections of tree trunks such as pine and juniper.

Above all, choose a sunny location with good drainage. And decide how big a foundation planting bed you want for low, compact vegetables (such as peppers, cabbages, and lettuces), placing them where they will not be perpetually shaded by the tall growing vines.

Selecting the Support

The amount of space that a vertical planting requires depends on whether you want a wall-mounted unit or a freestanding one. When you attach a trellis or garden netting to a wall, for example, just 12 inches of width from the wall is all that most plants will need. For a freestanding unit where you wish to grow vining plants up both sides of a trellis or netting, then 24 inches width is all the space you need—12 inches for each side of vines.

The actual length of the trellis or netting depends on how many vining plants you wish to grow. I like to estimate 12-inch spacing for most vining plants, although many pole beans and vining peas will tolerate closer spacing, such as 6 inches for pole beans and even 4 inches for peas.

The minimum width I like to consider, especially if I'm starting a new vegetable bed, is 4 feet and then multiples of 4 feet, because ready-made trellis and garden netting usually comes in 4 feet widths. Height depends on how high the chosen plants can grow and how high you can reach. For garden peas, I like to provide 6 feet of support, but pole beans can easily reach a productive height of 10 to 12 feet, requiring a stepladder to harvest the topmost yields.

In the following section I have focused on vegetables, since most gardeners are interested in achieving maximum yields in minimum space and may want to test my vertical gardening methods on them first. Then with a season of vertical vegetables under your belt, you can quickly start planning your vertical gardens for fruits and flowers, too.

Creating the Bed

Once you have decided whether to have a freestanding vertical garden or one that is positioned against a wall, you need to sketch out a rough plan to show the placement and dimensions of varieties, whether you wish to grow vegetables, fruits, or flowers. This helps you to decide how many seed packets or transplants to purchase, and what accessories to obtain—such as do-it-yourself supports (such as bamboo canes) or other commercially available ones.

Graph paper is very useful for laying out a garden plan. Allow each square to represent 12 square inches of garden space. Simply take a pencil or a colored felt-tipped pen and make a bold line where your vertical supports cross the bed. Color the supports black or brown, then shade on either side of the line to show individual planting strips. Use a different color for each plant (for example, red for a tomato vine, green for pole beans, and yellow for 'Sugar Snap' peas). Most vines, like pole beans, prefer 12-inch spacing, but some will tolerate crowding. Peas can be closely planted; space three pea vines 4 inches apart and three to each square of graph paper.

TYPES OF PLANTS

Not all plants suitable for vertical gardening need to be self-climbing, meaning those with a twining habit or grasping tendrils. Some, like indeterminate (vining) tomatoes, will need their long stems tied up using string or twist ties. Others, like strawberries, produce runners with a cascading habit, so these plants can be used in tower pots to drape their fruiting stems down, forming a curtain of foliage and fruit. Even low-growing plants like lettuces and peppers can be grown in a space-saving column by using tower pots that stack one on top of the other. I've included information on sweet corn and okra, which are tall-growing plants that can themselves be used as supports for other plants. For the plant listings in the Vegetables for Vertical Gardens chapter, I've developed a set of four symbols (shown on the next two pages) as a ready reference to identify the four basic kinds of vegetable plants to grow vertically: climber, foundation, container and tower pot, and support.

Climber Plants

The vegetables most suited for vertical gardening are vining-type vegetables. Even with their natural tendency for vining, most of the vegetables I recommend need assistance to climb, so train their stems to grow upward using string or twist ties. You'll need to match the weight of the vegetable you're growing to an appropriate-strength support. Cucumbers, English peas, Malabar spinach, sweet potatoes, and pole beans need only a lightweight support like willow branches, netting, or string in order to climb. Other vegetables, such as edible gourds (including chayote), melons (especially cantaloupe), pumpkins (especially miniatures), squash (including climbing zucchini, vegetable spaghetti, and small winter types), watermelons, and yams (especially Chinese climbing) need stronger supports like tree branches, bamboo, and builder's wire. When searching seed racks or garden catalogs for your flower selection, be sure to check heights. Plant breeders have introduced dwarf varieties of traditionally tall plants like sweet peas and nasturtiums, so be sure to choose tall varieties for your vertical gardening beds.

Foundation Plants

These are low-growing plants that do not climb, but can be planted at the base of climbers; I call these plants foundation plants. They share space congenially with the roots of climbing plants, and their foliage nestles in comfortably with the vines and stems of these skyward neighbors. Some of my favorites are beets, cabbages, carrots, Swiss chard, eggplants, herbs, lettuces, onions, peppers, and turnips. These work well in raised beds and containers to accent climbers. Also consider a foundation planting of low-growing French marigolds as a natural insect repellent. When growing flowers vertically, other good low-growing foundation plants include wax begonias, multiflora petunias, and 'Profusion' cushion-type zinnias.

Container and Tower Pot Plants

Containers, cascade planters (usually three tiers high), and tower pots (pots that stack one on top of another up a central column) are perfect for vertical small-space growing, especially on an impervious surface like a wooden deck or brick patio. Most containers (especially dish planters) and cascade planters with bowl-shaped receptacles allow room for a central climbing plant like a pole bean or cucumber in the middle, and several more plants positioned around the rim. Parsley and mini lettuce, for example, are ideal for surrounding a central climber. For planting around the rim, also consider edibles that cascade such as strawberries, sweet potatoes, and New Zealand spinach. Of course, these planters can be devoted to flowers or a combination of vegetables and flowers. In particular, it's good to choose everbearing plants (like day-neutral strawberries) or ever-blooming annuals like nasturtiums.

Support Plants

There are two tall plants with strong stems that I've found can be used to support some of the climbing plants in a vertical garden. I've grown early-maturing sweet corn as a support plant in my own garden and have seen okra used as a support plant in Southern gardens. Because these plants are so sturdy, they can support many types of climbers, including pole beans, cucumbers, and single serving–size melons like 'Tigger', which will wrap around the stem of the support plant and shoot skyward.

Choosing a Site
and Preparing
the Soil

Good soil is the foundation of gardening success. Soil not only anchors plants; it also provides all the nutrients necessary for bountiful harvests of vegetables, fruits, and flowers. By adding compost or commercial organic fertilizers, you can enrich your soil with the nutrients needed for superior growth.

One of the supreme benefits of vertical gardening is that you need less soil and garden space for growing your desired plants. You may only need to prepare a narrow strip of soil 1 to 2 feet wide and 6 to 12 inches deep to grow plants with spectacular results.

SITE SELECTION

Vertical gardening offers a wide array of choices in selecting a site. Once you decide what you want to grow and which supports those plants will need, you can choose a site that's suited for either freestanding supports or wall-mounted supports. The soil requirements are basically the same for all types of vertical growing: The site must drain well; it must provide at least 6 hours of direct sunlight per day for sun-loving plants like tomatoes and pole beans; and the soil must not be too alkaline or too acidic (although a slightly acid soil suits most vining plants). You should also be aware of any areas in your yard that need frost and wind protection; most gardens have microclimates where even a light, late spring frost may strike and kill tender plants like tomatoes. A vertical garden against the house may benefit from house heat, so that early fall frosts need not be as harmful there to still-producing plants as they might be in a freestanding vertical garden out in an open garden space.

DRAINAGE

To test for drainage at your chosen site, dig a hole 6 inches deep and 6 inches wide and pour in a bucket of water. If the hole puddles and takes several hours to drain completely, then the site has poor drainage. You should either choose another site, or consider one of three ways to improve drainage: make a raised bed above the indigenous soil, drain the site, or improve soil texture. For a raised bed (with or without a frame), lay down a foundation of crushed stones and add screened topsoil to a depth of at least 6 inches (the deeper the soil, the more plants like it). If you choose to drain the site, you'll need to dig down and lay drainage pipes to direct excess water away from the specific growing area. In many instances, draining a site can be too labor-intensive because of the digging involved, so a better alternative is to improve soil tilth (texture) in that area. Often, soil will drain poorly because it has a clay consistency; if you add soil amendments (see page 24), you may be able to solve the problem.

SUNLIGHT

Light intensity plays such an important part in plant growth that university studies have shown that just one-tenth of a second less light per day can produce a noticeable difference in the performance of tomato plants. Although a minimum of 6 hours of direct sunlight is recommended for most vegetable crops, early morning sunlight and noonday sunlight are most important. Midday sunlight is especially important for warm season crops like tomatoes and peppers.

If a site is shaded by trees, the removal of a single tree branch can mean

Schoolchildren in Orlando received help from the nonprofit Green Education Foundation, Walpole, Massachusetts, to install a series of raised beds with Skyscraper Gardens at the head of each raised bed.

the difference between fruit and no fruit or flowers and no flowers. If a site is shaded by a tall building, it might be possible to improve the amount of light by painting a nearby wall white. Mirrors, especially in small city gardens, can also help to reflect or direct light to a particular site.

When growing edibles against a wall, avoid a north-facing exposure because of the limited direct sunlight available. Rather, use a shade-loving ornamental vine like clematis or climbing hydrangea for flowering effect, or euonymus or ivy for evergreen foliage interest—and save sun-loving vegetables for areas with more light.

FROST PROTECTION

Exposed low areas are more prone to frost than sheltered sites. You can detect frost pockets simply by walking your property after a snowfall or heavy frost and observing where the snow or frost lingers. If you have spots where snow or frost melts first on a sunny day, these areas could be considered a sun trap and are especially beneficial to warm season crops like tomatoes. Usually the first place snow melts is against the south wall of the house. In such a location, I have been able to overwinter calla lilies out-doors, even though I am in a plant hardiness zone considered too cold for them. When growing against a wall, remember that brick or stone will reflect more heat than wood or aluminum siding.

In spring, when frosts can occur right up to the last frost date (see "Hardiness Zones" below), be prepared to cover young transplants with overturned peach baskets, buckets, or horticultural fleece (a very inexpensive and lightweight see-through fabric available at garden centers). To lessen the risk of early frost damage, always harden off seedlings in a cold-frame for a week before transplanting into the garden, or buy transplants that have been hardened off at the nursery. If a tender plant is blackened by frost, you can trim off the blackened areas, but usually the plant will be too stressed to make a quick recovery. I find it is better to replace damaged plants with new transplants. When the fall forecast is for frost, again be prepared to protect plants, as a long period of pleasant frost-free weather often follows an early frost. Alternatively, pick frost-tender fruits like toma-toes and peppers to take indoors for further ripening.

HARDINESS ZONES

Learn your property's plant hardiness zone and note your first and last average frost dates. You can find the USDA Plant Hardiness Zone Map online or in gardening books and catalogs. However, be aware that since the USDA map features broad swaths of information, your local County Extension office or garden centers are generally a more reliable source for frost dates and advice.

My Pennsylvania property is a Zone 6 garden, with a last expected spring frost date of May 5, and a first expected fall frost date of October 15. That adds up to a frost-free growing period of 186 days, but some years we have had frost as late as May 15 in spring and as early as September 28 in fall. Cedaridge Farm South—my recent acquisition on Sanibel Island,

Florida—is a Zone 10 garden where most years are frost free, allowing for the growth of many exotic plants like coconut palms and mango trees outdoors.

SOIL TESTS

I always advise against testing your own soil with a do-it-yourself kit, since a professional soil testing laboratory can do a more accurate analysis of your soil samples and commonly charges less than $10. An analysis by a professional lab can not only tell you what imbalances there may be, but can also give you specific recommendations on how to correct the imbalances. In Pennsylvania, for example, virtually all soils are acidic, but when I moved to Cedaridge Farm, I needed to know *how* acidic, since an acid soil locks up nutrients. I obtained a soil test mailing pouch from a local garden center, collected several soil samples from my garden, and mailed the

To ready a garden spot for an arbor, level the site by removing sod. Use a spirit level to be sure the soil surface is even. Lay crushed stone as a base for the arbor legs. Place the prefabricated arbor flat with front legs on the stone, then tilt it upright so all four legs rest on the crushed stone.

pouch to my local Cooperative Extension Service, stating that I wished to grow vegetables. Back came an analysis saying that the soil lacked proper amounts of phosphorus and potassium, and it explained how to correct the imbalances. Since the third key plant nutrient—nitrogen—is unstable (here today and sometimes gone tomorrow after a heavy downpour), the analysis gave no reading for nitrogen, and based its recommendation on a typical deficiency in nitrogen.

Since the analysis showed a high acidity, the lab recommended a dose of dolomitic limestone. If my soil had been too alkaline, such as soil in a desert or seashore area, then sulfur or heavy applications of organic matter would have been recommended.

Even if you live in an acid soil area, do not assume all your soil is acidic, especially around house foundations and new construction. Leftover building materials like alkaline cement and lime are typically buried along the house foundation or may be under an open space where you wish to locate a flowerbed or vegetable plot. When the Obama White House decided to plant a vegetable garden in 2010, it was assumed that an open area of lawn would make a perfect site, but a soil analysis showed that the soil was toxic from turf having been treated with fertilizer derived from sewage sludge. While considered suitable for growing grass, the sludge fertilizer saturated the soil with toxins that could contaminate vegetable produce. Therefore, the entire area had to be dug up with a backhoe and replaced with toxin-free garden topsoil. As an extra precaution, the area was raised above the original soil level.

With professional soil analysis costing under $10, it's well worth the effort to identify the nutrients your soil contains and what amendments you can add for your particular plant preferences.

SOIL AMENDMENTS

You can tell the nature of your soil by scooping up a handful on a dry, sunny day and squeezing it in your hand. If the squeezed soil clings together in a lump and fails to break apart, it is clay. If you poke it and it crumbles, then the soil is likely to be loam (a mixture of clay and sand particles plus organic matter). If it trickles out of your hand easily and feels gritty, then it is probably sand.

Clay tends to bind up plant nutrients and can prevent plant roots from penetrating the soil. It is not a bad soil to begin with, but its fine granules must be forced apart and aerated with the addition of organic matter, especially garden compost. When planting a small space, I advise digging up the indigenous clay soil, placing it on a tarp, and mixing in an equal amount of garden compost and of sand. Do not simply add sand to try to improve clay, because adding sand without organic matter will create soil with the undesired consistency of peanut butter.

Loam soil is ideal for most garden plants. It has a soft, crumbly texture and allows water to drain at an even rate. Good loamy soil can also prevent plant disease problems, because most diseases spread in moist to wet soil conditions. Loam has a high proportion of organic matter. It not only provides aeration for plant roots to reach out freely in their search for nutrients; the loam particles also act as a sponge, absorbing moisture and holding it so the soil does not dry out too quickly and cause rapid plant wilting.

Sandy soil can be a real challenge, because water drains away quickly and often carries all nutrients away with it. Adding compost or rich, humusy matter will help improve moisture and nutrient retention.

With all types of soil, it is essential to keep adding organic matter. The action of wind and rain, thawing and freezing, and baking by the sun will often work negatively to bind clay soil particles back together. Similarly, in a sandy soil, even heavy applications of garden compost seem to disappear quickly as the organic material decomposes to almost nothing. Adding nutrients in the form of compost year-round or at the beginning or end of your gardening season is always a great way to improve the condition of your soil.

Arbors, Arches, Pergolas, and Trellises

3

The term *trellis* comes from the French *treillage*, meaning a support made of crisscrossed batons inside a sturdy frame for growing vining plants. Traditionally, you'll find plants like wisteria, clematis, and rambling roses climbing up trellises and other substantial supports. Supported by the latticework, climbing plants can produce a vertical curtain of foliage, flowers, and even fruit on a wide variety of beautiful and practical garden trellises.

Originally, trellises were made of wooden batons, but today they can be made of more durable metal or plastic. A trellis can be freestanding or placed flat against a wall or fence in order to break up monotonous expanses of stonework or wood. A section of trellis can be quite simple in design—usually a diamond or square pattern of slats inside a frame in the shape of a square, rectangle, inverted triangle or fan, or sometimes even a circle. Some trellises can be quite elaborate, combining a multitude of geometric shapes, even creating an exaggerated perspective called a tromp l'oeil—an illusion. The illusion makes a flat section of trellis appear to have depth. Trelliswork can be made from straight wooden slats to create a symmetrical design, or it can be made to look more rustic by using bamboo canes, willow whips, or even contorted sections of tree branches and twisted lengths of metal rods.

At Cedaridge Farm, there were a number of outbuildings that were functional but eyesores when I first purchased the property, including a garden shed (with a woodstove for burning trash) and a guest cottage. I very quickly made these look decorative by covering their walls with trellises and threading the slats with clematis, perennial sweet peas, and rambling roses to mingle their flowers.

HOMEMADE TRELLIS

Inexpensive ready-made sections of trellis can be purchased from lumberyards and garden centers for attaching to a wall or using as a freestanding unit supported by posts. When installing a store-bought trellis, it is best to keep the bottom above soil level, since the slats will easily rot if left in contact with the soil. After frost kills the vines on it, a store-bought trellis is best stored indoors for use in subsequent seasons, as its flimsy wooden slats can deteriorate quickly when exposed to wintry weather.

An assortment of wooden trellis is offered for sale as a cottage industry at a farm stand on a Pennsylvania country road.

Several types of trellis can be homemade at considerable savings and can offer easy gratification. For true cost savings, consider making your own trellis from bamboo canes that you grow yourself. Although there are dozens of varieties of bamboo in cultivation, the hardiest and most decorative variety is known as yellow-groove bamboo (*Phyllostachys aureosulcata*). It is actually a green-and-yellow striped variety that is evergreen and hardy from Zone 6 south, capable of growing 15 feet tall and producing strong, straight canes as wide as 2 inches. Even a relatively small grove— 15 feet × 15 feet—can produce a continuous harvest of canes to construct several designs of trellises. There is also an all-green variety, *P. nuda*. Be aware, however, that yellow-groove bamboo is a "runner" type; its roots spread out in all directions, doubling in area each year. Therefore, you need to confine your bamboo grove to a part of the garden where it will not become invasive, or else grow a clump in a large container to restrict its roots. Another bamboo that's suitable for trellises and supports is sold under the variety name 'Dragon's Head'; it is a hardy "clumping" bamboo and is not invasive.

When cutting bamboo to make trellises, consider their purpose and use; for instance, canes for pea vines do not need to be as strong as canes for taller and heavier pole lima beans. In my garden, I use ½- to 1-inch-wide canes for pea uprights and even thinner canes (¼ inch) for the crossbars; these thinner canes are sufficiently flexible to be woven between the uprights. Cut each bamboo cane as close to the ground as possible, and then measure off 6-foot lengths of it for pea uprights (this allows for 6 to 12 inches of the cane to be stuck into the soil for stability).

For heavier vines such as pole lima beans, I like to cut stronger and taller canes, from 1 to 2 inches in diameter. Also, for taller vines I measure twice the length of a pea stake—up to 12 feet. When you cut a length of bamboo, note that it is composed of equal segments with nodes. Each node sprouts a pair of side branches that must be trimmed. I like to leave about 1 inch of these side stems protruding, as they act as pegs to firmly hold the

ARBORS, ARCHES, PERGOLAS, AND TRELLISES

crosspieces of your trellis. Bamboo canes can be used to create a free-standing trellis or a trellis laid flat against a wall. Use twist ties to hold the crosspieces in place for a temporary structure; screws may be used to make a more substantial support.

Willow is another good, hardy plant for making homemade trellises. Many kinds of willow, especially pussy willow (*Salix discolor*), grow long, straight, whiplike branches that are pliable for weaving. These whips can be used to create a wicker trellis, weaving long horizontal branches between thicker wooden uprights.

Often, trelliswork can be incorporated into the design of arbors, arches, pergolas, and even the canopies for bridges to create more surfaces for climbing plants.

ARBORS

While arbors often incorporate an arch, they are usually more substantial and provide shade for a bench, hammock, or a swing seat. Arbors usually

The apple arbor at historic Eleutherian Mills, Delaware, presents a tunnel of apple blossoms in early spring, followed in fall by the fruit of heirloom apple varieties.

A house-shaped arbor made from store-bought trellis supports a planting of scarlet runner beans in the vegetable garden and vertically joins two raised beds.

incorporate trelliswork in their design and are generally backed by a hedge, wall, or fence. They can create an alluring focal point at the end of a path or vista, or serve as a transition between two garden spaces.

ARCHES

Arches are usually simple portals located between one garden space and another, and incorporate an arrangement of trellis. They define the entrance to a garden or mark a transition between different types of garden spaces. The top of an arch isn't always curved; it can be made from straight horizontal or peaked crossbars. When you visit a garden center and look at an assortment of arches, you will see that some are fairly light-weight and inexpensive, usually made from wood slats or wire. These simple arches are ideal to support quick-growing annuals like ornamental gourds and morning glories, but you should not use them for aggressive vines like wisteria. To test a more heavy-duty trellis for strength, grasp one of its crossbars and carefully pull down on it to see if you can trust it to support a heavy wisteria or trumpet creeper.

Plant a garden arch with two flowering vines, such as a climbing rose and a clematis, so their flowers intermingle to create a beautiful color harmony.

How Vines Climb

Twining stems
on pole beans

Tendrils on sweet peas

Holdfasts
on Virginia creeper

In order to determine the right support for a particular vining plant, it's important to understand how vines climb. Some have special climbing mechanisms that allow them to be self-supporting, while others need training vertically in order for them to climb.

Twining vines such as morning glories, pole beans, and honeysuckle have lead shoots that coil upward and encircle any kind of support, even a slippery bamboo cane. Some plants, including grapevines and sweet peas, climb by means of tendrils; these tendrils are slender, coiling appendages that will grasp any kind of support, allowing the lead shoot to grow skyward.

Virginia creeper produces holdfasts between leaf nodes; holdfasts are like suction pads that will adhere to any kind of rough surface. Another type of holdfast

These examples show how vines climb with different mechanisms.

is an aerial root. English ivy climbs by developing aerial roots at each leaf node, allowing the ivy to secure its vine to rough surfaces like stone and wood. These aerial roots can cause considerable damage to the pointing between bricks and to wooden surfaces.

A fifth type of climbing mechanism is thorns, like those on climbing roses. Thorns are not very efficient as climbing devices, because they need to hook onto other twiggy growth to become self-supporting. This is why climbing roses often need to be guided up a support and tied securely in place with string or twist ties. Twist ties and twine can also be used to aid other vines in climbing, especially those with weak climbing ability like clematis.

Aerial roots
on trumpet creeper

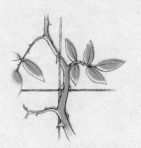

Thorns on rambler roses

Twine on climbing roses

Twist ties on tomatoes

This French-style festoon features repeating rectangular shapes and is the perfect showcase for the entwining rose 'American Pillar'.

CANOPIES

Usually a canopy extends from a doorway to provide cooling shade. Canvas canopies are unsuitable for covering with vines, but a canopy grid of beams and slats can make an attractive support for a substantial climber like a grapevine or wisteria. I also like canopies over footbridges: flat canopies if the bridge is flat, or arched if the bridge has an arched span. Generally, you should choose a metal bridge canopy for a heavy vine like wisteria, but a rot-resistant wooden canopy can still last a long time. If wisteria is too much plant for your canopy, consider clematis and climbing roses.

FESTOONS

While you may not be familiar with the term *festoon*, you'll recognize one instantly when you see it. Festoons are usually a series of frames that allow vining plants like climbing roses, ivy, and clematis to climb up supports and over cross members to create a portal of vines. These are very popular in French rose gardens, with some of the festoons extending to a considerable length, either arranged in a straight line like a fence or in a curve. One of the best examples of a series of festoons in America is at Longwood Gardens in Kennett Square, Pennsylvania, where a semicircle of arched festoons is decorated exclusively with 'American Pillar' roses. Festoons generally work best in a more formal space, but they can be used to create privacy in a more informal garden, too.

PERGOLAS

Pergolas are more substantial than either arbors or arches. A pergola is usually a series of arches connecting the house to an outbuilding or garden space, or connecting two garden spaces. Like an arch or an arbor, it can incorporate trelliswork to help vines climb up to form a canopy above head height. In home gardens, pergolas are often used to provide a shady green roof over a patio, with leafy vines clamoring over the top. Pergolas can run straight or they can curve. They can be placed on a level site or allowed to descend a slope. Pergolas can support a whole collection of vines; for example, sections of wisteria can alternate with sections of trumpet creeper, clematis, and roses. Or they can support a collection of one particular plant species, like several varieties of dessert grapes, a tunnel of climbing roses, or a dozen or more clematis varieties in different colors.

At Hearst Castle in San Simeon, California, the former home of newspaper magnate William Randolph Hearst, a pergola surrounding the garden is wide enough and high enough for a horse and rider to pass underneath.

The British architect Sir Edwin Lutyens designed pergolas with stone and brick pillars and substantial wooden crosspieces as extensions of his residences. The American architect Frank Lloyd Wright designed pergolas in metal and wood to create the sensation of "compression and release" for visitors during walks outdoors. The sense of "compression" is provided by a tunnel of pillars and crossbars supporting vines whose dense foliage creates a dark, shady, confined space for people to walk through; "release" happens when people step out of the tunnel into the open sunlight.

Planters
and Supports

4

The ways to garden vertically are limited only by your imagination. You can use a simple wooden trellis or garden netting to grow a fine crop of tomatoes, or you can stagger containers, such as window box planters and hanging baskets, up a wall for a mosaic of flowers and foliage. The heights you'll reach by growing vertically are amazing. I have seen 'American Pillar' climbing roses completely cover a barn, roof and all, and Virginia creeper extend 100 feet and more to cover the walls of a hotel. All that these plants needed was a little support.

In the home garden, climbing and cascading plants thrive in a variety of containers and planting areas. Some plants need just a little support, and others need more rigorous structures. In this chapter, discover the many ways I've experimented with growing plants vertically at Cedaridge Farms.

BAMBOO SUPPORTS

Bamboo canes are commonly used to help tomatoes grow vertically, but they are also a wonderful building material to make trellises and towers for many other types of plants in a vertical garden. Several hardy varieties of bamboo (such as the equally hardy 'Dragon's Head' and yellow-groove bamboos) will grow strong, upright canes to 12 feet tall and taller. The clusters of leaves at each node along the cane are easily stripped or pruned away to leave long, straight canes ideal for making a crisscrossed trellis pattern. I also construct scaffoldlike towers of bamboo to support tall, bushy plants like tomatoes. Where the crosspieces meet, you can usually use screws to secure them together, or you may find that long twist ties or zip ties are sufficient to hold

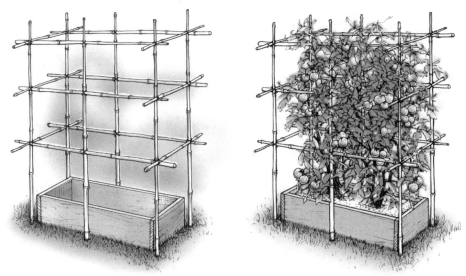

A scaffold made from inexpensive bamboo canes allows plants to grow inside and use the crosspieces for support.

A simple trellis made from bamboo canes is especially good for growing pole beans, tomatoes, and squash.

the canes firmly in place. See the "Tent Supports" section on page 51. Bamboo is especially good for supporting plants in containers, since the canes are strong and easily pushed down into soil within the container or outside next to it. If you're using a container on an impervious surface and need a rigid support for your climbing plants, secure the bamboo cane to the container with screws.

The simple crisscross pattern of bamboo canes adds sturdiness to a homemade bamboo trellis—ideal for 'Sugar Snap' peas.

This diamond pattern trellis uses bamboo canes and offers extra sturdiness, especially for heavy vines like indeterminate tomatoes and pole lima beans.

BUILDER'S WIRE

Use builder's wire mesh to grow gourds vertically on the wall of a shed; just staple 4-foot-wide sections of mesh to posts attached to the shed.

A product known as builder's wire, mostly used for reinforcing concrete floors, makes a strong, inexpensive trellis for mounting between two posts or attaching to a wall. Hardware stores sell it in 5 × 10-foot sheets and in 5 × 50-foot rolls costing about $25. The product uses a heavy-gauge #10 mesh, creating a framework of 6 × 6-inch reach-through mesh that plants can climb or twine through. If you buy builder's wire in rolls, cut the sections with bolt cutters to create a flat sheet ideal for heavy vines like pole beans and vining squash, or cut and roll it into a cylinder to support individual tomato vines.

A four-station support features builder's wire fastened between posts. This arrangement has room for eight 4-foot sections of vining plants in a small space.

CASCADE GARDENS ADJUSTABLE-HEIGHT TRELLIS

If you haven't seen a Cascade Gardens adjustable-height trellis in your local garden center or in a gardening catalog, take the time to search for one on the Internet. This handy device consists of a black metal bracket that attaches to a vertical surface (such as a fence, wall, or post) and five vertical weighted cords that can be adjusted from 1 to 6 feet in height for your plants to grasp and grow up. This product is ideal for supporting flowering annuals such as morning glories, perennials such as clematis, and also vining vegetables such as pole beans. It's beautifully designed, inexpensive (about $40), and worthy of any size vertical garden.

CHAIN-LINK AND OTHER FENCE SUPPORTS

Of course, many styles of fences can provide strong support for edible and ornamental vines, including chain-link, picket, and split-rail fencing—with split-rail being one of the most practical, in my opinion. Its thick log design will not rot as readily as a more flimsy structure like that of a picket fence, and its rough log surface texture is an ideal surface for climbing plants. Use split-rail fences as support for grapevines and kiwi vines, as well as flowering vines like rambling roses, clematis, trumpet creeper, and wisteria.

A common sight in neighborhood backyards, a chain-link fence is suitable for growing sweet peas, clematis, and other flowering vines to soften edges and provide a bit of privacy.

FAN TRELLIS

Made of wood or more durable metal, plastic, or vinyl, the prefabricated fan trellis is mostly used to grow plants against a wall, its splayed batons forming a pattern like the outstretched fingers of a hand. It is especially useful for growing flowering vines like clematis and roses, although it can also support any kind of vining vegetable. Traditionally, fan trellises were made of wood (and probably supported roses in your grandmother's garden), but today you'll find a wide variety of more durable trellis materials.

GARDENING IN BAGS

Vertical gardens needn't feature only the tried-and-true favorite supports; have some fun, experiment with new methods, and try growing plants in plastic pouches and bags that feature convenient planting holes. These can be attached to walls or posts to create a column or curtain of flowers, foliage, or fruit. Tomatoes and strawberries are perfect plants to grow in bags.

Plastic Pouches

In recent years, you may have seen flexible plastic pouches—open at the top and closed at the bottom—hanging from wall brackets (like hanging baskets do) and filled with healthy plants. These pouches have planting holes strategically placed in a checkerboard pattern and are ideal for growing mostly flowering plants in a column; they're even great for growing some fruits and vegetables, such as strawberries, cherry tomatoes, and hot peppers. Fill the pouch with an enriched potting soil or your fluffy, homemade garden compost. Avoid using garden soil, as it's too heavy and could collapse or tear the pouch. Pouches have drainage holes, are reusable when washed well between uses, and can be stored flat during colder months.

Pouches are most attractive using basal branching plants such as petunias and pansies or tomatoes and cucumbers, although compact vegetable varieties such as lettuce and parsley are also suitable. Since the pouch is suspended in midair and susceptible to drying out quickly, watering is generally necessary at least once a day through the open top and best accomplished with a watering wand or watering can with a long spout.

Upside-Down Planters

I don't believe any garden product has been more heavily advertised on television than the inverted planters! By far the most popular version is the Topsy Turvy upside-down planter. These bottoms-up planters are usually made of a flexible polypropylene fabric and are specially designed to grow a column of flowers and vegetables (typically tomatoes) upside down.

The moment I saw one, I obtained a sample and grew tomatoes at Cedaridge Farm. It worked well, as promised in the television commercial, but I quickly learned why some people might be disappointed if they do not follow directions properly. The growing bag needs to be filled with a commercial potting soil or light, fluffy, well-decomposed compost—*not* garden topsoil. (When watered, the garden topsoil becomes too heavy and can tear the bag off its hanger.)

Some potting soils are nutrient-enriched with essential plant foods, but others are not, so a granular fertilizer or a liquid fertilizer drench may be necessary to provide enough nutrients to produce a heavily bearing tomato vine. Even after adding a general purpose fertilizer, I found that I needed to give the vine a foliar feed at 3-week intervals to keep it green and fruiting continuously until fall frost.

Although the Topsy Turvy brand planter has a lid to help retain moisture, the lightness of the potting soil inside allowed water to drain away rather quickly, so I'd advise you to water daily, using a watering can with a long spout or a watering wand to ensure that the water pours through the watering hole.

For growing a tomato vine, I found the Topsy Turvy was a good way to save space and also was an amusing talking point for visitors to my garden. Yes, it really works! The instructions said that the Topsy Turvy could be used for other vining plants such as cucumbers, strawberries, and peppers, but in my tests none of these performed as well as a tomato vine.

If you decide to grow tomatoes in your upside-down planter, take care not to break or damage your transplant when you insert it. A sponge collar holds the neck of the transplant in place, but it can be tricky holding the bag and inserting the tomato plant so that it fits snugly, with its roots in the potting soil inside the bag and its green stem and leaves outside in the sunlight.

As I suspected would happen in my tests, the young transplants at first have a tendency to grow upward rather than downward. However, as the vine grows longer, the weight of its stems, leaves, and flower trusses will cause the vine to straighten down to create a pillar of cascading fruit.

For best results, I found that 'Sungold', 'Sweet 100', and other cherry tomatoes were highly productive, as was a medium-fruited variety like 'Early Cascade', with fruit about the size of a billiard ball. The larger varieties like 'Beefsteak' did produce fruit, but the fruits were not plentiful. Use indeterminate varieties (those with long vines) exclusively for best results; some indeterminates (such as 'Better Boy') can reach 15 feet. Avoid determinate tomatoes (those with short vines), like 'Patio'.

Make sure you use a strong bracket to secure the planter to a height you can reach (say 6 feet). If secured to a south-facing wall, the reflected heat from the wall will not only promote earliness, but also deter frost damage if an unexpected late frost occurs.

GARDEN NETTING

There are different kinds of garden netting in different widths and lengths for rolling out and cutting to suit your needs. It is mostly made of durable plastic and is reusable season to season. Some garden netting has a fine mesh, often used for protecting plants from birds and deer, and is suitable for growing ornamentals. For supporting fruits and vegetables, you need a larger mesh with a 4- to 6-inch-wide grid, which allows you to reach through it to harvest.

You'll need to drape or hang garden netting from a crossbar of wood, metal, or plastic—anything sufficiently sturdy to resist breaking when weighted down by heavy yields of fruit. Attach crossbars to upright garden supports, brackets on a wall, or posts drilled with facing holes. The netting also needs to be held taut to the ground, using metal or plastic pegs, so it doesn't collapse on itself; you can find pegs at garden centers.

The length of garden netting needed depends on the plants you wish to grow. Pole lima beans, for example, can grow to 15 feet high in a single season. I normally don't use poles taller than I can reach with a short stepladder—no higher than 10 feet. For sugar snap peas, 6 feet of netting is fine.

For most annuals and herbaceous perennials, garden netting is a perfectly suitable vertical growing material. However, vigorous woody plants like wisteria and trumpet creeper generally need a stronger wooden or wire trellis. Builder's wire can make a strong substitute for plastic netting. I use it for heavy vines like climbing roses and grapevines. Builder's wire comes in rolls and can be bent into a cylinder to create a tower for growing tomatoes or clematis. It can also be rolled out flat for mounting against a wall or between posts to serve as a climbing surface for plants.

Garden Netting against a Wall

Using garden netting is an easy and inexpensive method for growing vines up a wall. Simply choose metal or wooden brackets and secure them at least 6 feet high (the height an average person can reach) on the wall. Hang the garden netting from strong bamboo canes, strong wire, or tightly drawn string attached to the brackets. By using pegs to hold the netting taut to the ground, you can create a curtain of mesh for vining plants to climb. Avoid bird netting or deer netting for wall applications, because the mesh is too small to allow you to reach through to harvest vegetables or flowers if they grow on the backside of the net. When mounting a garden netting system against a wall, provide a planting bed area beneath it at least 12 inches out from the wall with a soil depth of at least 6 inches.

Garden Netting as Part of a Freestanding Unit

The easiest way to create support for a freestanding vertical garden is to string a wire between two strong posts or bamboo canes and drape garden netting from it, holding the netting taut to the ground by pegs. You'll need at least 12 inches of planting space on either side of the netting to grow a double row of plants, such as pole beans. Minimum height for pole snap beans should be 6 feet, but you can extend the height to 10 to 12 feet if you have tall enough supports and a means to harvest at that height. A free-standing unit with a garden netting surface can be featured in ornamental beds as a background to low-growing plants, and also in the middle of an island bed for a tall accent surrounded by low growers. You also can use garden netting to create privacy for a patio, between adjoining driveways, or between twin decks of townhouses or condos.

Garden Netting Using PVC Pipe for Support

PVC pipe makes a great support system for garden netting. You'll need two pipes for the upright posts, one pipe for the top bar, and two elbow connectors. Thread the top bar through the top row of the mesh, then connect the elbows and the upright posts to create a U-shaped support. The ideal width of a section is 4 feet, although you can extend the length by adding T-joints and upright supports every 4 feet. My only reservation with PVC pipe is its rather utilitarian appearance compared with more attractive wooden or metal trellis.

MAYPOLES

A maypole is simply a sturdy pole with strands of string that radiate down from the top, creating a tepee support for twining plants like pole beans and clematis. The strings are held taut to the ground by pegs. One of the most attractive garden supports for vegetable gardens, maypoles work well in ornamental gardens, too, especially for flowering annuals such as morning glories and climbing nasturtiums.

Cucumber vines grow up a maypole support where strings splay out from a central pole.

OBELISKS

Obelisks are garden towers with lattice sides that reach to a peak to create a steep pyramid; you'll find them in bamboo, willow, wood, metal, and plastic. These sturdy supports are decorative and popular for displaying flowering vines like clematis and climbing roses. At Cedaridge Farm, I have an herb garden with a metal obelisk positioned in the middle of each quadrant, so I can plant and grow hop vines, scented-leaf geraniums, and clematis vertically for purely ornamental effect.

A simple obelisk or tripod made from wooden slats can be angled to form a three-cornered pyramid. Add rustic crosspieces at an angle for extra strength.

SKYSCRAPER GARDENS

Many people resist purchasing commercial products to garden vertically because of their expense, but a vertical gardening kit or a sturdy section of prefabricated wooden trellis purchased from a store can cost less than $40. By growing just two edible plants—a vegetable spaghetti squash yielding a dozen fruits and a 'Better Boy' hybrid tomato vine yielding a hundred fruits, the cost can be recovered easily in one season. If you're a vegetable gardener, you clearly enjoy the delicious homegrown bounty you harvest from your garden, and you appreciate that you only need to step outside to gather ingredients for your meals. But if you're buying at a produce counter instead, here's the reality: A dozen vegetable spaghetti fruits averaging 5 pounds each at $1.67 per pound can cost about $100, and 100 'Better Boys' (averaging three fruits per pound and retailing for $3 a pound) can cost another $100. That demonstrates an extremely good return on an initial investment in a vertical support.

The Skyscraper Garden is a convenient commercial system that I've designed for growing plants vertically. At its most basic, it consists of a pair of cedar brackets that attach to a wall or between two posts, a metal cross-bar, a 4-foot-wide × 6-foot-tall section of durable garden netting that hangs from the crossbar like a curtain, and pegs to hold the netting taut to the ground. Plants can climb the netting whether it's positioned against a wall or fence, or is a freestanding unit between a pair of posts set 4 feet apart. Multiples of the 4-foot-wide unit can extend the vertical garden to an indefinite width, so that the entire expanse of a long wall or long, narrow bed can be used. And, believe me, multiple units can have a stunning effect when overflowing with flowers and bounty.

After I perfected the design for the Skyscraper Garden, I realized that I wanted to share this innovative idea with other gardeners. So now the Sky-scraper Garden is available for purchase from cedarstore.com. I'm sure you'll agree that it's reasonably priced at $40 and has all the components you'll need in one package. It's easy to install and will last indefinitely, even if it's left in place over winter. Of course, you can buy materials (you'll need mounting brackets, a crosspiece, pegs, and netting) and make your own, too.

A Skyscraper Garden offers additional vertical growing benefits when it's affixed to a south- or southeast-facing wall. Reflected heat and light from a wall will promote early, vigorous growth. Heat from a house wall will also protect against late frosts. The size of a planting strip along a wall foundation can be as little as 1 foot wide × 4 feet long, reducing the amount of bed space for a normal horizontal 4 × 6-foot garden plot from 24 square feet to 4 square feet. This means that you'll have only a very small surface that you'll need to cultivate, with less to dig, less to fertilize, less to irrigate, and less to weed. Digging can be avoided altogether by in situ composting (see page 75); fertilizing can be less wasteful (see page 128); irrigation can be made easy and less wasteful (see page 127); and weeding can be avoided by mulching (see page 123).

With a freestanding Skyscraper Garden unit attached to two posts (instead of attached to a wall) and centered over a 2 × 4-foot planting bed,

To prepare a bed for a no-dig Skyscraper Garden, lay newspaper over the indigenous soil as a weed barrier, then add homemade compost and a wooden barrier to contain the soil. Attach rot-resistant cedar brackets to a wall 4 feet apart, then insert a crossbar between the brackets to hold a 4 × 6-foot length of reach-through garden netting. Use garden pegs to hold the garden netting taut to the ground.

the net between the posts can be planted on both sides. Sprawling plants like vining cucumbers and melons can be grown vertically in just 8 square feet (2 × 4 feet) of garden space, rather than the 24 square feet (4 × 6 feet) of planting space they would normally occupy in a horizontal garden bed.

The Skyscraper Garden system works equally well for most flowers and vegetables that have the ability to climb. The list of edibles and ornamentals is impressive, including both cool season and warm season crops. It includes plants not normally associated with vertical gardening, such as the gourmet French 'Charentais' melon, the burpless (bitter-free) cucumber 'Orient Express', a climbing Trombone-type zucchini ('Trombocino'), climbing 'Wave' petunias, morning glories, and climbing nasturtiums. Most other climbing systems are expensive or must be fixed flat against a wall. The Skyscraper Garden system features brackets that project the netting 12 inches away from a wall. This provides air circulation to prevent rotting, and it allows flowers and fruit to set all around the plant, rather than on just one side. It allows most vines to grow more easily, because they have room to climb and twine; bear more abundantly, because the flowers are more easily seen by pollinators; and grip the flexible netting support more firmly than they could a flat wooden trellis. The wide mesh also allows gardeners' hands to reach through the netting for harvesting flowers and fruit on the back side. And, best of all for almost any-age gardener, the Skyscraper Garden system is a pleasure to use, since plant maintenance is minimal and harvesting does not require stooping.

TENT SUPPORTS

There's nothing easier than this! Lean two sections of square or rectangular preassembled trellis against each other to create a tent support that's ideal for vining cucumbers, melons, and winter squash. You can

Homemade cucumber trellis made from wooden slats helps keep fruit off the ground and perfectly formed.

also lean pairs of bamboo canes into each other by crisscrossing their ends and securing them with long twist ties or twine to a long single cane running across the top. Use two people to set up this quick bamboo tent system, with one person holding the horizontal cane and a second person crisscrossing and securing the vertical canes.

A tent-style support made by leaning bamboo canes into each other is ideal to support climbing 'Trombone' zucchini.

TEPEE SUPPORTS

The tepee support is as old as gardening itself. Most commonly, tepees consist of three strong poles, such as bamboo canes, arranged in a tripod shape to form a point. The point, or an area slightly below the point, is secured by wire, twist ties, or string. The three poles can be increased to four or even

A simple tripod or teepee structure made from rustic tree branches makes an especially attractive support for pole beans.

Use pliable willow whips to create a circular tepee for climbing bean vines.

a dozen, in order to accommodate more vines. Vines planted at the base of each pole can be allowed to twine upward; pole beans in particular like this method of support. When there are many poles close together in a tepee, the vines will knit together to form a tepee of foliage. (Children love to cut a gap in the foliage between two poles to play inside.)

TOMATO TOWERS

Gardeners have tried improving tomato towers for decades, but these structures all basically lend their support in the same way—with flexible builder's wire mesh curved into a cylinder. Commerical towers come preformed as upside-down wire cones that stand up to 6 feet; you'll find square, zigzag, and V-shaped ladder towers, too. Plant a single tomato vine inside a cone or alongside a tower and allow it to grow up and push its branches through the openings to become self-supporting. Shorter 3-foot towers are suitable for determinate (bushy) tomatoes, peppers, eggplants, and squash.

Tomato towers are multipurpose supports—use them for bush-type tomatoes, tall pepper varieties, and sprawling zucchini and squash.

TOWER SYSTEMS

I love to see vertical garden towers. They can be special containers that fit snugly into vertical holders, or tiered shelves that become hidden by your pots full of flowers and foliage—perfect for confined spaces like a deck or patio. Tower plantings create an exceedingly decorative accent that's more appealing than a collection of potted plants clustered at ground level. A number of manufacturers produce tower growing units, from tiered stands to cascading planters (see below), which allow you to create a vertical display in a small space.

Many of the stackable containers used for these tower systems are made of plastic, wire, or Styrofoam, lightweight enough to work well in a tall tower grouping. Some containers known as strawberry pots feature cupped openings on the sides for plants to grow out of and cascade down from. These openings allow plants, such as strawberries and 'Tumbling Tom' tomatoes, to arch out and form a curtain of foliage and stems.

Cascade Planters

One version of a tower system is the three-tier cascade planter, composed of three metal wire bowls or baskets supported by a central metal pillar. The bowls of these cage-style plant stands need to be lined with coco fiber to hold potting soil. I find that a 50-pound bag of potting soil fills the three bowls perfectly. Each bowl planter is progressively larger from top to bottom, allowing a large assortment of flowers, herbs, or vegetables (or a mixture of all three) to be grown in a sunny location on a deck or patio. I've found that the entire unit can accommodate up to 18 bushy plants. Moreover, the base bowl requires a space of only 2 square feet, and the stand's elegant legs elevate the bottom bowl off the ground, creating a compact tower 36 inches high. The planting tiers can be watered by hand, or you can use a drip irrigation system to water the planter automatically at timely intervals.

Other types of cascade planters feature a metal hanging rod; clamps attached to the metal rod allow the pots to be held aloft, one above the other.

Hydroponic Towers

Most of the commercial systems I have seen for hydroponic cultivation are unsuitable for home gardeners, as they are expensive and require a lot of plumbing and maintenance. But there is one exception that is cost efficient, even for a small backyard: a system of five stackable, boxlike Styrofoam "pots" made by Hydro Harvest Farms, of Ruskin, Florida, that uses a soilless growing medium and a liquid fertilizer.

The basic Hydro Harvest unit consists of a 2-foot-square ground pot suitable for growing foundation (or root) crops like radishes, turnips, carrots, and beets, as well as flowers for cutting like snapdragons, zinnias, and marigolds. This ground pot provides stability for four tower planters that cross-stack one on top of the other to create a vertical column. One kit (consisting of the foundation pot, four tower pots, and the hydroponic mechanisms) costs $100 and is easily assembled. A four-tower set with automatic feeding and recirculating pipes costs $400 and features planting stations to accommodate 64 plants. The stations are filled with a soilless, sterile planting medium—a combination of vermiculite and perlite (both by-products of ancient volcanic action)—with excellent moisture-holding ability. Each tower uses only 1 gallon of nutrient solution per day. All the pots spin for easy access. The system is reusable, and the company reports that some towers are going strong after 10 years of continuous use.

I visited the Hydro Harvest demonstration farm in Florida and learned that their hydroponic systems use 80 percent less water than conventional irrigation systems and produce six times greater yields compared with horizontal production. They use a regimen of integrated pest management with no chemical pesticides, and when I inspected their demonstration plot, I didn't see a single bug bite on anything. Insects and diseases are

These strawberries are starting to fruit in a hydroponic system that uses tower pots.

VERTICAL GARDENING

controlled by using natural solutions—predatory bugs like preying mantises and ladybugs, for example, with an assortment of organic controls like natural pyrethrin and a neem-insecticidal soap concentrate. The fact that plants are not grown in soil that can be contaminated with disease organisms or pest larvae or eggs means that a minimum amount of pest control is needed.

The inventors, John and Terrie Lawson, got the idea to start a backyard vertical hydroponic system after they read about a Florida farmer growing strawberries hydroponically. They took a small parcel of land they owned in Ruskin and turned it into Hydro Harvest Farms. They grow and sell up to 40 varieties of vegetables and small fruits at their farm stand. Their large-scale system is fully automated, with the nutrient solution fed by a timer, allowing 21,000 plants to be grown vertically without soil in only a half-acre of space. The Lawsons claim that the system, once installed, requires just 15 minutes a week to maintain. Growing 100 tomato plants requires just 4 gallons of water a day. Besides strawberries and tomatoes (their most profitable crops), the Lawsons grow lettuce, zucchini, eggplant, peppers, and even dwarf okra vertically.

Their system promotes earliness by avoiding stress. Plants in a traditional garden are subject to fluctuations in weather patterns—cold nights, dry spells, and erratic feeding. The Hydro Harvest system allows strawberries (day-neutral varieties, see page 253) to ripen 2 weeks earlier in spring and continue producing crops up to 4 weeks later in fall. For more information, see hydroharvestfarms.com.

Tiered Plant Stands

One of my favorite tower systems in the good-looks department is the tiered plant stand, which is available in a variety of forms—from rectangular metal shelving to curved and semicircle wire tiers that support your collection of pots. These tiered stands are ideal for placing on a deck or patio to help decorate a space vertically. Plants growing in pots on tiered stands can be hand watered with a watering wand or watering can, or a drip hose can be set up to apply water automatically. Be sure to check the moisture content of the potting soil daily, as these tower pots, raised up in the air, have a tendency to dry out quickly. Tiered plant stands are well suited for growing vegetables, herbs, and flowering annuals and perennials.

Swiss chard and herbs grow in pots that are part of a tiered display.

WALL UNITS USING FOUND OBJECTS

Visit any junkyard and you are bound to find discarded machine parts that may be suitable for offbeat trellises. My favorite is rusted bicycle wheels, offset and secured together by wire, laid flat against a wall up to the roofline. Flowering vines in particular can be beautiful when grown up bicycle wheels for support; try blue morning glories and orange climbing nasturtiums allowed to knit together for a colorful mosaic. While bicycle rims make eye-catching circular pieces of art, I have also seen orchard ladders and sections of rusty metal fencing used to support climbing vines.

Mount found objects like bicycle wheels against a brick wall and allow fast-growing gourd vines to provide the art.

WIRE STRANDS

Wire strands, strung horizontally between two T-shaped posts, are mostly used to support heavy vines like grapes and kiwi, and arching canes like those of raspberries and blackberries. Usually it's best if the posts are sunk into concrete for stability, with wire strands stretching between both ends of the T-forming crossbars on top. With raspberries and blackberries, a pair of crossbars—one pair at the top of the posts and a second pair halfway down—can efficiently support an abundance of long arching canes.

LARGE-SCALE IDEAS

At Cedaridge Farm, we have a toolshed with a tall brick chimney that was used to vent a stove I no longer use. I considered the tall expanse of brick an eyesore, so I planted a single trumpet creeper at the base, allowing it to climb to the top of the chimney, sinking aerial roots into the porous brick in order to climb without additional support. The vine reached the top of the chimney by the second season, and attracts scores of hummingbirds each summer. We also have a wide, high stone wall of our three-story farmhouse covered with a Virginia creeper vine, and a south-facing wall of a barn planted with a Cayuga dessert-quality grapevine. Other hardy candidates for covering large expanses include wisteria, Arctic kiwi, Boston ivy, silver fleece vine, and climbing roses. For those who live in frost-free areas, the choices are even better because they include tender bougainvillea and black-eyed Susan vine.

The French Impressionist artist Claude Monet not only covered the gables of his house with Boston ivy; he also had a metalworker construct long, tall metal trellises to run across the entire front of his house above the front door, and planted climbing roses (such as yellow 'Mermaid' and pink 'Belle Vichyssoise') on them to ramble horizontally between the first and second floors and drape their blossoms toward the ground like lace.

Green Walls

A French botanist, Patrick Blanc, has made a profession out of installing *murs verts* (green walls), mostly for commercial spaces like hotels and public gardens. I saw a real beauty covering the wall of a courtyard of the Hotel Pershing Hall in Paris. These green walls are made from a special felt "blanket" suspended from a wall to hang like a curtain. Plants are set into the felt, where their roots anchor themselves. A special liquid nutrient solution drips down through the felt to provide nourishment. This is recirculated by a system of pipes.

Blanc got the idea of making green walls from studying plants in tropical rainforests, where sufficient moisture and nutrients allow plants to cling to vertical cliffs, creating a tapestry of color from different leaf colors, shapes, and textures. These plants can be tropical, as in the case of the Hotel Pershing Hall, where the roof of the courtyard is covered with glass and the interior space heated to exclude frost. In temperate outdoor locations, the plants used can be hardy evergreens or deciduous species that go dormant during winter or are replaced each season.

The Blanc system is not really practical for a home environment, as it is costly to install and costly to maintain, but it's an example of the multiple ways you can garden vertically. Several US manufacturers are now producing "living walls" for home use (see them online) that are less costly than the aforementioned system. However, even these simplified systems are expensive when compared with creating your own living walls using baskets of cascading plants and window box planters of erect vining plants.

Vertical Tapestry Gardens

While the sophisticated commercial green wall systems may not be suited for home gardens, I have been able to create simple green walls at Cedaridge Farm without the complex plumbing typically needed for a *mur vert*. I call my version a vertical tapestry garden.

There are several easy ways to create a vertical tapestry garden, depending on your location. If you have a deck, terrace, or balcony, for example, you can position plants in window box planters to cascade down to meet erect vining plants that are growing up from the ground, supported by trellises. The two sets of plants—cascading and upright—then create a tight knit of foliage and flowers and a beautiful curtain when they meet in the middle. It's the ultimate top-down and bottom-up vertical garden.

A vertical tapestry garden is also possible using tiers of shelves or hanging baskets. A flight of steps can accommodate containers of plants at its side for a vertical accent, or a pair of stepladders holding up planks for shelves can support hanging baskets of petunias and trailing verbena, for example, so the plantings intermingle. Even on a solid wall, brackets can be placed at strategic intervals to accommodate a collection of hanging baskets, so the flowering effect is like a curtain of color. Be sure to use a watering wand, so you can poke its spout through the dense foliage and flowers and easily apply water to the root zone of each basket.

When creating a vertical tapestry garden, don't limit yourself to just flowers. Some of the best tapestry gardens use plants with interesting foliage, particularly the heart-shaped leaves of Dutchman's pipe; the colorful ivy-shaped leaves of heuchera; and the silvery, heavily veined leaves of brunnera 'Jack Frost'. Even common lamb's ears looks sensational placed in a tapestry garden.

Containers
and Hanging
Planters

5

Gardening in any of the many types of standing and hanging containers (some of which were mentioned in the previous chapter) has many advantages over gardening in the ground. First, you have the ability to create incredible small-space gardens that grow both bottom up and top down. They can bring a sense of intimacy and privacy to patios and porches with their cascades of blooms and foliage. With a little imagination, you can grow a large number of plants—both ornamental and edible—in a relatively small space.

Second, you do not need to contend with weeds in container gardens. Potting soils are sterile and don't have any weed seeds to germinate or weed roots to sprout. Even if you mix a commercial potting soil with your own garden topsoil to make it go further (as I do), the few weeds that do come up are easily eliminated.

Third, watering is easy if you use a watering wand—a long-handled hose extension tube with a trigger grip that allows you to poke its nozzle in between foliage and water generously at the root zone. It was the best investment I ever made when I began container gardening. If you have only a few containers, a 2-gallon watering can with a long, thin spout is helpful. Container plantings tend to dry out quickly, so if you have an abundance of

Be inspired to create vertical gardens with containers: Use a tripod of bamboo canes for a climbing rose and clematis to intertwine, and stack clay strawberry pots one atop another to form a tower for planting an assortment of herbs and vegetables.

pots, consider investing in a hose drip system (many are simple to install and very affordable) to water pots at the turn of a faucet.

Containers and hanging baskets allow you to feature both foundation plants and climbers, as mentioned throughout this book, including a plethora of annuals and perennials. For an edible bottom-up and top-down presentation, pair a container of 'Sungold' cherry tomatoes with a hanging basket of day-neutral (everbearing) strawberries such as 'Tristar'. For an ornamental bottom-up and top-down presentation, pair a container of climbing nasturtiums with a hanging basket of 'Million Bells' mini-petunias (botanically known as *Calibrachoa*, closely related to petunias). Try pairing a container of 'Galaxy' climbing sweet peas with trailing verbena in an elevated dish planter.

When choosing containers, remember that a vining plant needs a stronger root system than a dwarf, low-growing plant, so the bigger the container, the more successful you are likely to be. A large container is especially necessary if you plan to grow vigorous vines loaded with produce, like pole lima beans, or need to use a trellis or support in the pot. Moreover, you must ensure that the vertical vines do not act like a sail that will tip over in a gusty wind. You can secure containers by partially burying the container in soil or by stabilizing the sides with bricks.

CASCADING PLANTS FOR VERTICAL GARDENS

Bacopa (*Bacopa* 'Snowflake')

Begonia (*Begonia boliviensis* 'Bonfire')

Coleus (*Solenostemon* 'Solaris')

Creeping Jenny (*Lysimachia nummularia*)

Creeping phlox (*Phlox subulata*)

Cup flower (*Nierembergia*)

Fan flower (*Scaevola*)

Fuchsia, weeping (*Fuchsia* hybrids)

Geranium, ivy-leaf (*Pelargonium peltatum*)

Impatiens, trailing (*Impatiens* hybrids)

Lantana (*Lantana camara*)

Lobelia (*Lobelia erinus* cultivars, Cascade Series)

Nasturtiums, vining (*Tropaeolum majus*)

Osteospermum, trailing African daisy (*Osteospermum ecklonis*)

Petunia (*Petunia* 'Purple Wave')

Petunias, mini (*Calibrachoa* 'Million Bells')

Sedum (*Sedum rupestre* 'Angelina')

Sweet potato vine (*Ipomoea batatas*)

Tickseed (*Bidens ferulifolia*, also sold as *ferulaefolia*)

Verbena, trailing (*Verbena x hybrida*)

DISH PLANTERS

Dish planters are wide, shallow containers that can accommodate a cluster of vines to drape down the sides like a curtain. These dishes are especially beautiful when placed high up on a pedestal or at the edge of a balcony. Since most dish planters are shallow, I would not use them with trellises; they are more effective when vines are allowed to spill over their sides to create a vertical column of flowers and foliage. In the following lists, a "skyscraper" plant means a vine that grows up and stands erect; a "trailing" plant means a vining plant that spreads out and arches down to create a curtain of flowers or foliage. Remember that in many containers, it's possible to include some foundation plants around the rim. For example, in a dish planter, low-growing edible plants like lettuce, parsley, and cabbage can encircle the other plants so that three tiers are featured—the skyscraper plant, the cascading plant, and the foundation plant around the edge. When using edibles, consider miniature varieties like 'Tom Thumb' lettuce and 'Gonzales' cabbage. Some excellent flowering foundation plants include alyssum, aubrieta, ornamental pepper, and 'Petite' marigolds.

TOP 10 SKYSCRAPER PLANTS

Clematis (*Clematis*)
Cup and saucer vine (*Cobaea scandens*)
Flame vine, Mexican (*Mina lobata, Ipomoea lobata*)
Gloriosa climbing lily (*Gloriosa superba*)
Moonflower (*Ipomoea alba*)
Morning glories, tall kinds (*Ipomoea purpurea*)
Nasturtiums, climbing (*Tropaeolum majus*)
Passion vine (blue is *Passiflora caerulea*, red is *P. coccinea*)
Roses, climbing (*Rosea*)
Sweet peas, tall kinds (*Lathyrus odoratus*)

TOP 10 TRAILING PLANTS

Bacopa (*Bacopa*; 'Snowflake' is one example)

Begonia (*Begonia boliviensis* 'Bonfire')

Fuchsias (*Fuchsia*)

Geranium, ivy-leaf (*Pelargonium peltatum*)

Ivy, Swedish, variegated (*Plectranthus australis*)

Lobelia (*Lobelia erinus* cultivars, Cascade Series)

Petunias, mini (*Calibrachoa* 'Million Bells')

Strawberries, day-neutral (everblooming), 'Tristar'

Tomatoes, 'Tumbling Tom'

Verbena, trailing (*Verbena* x *hybrida*)

HANGING BASKETS

Used mostly by home gardeners for hanging under the eaves bordering a patio or from metal shepherd's crooks, traditional hanging baskets are especially good for creating a column of color. Many flowering plants like climbing nasturtiums, morning glories, trailing verbena, and cascading petunias can drape around the edges of a basket to produce a curtain of flowers. Even vining cherry tomatoes, strawberries with long runners, and climbing cucumbers can be planted in baskets to drape their stems or runners from head height toward the ground. See Cascading Plants for Vertical Gardens on page 63 for my favorite plants for hanging baskets.

In general, you will find three choices of basket: wood, wire, and plastic. Wood baskets look good and have good insulation, preventing the soil from overheating on a hot day. Wire baskets are even better, because they must be lined with coco fiber or sphagnum moss to form a nest for potting soil; these liners keep the soil cool. In wire baskets, you can often plant the gaps around the sides, as well as along the top of the basket, for a fuller, more rounded look. Plastic is my least favorite basket, because it often looks cheap and does not have such good insulation. Plants in plastic baskets will dry out much more quickly than those in wood or wire baskets, so take that into consideration when choosing a hanging basket.

HAYRACK PLANTERS

I particularly like hayrack planters that can be attached to the side of a house; they present a long, troughlike cradle for massing an assortment of plants, which can even be a mix of ornamentals and edibles. Hayracks can be mounted at head height and higher and planted with long trailing plants, like variegated perennial vinca and annual sweet potato vine, that will touch the ground by midsummer. Or hayracks can be attached at windowsill height and planted with a mix of foundation plants and cascading vines. See Cascading Plants for Vertical Gardens on page 63 for the best choices for hayrack planters.

PEACH AND WICKER BASKETS

Bushel baskets used to display peaches and other fruits can be lined with plastic (punch some holes for drainage) and filled with potting soil. A bushel of soil can grow several pole bean plants with ease. Insert a trellis inside the basket or in the ground behind the basket so there will be less risk of it tipping over. For skyscraper and cascading plant choices, see the lists earlier in this chapter.

Wicker baskets make attractive containers; line them with plastic, then poke holes to allow for drainage. Plant an assortment of compact vegetables and vining pole beans.

TERRA-COTTA POTS

You cannot go wrong with terra-cotta clay pots. Their earthy color looks good anywhere, and they suit any kind of vine because they are available in all sizes, even up to 25 gallons in capacity, and in a pleasing variety of shapes. However, terra-cotta containers are breakable and are easily damaged by freezing, so you'll need to empty pots after the growing season in colder regions or move them to a frost-free location to prevent cracking. In a vertical garden, terra-cotta pots are ideal for

Both decorative and edible, these day-neutral strawberries cascade from the pockets of a strawberry planter.

creating a sense of height on stair steps, nestled in with bedding plants, or displayed on a tiered plant shelf. For skyscraper and cascading plant choices, see the lists earlier in this chapter.

URNS

Urns can be made of clay, concrete, or metal, and they can be plain or fancy. The fancy metal urns can look ostentatious, but simple urns can look good on pedestals, with their plants draping down the sides like a curtain.

Urns add a higher level of sophistication to a garden than other containers, not only in their often ornate design, but also because they provide sufficient room for you to choose weeping woody plants—like weeping forsythia or even a weeping bonsai spruce. Since urns can be large, consider growing one of my top choices for spectacular weeping plants (see below).

Urns can be used as matching pairs on pedestals at the entrance to a property to create height and a sense of grandeur. An appropriate single urn on a pedestal can help create an ethnic theme in a French, Italian, Chinese, or Japanese garden, as well. French urns tend to be decorated with fleurs de lis, nymphs, and garlands; Italian urns tend to be bronze, show figures from Greek and Roman mythology like Bacchus and Medusa, and include elaborate handles in the form of snakes and breaching dolphins. Many Chinese urns feature blue and white designs of willow trees—a favorite of the French artist Claude Monet—and of tall bamboo as a vertical accent. A Japanese urn may be shaped like a bonsai dish and have Japanese word characters and depictions of bonsai trees as decorations. For skyscraper and cascading plant choices to use in urns, see the lists earlier in this chapter.

TOP 5 WEEPING PLANTS FOR URNS

Beautybush, weeping (*Kolkwitzia amabilis* 'Dream Catcher')

Butterfly bush, weeping (*Buddleja lindleyana*)

Curry plant (*Helichrysum petiolare*)

Ninebark, weeping (*Physocarpus opulifolius* 'Seward', 'Summer Wine')

Willow, dappled (*Salix integra* 'Hakuro Nashiki')

VERSAILLES PLANTERS

Versailles planters are box-shaped containers on casters so they can be moved about easily. They were first used at Versailles Palace in France to grow orange trees and palms. They used to be painted gray or green, but you can now buy them in just about any color, including blue and white. Because the square shape helps to stabilize the container, tall trellises can be used in them to grow heavy vines, such as wisteria and climbing roses. Versailles planters are especially good to use as sentinels at the entrance to a house or a garden. For sentinel plantings, consider standards—woody plants in tree form—with a slender trunk and topknot of leaves or flowers. See my choices for these foundation standards below. They can be expensive, but they are a sensational way to say "Welcome" when located on both sides of a front entrance. For cascading plant choices to pair with standards, see the list earlier in this chapter.

TOP FOUNDATION PLANTS FOR VERSAILLES PLANTERS

Bay laurel standard (*Laurus nobilis*)

Butterfly bush standard (*Buddleja*)

Coleus standard (*Solenostemon*)

Fuchsia standard (*Fuchsia*)

Geranium standard (*Pelargonium peltatum*)

Hibiscus standard, both hardy and tropical (*Hibiscus*)

Mandevilla standard (*Mandevilla*)

Marguerite daisy standard (*Chrysanthemum leucanthemum*) or (*Argyranthemum*)

Rose standard (*Rosa*, everblooming 'Scarlet Meidiland')

WINDOW BOX PLANTERS

Long, narrow window box containers are not only useful for decorating a window ledge; they are also terrific for placing on balconies, along railings, or around the edges of a patio, pool, or deck. The larger, heavier window box planters can be fitted with trellises for vines to climb up; everblooming annuals such as sweet peas and morning glories are good plant choices. A window box planter can also be placed at the foot of a vine and planted with low-growing plants like lettuces or marigolds. Window box planters are especially useful for decorating the entire width of a window. Because they are longer than they are wide, you can feature a much wider assortment of plants in them than in other types of containers. Try growing skyscraper plants, foundation plants, and cascading plants for a dramatic, multilayered planting. For skyscraper and cascading plant choices, see the lists earlier in this chapter.

Composting

6

One of the benefits of vertical gardening is that you can use less compost on a smaller garden area, applying it generously to make a thick, highly nutritious layer. When you're working with a traditional horizontal garden, you're often inclined to spread too thin a layer of compost in order to cover a large area with the amount of compost you have.

The term *compost* can be misleading. To most gardeners it means the end product of a compost pile, and since most compost piles are made from various organic ingredients, such as grass clippings, shredded leaves, kitchen waste, and wood ashes, the result is a nutritious, dark brown, crumbly substance called humus that plant roots can penetrate easily. In such a mix you'll find three essential plant nutrients: nitrogen for healthy foliage, phosphorus for healthy roots and flower initiation, and potassium (or potash) for overall vigor and disease resistance. You'll also find a number of micronutrients, such as calcium, and a healthy population of beneficial microorganisms that continue working to turn a depleted soil into a rich one.

Compost, however, can also mean the by-product of a single organic ingredient. Stable manure compost, for example, is generally high in nitrogen; cottonseed meal is also high in nitrogen; bonemeal is high in phosphorus; and greensand, an olive-green sandstone that was originally part of the ocean floor, is high in potassium. Compost from these single sources is

COMPOSTING

usually sold in packages or bags at garden centers, but individually they do not necessarily make a balanced nutrient mix. You can combine these ingredients to add the three major plant nutrients (nitrogen, phosphorus, and potassium) to your soil, or you can add ingredients to a compost pile of mixed ingredients, where they will form a potent soil conditioner and general purpose fertilizer.

HOT AND COLD COMPOST

There are many ways to make homemade compost. You can make it in a compost heap or in a compost bin that you build yourself or buy commercially. There's a "hot" method of composting and a "cold" method. Hot composting is the preferred method for vegetable and flower gardens, because it allows the heap to generate high temperatures that are sufficient to kill harmful weed seeds and disease organisms. High heat also speeds decomposition. To achieve hot composting in a compost bin or pile, you add the ingredients in layers; for example, you add a layer of shredded leaves, then a layer of kitchen waste, a layer of grass clippings, a layer of sawdust, a layer of wood ashes, and so on. The most efficient compost piles have both "brown" and "green" ingredients; the browns are usually plant materials like straw, dry leaves, and pine needles, and the greens are

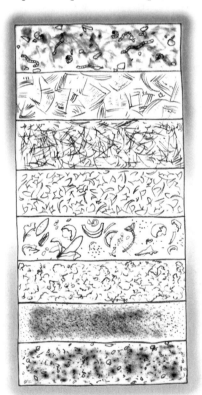

A cross section of a layered compost pile shows how different organic ingredients are piled in order to generate heat for fast, efficient decomposition.

usually moist like kitchen scraps, grass clippings, and spoiled fruit. Moisture and aeration also help a compost pile heat up, so try to fluff and turn the pile regularly. Steam rising from the heap indicates that hot decomposition is taking place.

Cold composting usually occurs when the ingredients are added to a compost bin or pile without any attempt at layering. Given time, the ingredients break down into humus—the nutritious, crumbly substance resembling soil. A cold pile may generate some heat, but not the high temperatures of a layered compost pile. In both the hot and cold processes, the ratio of fresh green material (which is high in nitrogen) to dried material is important. I consider a one-half brown to one-half green ratio ideal, but other gardeners find that a two-thirds brown to one-third green ratio works fine. Usually a compost pile will fail to heat if it has inadequate green material; if you don't have enough green material, try adding an activator that's rich in nitrogen, such as rotted manure, blood meal, or alfalfa meal. However, do not use pet manure like dog or cat droppings, as these ingredients can contain parasitic worms harmful to humans.

Earthworms and Compost

Of all the beneficial organisms present in healthy soil, one of the most important is the earthworm. Most cultivated soils already contain earthworms, although they're more plentiful in rich soils. If you make sure your compost pile contains plenty of kitchen waste—such as potato peelings, spoiled vegetables, overripe fruit, stale bread, banana peels, eggshells, and even shredded newspapers—earthworms will enter from the indigenous soil and create a population explosion.

Earthworms will eat the decaying organic matter, pass it through their bodies, and expel it as waste far more nutritious than what they ingested. Furthermore, what earthworms do on a scale you can observe, microorganisms (such as beneficial bacteria) can also do on a scale that is invisible.

Compost Tea

Except for carnivorous plants, most plants can absorb nutrients only in soluble form. So it's not surprising that growers of giant vegetables generally have special formulas for compost tea—formulas that they typically keep secret. When you see giant pumpkins that weigh more than 1,000 pounds at the Ohio State Fair or 100-pound cabbages at the Alaska State Fair, it's not just the variety of vegetable the grower selected that's responsible for these whoppers. A key to this phenomenal growth is usually an organically rich soil and the use of compost tea. The secret ingredient in an Ohio friend's garden is buffalo manure from a local farm. For another friend in Alaska, it's fish and crab waste. Yet another friend, in New Zealand, uses

Derek's No-Longer-Secret Compost Tea

Crushed eggshells

Fish bones (very important)

Kitchen waste

Stable manure

Wood ashes

Combine eggshells, bones, kitchen waste, manure, and ashes in a compost bin and allow to rot down until dark and fluffy with a yeasty aroma. From the bottom of the bin, extract three bucketsful of finished or partially finished compost and empty it into a trash barrel. Fill the barrel with warm water and allow it to steep for 3 days. Stir and pour the brown, soupy liquid into a 2-gallon watering can and apply it directly to the root zone of plants. Stir the liquid before each application. When you reach the bottom of the barrel, empty the slurry onto your compost pile or use it as a mulch around plants.

Note: I obtain the fish bones for this recipe from fishmongers or from walking the shorelines of rivers, lakes, and the sea. You can also save fish bones from seafood meals and the peelings from shrimp.

"daggy" wool (discarded sheepskins, such as bobbed tails) from a local sheep station.

I'm happy to share the recipe for my own compost tea, which is responsible for my high yields of produce, such as 500 'King of the Garden' lima beans from a single vine, 3-pound 'Supersteak' tomato fruits, and 2-foot-wide 'Simpson Elite' lettuce. This tea is a powerhouse of energy that flower and vegetable roots can absorb quickly. I apply this to the root zone of my vegetable plants once a week for best results.

NONLAYERED METHOD OF COMPOSTING

If all that compost bin layering and turning and mixing in additives sounds like a lot of work, don't worry. You can still make excellent compost by simply dumping waste material haphazardly into a heap and letting nature take its course. Decomposition will still occur; it just takes a little longer. This nonlayering system is the one used by most people to compost in situ (in place). Composting in situ works especially well if you create a raised bed of wooden boards, landscape ties, or stones so the ingredients stay contained.

If you do not layer your ingredients, simply try to ensure you make your compost pile from as many waste products as possible. For example, the average homeowner has little problem acquiring kitchen waste, shredded leaves, grass clippings, and wood ashes. It's even better if you can add a manageable amount of stable manure (many stables are only too pleased to share their excess manure). Dairies, chicken farms, and pig farms also are potential sources for manure. If the manure is still fresh and steaming when you receive it, you need to set it aside to let it decompose a bit before adding it to a nonlayered compost pile. If you have no place to allow the manure to "mature" separately, then simply add it over the entire heap, and it will eventually break down into a brown, crumbly, clean, fluffy soil-like texture. Cover fresh manure with a tarp if it might offend neighbors, or quickly add a cap of grass clippings or shredded leaves to contain the odor.

SHEET COMPOSTING

Another type of in situ composting is called sheet composting. It is a perfect alternative if you are unable to dig your soil or you find it difficult or inconvenient to cart compost from a compost heap to your planting beds. In truth, it's a legitimate method of growing for all gardeners. Even though I mostly make compost in heaps for spreading in beds in spring and fall, I also have several sites where I grow plants directly in the compost.

Sheet composting works especially well when you have an abundance of shredded leaves, which can nourish vegetables that are greedy feeders. When leaves break down, they create a nutrient-rich compost called leaf mold that's soft and crumbly. Try growing pumpkins, melons, edible gourds, large winter squash (such as orange 'Boston Marrow' and blue 'Jarrahdale'), and large fruiting tomatoes like 'Beefsteaks' in this way, and you'll be amazed at their stellar growth.

The most impressive sheet composting I have ever seen was in the historic Chelsea Physic Garden in London, where three roomy, square, slatted compost bins were growing tomatoes, pole beans, and potatoes. The tomato and pole bean bins each had a tripod to which the plants were staked to keep the fruit and pods clean. Each bin was about 4 feet square × 4 feet high, allowing for good drainage and plenty of room for root development. The 4-foot height was what I found most impressive; in my own garden I've found that large yields are possible in a 2-foot depth of pure compost, so imagine what a 4-foot depth would yield.

HOMEMADE COMPOST BINS

Lots of organic gardeners simply pile their organic waste in a heap and allow it to decompose naturally. But I like a garden to be tidy, so I've made different bins to meet my needs. Homemade compost bins are easy to construct, and there are many commercial bins that may be suited for your garden space and conditions, too. When it comes to compost, you can never

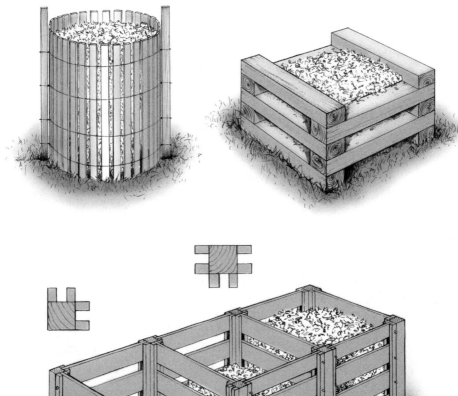

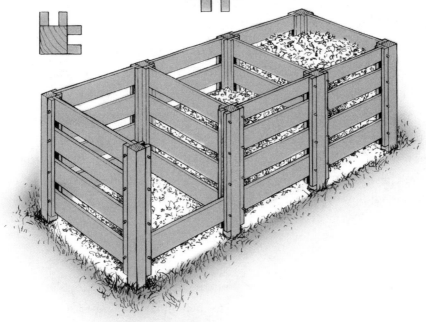

These three kinds of compost bins are ideally suited for making compost for vertical gardens: a cylinder made from slatted snow fencing; a square bin made from interlocking landscape ties; and a three-compartment compost bin I designed for CedarStore.com.

make too much, since even a small garden space can consume large amounts of compost. Your soil needs constant replenishment, because Mother Nature continues to break down organic matter, and even light rainfalls can wash away soil nutrients.

The most efficient bin systems use three compartments. Three compartments are better than one, because one compartment can contain finished compost, the second can contain compost in the process of decomposition, and the third can be a pile of fresh compost ingredients. A three-bin system allows you to have usable compost on a continuous basis: When one compartment of compost is used up, a new pile is started in its place, so you always have three piles in different stages of decomposition.

Cinder Block Bins

Cinder blocks can be costly and unsightly, but they will make a sturdy, rot-resistant enclosure for making compost. To create a stable base for a cinder block bin, it is best to build it on a foundation of crushed stone. To allow for adequate air circulation in a cinder block bin, lay the cinder blocks so the holes face sideways, rather than up and down. To allow earthworms to move up through the crushed stone into the compost, I make the crushed stone layer no more than 2 inches thick, just enough to give the cinder blocks stability.

Wire Bins

For a roomy and movable compost bin, bend and roll a rectangular section of chicken wire or builder's wire to form an upright cylinder shape. Cylindrical bins are especially ideal for fallen leaves, because unshredded leaves can take up quite a bit of room in an all-purpose compost pile and can delay decomposition. When it's time to turn the pile of leaves, just lift off the cylinder, set it next to the pile, and shovel or fork the decomposing leaves (leaf mold) back into the cylinder for a few more weeks of decomposition.

You can also join panels of wire mesh fencing to create a three- or four-sided compost bin, tying the panels together with wire, twine, or plastic ties. This type of bin allows for generous air circulation.

Wooden Bins

Wooden compost bins can be made from 2 × 4 lumber or from straight sections of tree trunks such as juniper; you can join or stack these wood lengths to create a bin. Allow gaps between the cross members for aeration. You can also make an inexpensive compost bin from wooden pallets, often available free from local businesses such as garden centers. Three upended pallets can form the sides, with the front left open for access to the pile. Some gardeners use a pallet for the floor, but I find that a wooden pallet soon rots under the weight of moist compost; in any case, I like earthworms and soil bacteria to be able to enter the heap without restriction.

COMMERCIAL COMPOST BINS

Commercial compost bins are quite attractive and can have features like lids, wheels, and handles to tumble the contents. Go online and read reviews to find the bin that's right for your garden and your budget. The following three types of bins offer a good mix of looks, quality, and price.

Many commercial compost bins are made from durable plastic; just open the top of the bin to add organic waste material, then lift the bottom panels to extract finished compost.

This three-compartment compost bin is used at Cedaridge Farm. The bins hold finished compost, compost in the process of decomposition, and a new heap for a continuous supply.

Compost Tumbler

The compost tumbler consists of a barrel-shaped drum on legs. A crank handle or indented grooves allow the drum to be rotated daily or weekly, depending on how often compost material is added. The benefit of tumbling compost is speedy decomposition. Useful compost made in a tumbler can be ready within a month during the hot summer months. The ComposTumbler unit was invented by an Australian home gardener and is used worldwide for fast, efficient composting. Go to compostumbler.com for more information.

Renoir's Three-Compartment Compost Bin

After making a study of commercially available compost bins, I realized that most commercial units are for small-scale composting. But if you want a continuous supply of compost, you would have to purchase three units: one for finished compost, one for the process of decomposing, and one for starting compost. So I devised an alternative three-compartment compost bin that I use at Cedaridge Farm. I first saw this type of three-compartment compost bin used in the master painter Pierre-Auguste Renoir's garden in the south of France, and was inspired by its removable wooden slats that give access to the three heaps from the front or back. This unit is now available from the Cedar Store, Gibsonia, Pennsylvania, as one of a series of structures inspired by Impressionist painters (cedarstore.com).

BlueStone Master Composter

The BlueStone Master Composter is essentially a square-shaped, lidded black bin that's assembled by locking together four sides. It features a folding door at the bottom of one side for the removal of finished compost. It's 2 feet square at the base and 3 feet tall, so it's easily tucked into a corner of the garden to be unobtrusive. Yet it's capable of making a generous amount of compost. The tight construction keeps out larger foraging animals, such as raccoons. Visit bluestonegarden.com for more details. Presently retailing for $50, it's the least expensive compost bin I've seen.

Even though I have a three-compartment compost bin, I still have a compost bin like the BlueStone next to it. I make a special compost in this bin for my most treasured plants, like my sugar snap peas and lima beans. I'm more careful with what I put into this bin, more precisely measuring out generous amounts of wood ashes, shredded leaves, and kitchen waste, and—most importantly—combining it all with coffee grounds obtained from my local Starbucks coffeehouse. (Starbucks has a policy of donating its coffee grounds to home gardeners on a first-come basis.) The coffee grounds are free of soil-borne disease organisms, and when mixed with other compost ingredients in a compost pile, help to create a perfect consistency for finished compost. Just a note about coffee grounds: Do not use coffee grounds in the garden without first mixing them with soil or compost; I've found that when used alone, the grounds can inhibit seed germination. I pamper my sugar snap peas and lima beans with this special compost because I believe it helps to give them extra energy to fill their pods and deliver their best flavor.

Seed Starting
and Propagating

7

There are few pleasures in life that can match the satisfaction you feel at planting a tiny seed and being responsible for its germination, maturity, and fruitfulness. With many woody plants—especially vines—there is also endless pleasure to be gained from propagating a new plant by root division, cuttings, soil layering, and—miracle of all nature's miracles—air layering.

The key to a vertical garden is growing the variety of plants that have climbing tendencies, and a large number of these climbing plants can be grown from seed. In fact, for most annuals and vegetables, seed starting is the best way to grow new plants, not only because packets of seed containing dozens, even hundreds, of seeds can be purchased for the cost of a single nursery-grown potted transplant, but also because many climbing vegetables—such as climbing spinach, climbing 'Trombone' zucchini, and vegetable spaghetti—are almost impossible to find as transplants at local garden centers. New varieties are especially difficult to find as transplants, since it can take a long time for garden centers to feel sufficiently confident of public demand to offer them.

Seed is inexpensive, and its germination is likely if you purchase it from a reliable source and use it by the date stamped on its package. If you are unsure about a seed source, search the Internet for information about the company and check for any complaints regarding germination percentages. I never worry about a few complaints, because it's impossible to satisfy all people, but if there are a lot of complaints about seed not being viable, then it may be best to buy elsewhere.

Of course, certain problems can cause poor germination even if the seed is viable. Soil diseases like damping off can kill seedlings as soon as they emerge, making them keel over at the soil line and die. Hidden in soil are many potential spoilers like cutworms that will eat the sprouted seed before it even emerges from the soil and also after the sprouts break through the surface. Slugs and snails can deplete a sowing of germinating seed as soon as the first leaves emerge, and a period of cold, damp weather can cause seeds to rot before they even have a chance to sprout. Peas and beans are especially vulnerable to cold, damp conditions.

PREGERMINATING SEED

When planting seed that is prone to rotting (like peas and beans) or seed that could use a head start in the growing season, I like to pregerminate half the packet and save the other as insurance. This easy procedure is called chitting and does not even involve potting soil. Simply moisten a thin layer of paper napkins, arrange half the seeds on it, and cover lightly with another damp napkin. Kept moist with misting, the seed coats will split, each sending out a root and a pair of cotyledons (first leaves). For a head start, these pregerminated seeds can be taken to the garden and planted with the leaves poking through the soil. I even practice chitting with some ornamentals—especially morning glories, sweet peas, and nasturtiums.

DIRECT SEEDING

Some plants, such as pole beans, prefer to be direct-seeded into the garden bed, as they resent any kind of root disturbance. When direct seeding, a rule of thumb is to plant the seed at a depth equal to three times its size, but always check the seed envelope for information. Since most pole bean seeds are about ⅓ inch long, they should be planted at a depth of 1 inch. At the other extreme, tiny seeds like lettuce and carrot are so small they will blow away if you even breathe on them. This type of seed needs planting with just enough soil covering to anchor it. Large seeds like pole beans are easy to space at correct distances (for example, 6 to 12 inches apart). Small seeds are more difficult, so when I direct-seed small seeds, I prefer to scatter them thinly in a broad row. Some thinning will be necessary later in order to prevent plants from crowding each other and preventing full development. This is especially important when growing carrots, turnips, and lettuce.

When you're gardening vertically, it pays to take extra care in preparing seed beds for direct seeding. I like to create rows at least 2 feet wide, slightly raised above the indigenous soil level to aid drainage. I smooth the top of the bed flat with the back of a rake and ensure that the bed surface is weed free.

For large seeds like pole beans, I use a hoe to create a furrow and then sow the seeds into the furrow. For melon seeds, I plant them in groups: I use a hand trowel to make a depression, then I sow four or five seeds, later thinning them to the healthiest seedlings. For fine seeds like carrot and lettuce, I sow seeds on top of the soil surface and dust a fine layer of screened soil over them, just enough to anchor the seed. This thin layer helps prevent crusting of the soil surface, which can prevent seedlings from poking through. And, even if rain is predicted, I water all direct-sown seeds.

POTTING SOILS

A healthy potting soil is as vital to seeds and transplants as water is. Ready-made sterile potting soils are available from garden centers and will give you good results, but I find that making my own potting soil is rewarding—and free! I combine equal amounts of baked garden topsoil (see directions below) and coffee grounds from Starbucks to create an excellent home-made potting soil.

If you plan to start seeds indoors in pots saved from a previous year, be sure to thoroughly wash the pots with bleach and rinse them well before reusing them. Grains of soil from a previous planting can contain fungus diseases like damping off.

If you plan to use garden topsoil for starting seedlings, you must bake it first to kill all harmful soil organisms. Spread the topsoil in a disposable aluminum turkey roasting pan and bake at 450°F for 40 minutes. I will even bake bigger batches of garden soil outdoors in a cauldron over a burn pile, for special disease-free planting beds when I'm planning to grow disease-prone sweet peas.

SEED STARTING

Even with varieties that can be direct-seeded, I prefer to start some seeds indoors in order to have transplants ready to go into the ground extra early. This is always a good idea for pole lima beans, since they are at high risk for rot if cold weather and heavy rains follow planting. With a large seed like a lima bean, I simply plant one seed in a transplant pot (usually a peat pot). At transplant time, I carefully peel away the peat bottom to release the roots with as little disturbance as possible and plant the seedling in a vertical gardening bed. This two-step seed starting can advance harvests by up to 2 weeks compared with direct seeding.

Garden centers are full of high-quality seed starting supplies that can make seed starting tidy and streamlined, but I prefer to reuse materials I already have at home. I find discarded food packages such as yogurt packs and cardboard milk cartons ideal for growing tomato, squash, and pepper transplants. The depth of a pint or quart capacity milk carton allows for a vigorous root system to develop, and the cardboard sides are easily removed at transplant time. Before transferring frost-sensitive plants to the garden, be sure to harden them off by placing them outdoors for 5 days in a coldframe or a box that you can cover with a lid during the night to keep the temperature more consistent.

Many small-seeded varieties, like lettuce and impatiens, prefer to be sown in a seed tray filled with potting soil, then transferred to individual pots after they are large enough to handle. When the roots fill the pot, creating a rootball, the plant is ready to transplant. This is a three-step method of seed starting. Again, garden centers sell seed trays for this

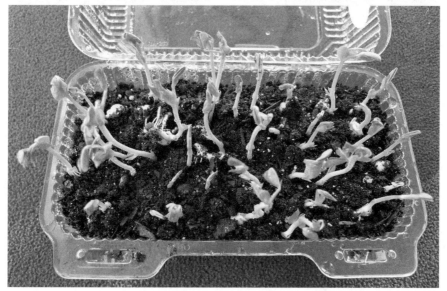

Recycled plastic bubble containers (like those used for strawberries) make great mini greenhouses for seedlings; just close the clear plastic lid to trap humidity and prevent moisture loss. Within a week, these pea seeds germinated and were ready to be transplanted in the garden.

purpose, but I prefer to use empty clamshell-style plastic food containers like those used for strawberries and bakery goods. These clamshell containers have clear plastic lids (with slotted air holes) that can be closed to create a moist, humid environment that seeds relish. The smallest seeds will germinate at a high percentage rate. As soon as they are large enough to handle, I use a pointed pencil to tease the seedlings out of the container, and then I plant them in individual transplant pots with as much potting soil attached to their roots as possible. Three or four weeks in the transplant pot can be enough to produce a healthy transplant that's ready for the garden. I err on the side of planting the rootball slightly below the soil surface outdoors; if the rootball sticks up and is exposed (or even if it's level with the top of the soil), it can quickly suffer from dehydration.

A special commercial electric heating pad is a useful accessory for starting seeds. These flat, water-repellent pads provide bottom heat to seed-starting pots and trays. Seeds—especially warm season crops that need a high temperature to germinate, and many woody vines—respond well to bottom heat.

WATERING SEEDLINGS

When watering seed trays or homemade seed containers, use a spray bottle to spray potting soils with a fine, gentle mist. Any cleaner spray bottle rinsed of its contents will do. In bright light, potting soils can dry out quickly, so cover seed trays or seed containers with a clear plastic lid or clear plastic wrap stretched across the top above the soil surface, and check for moistness daily. Do not use a watering can to water seed trays or small seedlings, as the water flow can disrupt the soil, delay germination, and uproot seedlings.

Lukewarm water is best for both seed trays and transplants. Avoid water direct from a well for watering seedlings, as this can be icy cold and shock them. If you're experiencing cold temperatures and need to water seedlings, be aware that rain barrel water can also be freezing cold. Fill a spray bottle and let the water come to room temperature first.

STRETCHED SEEDLINGS

Be sure that your seedlings receive enough light when grown indoors. Seedlings that must stretch toward the sun become stressed and can take a long time to recover when transplanted. (Stretching will also occur when a seedling becomes rootbound.) Don't place seedlings in a position where they must stretch toward a light source, such as in a kitchen window. When starting seeds in a window or on a table near the window, elevate the pot or seed tray so it is above the windowsill and place a reflector (aluminum foil over a shirt cardboard will do) opposite the window so that there is all-around light. If you cannot provide good all-around light, consider the use of a grow light, such as a fluorescent shop light.

HARDENING OFF

Before you transfer seedlings to the garden, harden them off in a cold-frame. Hardening off means toughening up your plants for outdoor growing conditions by exposing them little by little to outdoor temperatures, light, and wind conditions.

You have many options for hardening off. You can leave seedlings (in their trays or containers) outdoors for 1 hour on the first day, then 2 hours on the second day, then a full morning until they are accustomed to your garden conditions. You can also harden off seedlings in an inexpensive assemble-it-yourself coldframe. Or you can make your own coldframe by using a plastic storage box or a wooden crate and a pane of glass. Cover the box with its lid or the wooden crate with the glass at night and remove it during the day, or the coldframe may cook the seedlings. Another option for hardening off seedlings is to place them in an unheated garage or an unheated closed-in porch during the night.

TRANSPLANTING

Transplanting is easy as long as you know the basics. First, know your weather conditions. When you transplant seedlings, be sure you know whether the variety you're planting is tolerant of light frosts or susceptible to frost damage. Cool season plants tend to be tolerant of light frosts and therefore can be planted out several weeks before your expected frost date; for more on frost dates, see Hardiness Zones on page 22. Warm season plants tend to be frost sensitive; therefore, transplants should not be set into the garden until frost danger is past. If possible, it's best to transplant on a cloudy day or during cooler evening hours, so the transplants have a little time to get acclimated.

Second, dig the planting hole slightly wider than the seedling container, but keep it at the same depth. The exception is for tomatoes, which should be planted deeper so roots form along their stems.

Third, always handle transplants carefully, because root disturbance can cause stress. If your transplants are in plastic pots or recycled containers, gently turn the pot or container on its side (or upside down, if necessary) and slide out the plant—soil, rootball, and all. If the soil seems trapped in the container, gently tap the bottom of the pot until it releases. Always support seedlings and transplants with your hand when removing them from pots. When transplanting from peat pots, I prefer to remove the peat pot, since the peat can take too much time to decompose and can restrict plant roots.

Fourth, water transplants daily.

When planting seedlings or plants against a trellis or netting in a vertical garden, plant as close as possible to the support and guide the lead shoot toward the support as it grows, using plant ties when necessary.

Seedlings and transplants are vulnerable to pests right from the start. Grubs and cutworms in the soil emerge at night and can eat young transplants. You can deter them by sprinkling wood ashes around and over young leaves. Another way to protect seedlings is to give them a collar, made from an overturned plastic or paper drinking cup. Make a slit up one side of the cup, cut out the cup's bottom, then push the cup into the soil up to the rim to create a barrier around the transplant. For the seedling stage, you can also take the precaution of repelling insect pests like aphids and slugs by dusting plants with diatomaceous earth or spraying with an insecticidal soap solution. Plants raised off the ground in pots of commercial potting soil usually will not need this treatment. See the Controlling Pests and Diseases chapter on page 103 for more information.

TYPES OF SEED

Everyone knows what a seed does—you plant it, water it to break dormancy, and it will grow. A seed is actually a plant embryo with its own supply of nutrients surrounded by a protective skin. Seeds come in all shapes, colors, and sizes, but you can't tell if they're viable simply by looking at them. That's why it's important to buy your seeds from a reliable source. When seeds are kept cool and dry, they can have a shelf life of 1 year to several years to several hundred years or more (as proven by archaeological excavations). You'll find that you can buy (or trade) different types of seed, ranging from open-pollinated standard varieties (such as heirlooms) to hybrids, patented, or genetically modified varieties. It's important to know the differences among them, especially if you plan on saving your own seed from one season to the next.

Open-Pollinated or Standard Seed

Open-pollinated seed is produced by natural means, such as when bees or wind transfer pollen from one flower to another. It is seed that will grow true to type from one generation to the next, allowing you to save the seed with confidence. Some open-pollinated varieties have patent protection and are identified by the initials PVP for Plant Variety Protection (see Patented Seed on page 93).

Heirloom Seed

There is a lot of confusion over what constitutes an heirloom seed. One definition says it is any variety that was in cultivation before World War II; another says it is any variety that has been in commerce more than 50 years; another claims it can be any open-pollinated variety capable of growing "true to seed" and therefore capable of being "saved." I don't agree with that last definition. I believe that for a variety to be declared an heirloom, it needs to be around for at least 50 years, since many new open-pollinated varieties prove to be disappointing and quickly fade from the marketplace.

For anyone interested in heirloom seeds, the Seed Savers Exchange is the place to start learning about and buying heirloom seeds. They publish a catalog of numerous varieties, most saved and offered to the public by dedicated gardeners and farmers. Because thousands of home gardeners thought enough of particular varieties and saved seed from them season after season, heirloom seeds are available for us to enjoy today. There are some heirloom varieties I would never want to be without. For example, the 'Big Rainbow' (also called 'Striped German') tomato is a sensational, fine-flavored, giant-fruited, yellow and red variety that I prefer to most other giant-fruited tomatoes. Similarly, I find 'King of the Garden' lima beans still among the best for high yields and large, meaty beans. You can buy these varieties on the Internet.

However, just because a variety is listed as an heirloom doesn't make it worth growing. Many heirloom fruits and vegetables have qualities we don't always treasure today—such as a short shelf life, an odd appearance, or a variable ripening timeline. Some old varieties of pole beans are fibrous or highly prone to disease compared with modern varieties, and many heirloom tomatoes take too long to reach maturity in northern gardens. 'Moon and Stars' watermelon is an interesting heirloom oddity on account of its dark green skin color and yellow spots that represent the moon and a constellation of stars; but to my taste, the pink flesh has a rather insipid flavor compared with most red-fleshed watermelons like 'Crimson Sweet'.

Hybrid Seed

Hybrid seed tends to be more expensive than standard seed (open-pollinated), because the two parent plants that make the cross must be isolated and a human workforce used to cross-pollinate hundreds—even thousands—of plants. There is a lot of misinformation published about hybrid seed, as though it is unnatural and endangers heirlooms. Some companies, as a marketing policy, do not sell hybrid or patented seed, but in my opinion that is shortsighted. It's a myth that plant hybrids are only the result of human invention. Some hybrids do occur naturally: At Cedaridge Farm, I have dozens of hybrid oaks—white oaks that have crossed with red oaks, and pin oaks that have crossed with scarlet oaks.

The use of hybrid seed is an organically approved way of ensuring higher yields and disease resistance, since hybrids tend to be more vigorous than standard varieties. Seedless watermelon hybrids, for example, have more flavor than standard watermelons, because the energy that would have been used to produce seed goes into producing a tastier fruit. 'Gypsy Hybrid' pepper has greater cold tolerance than standard peppers, and a hybrid tomato like 'Better Boy' will outyield any standard variety and possesses disease resistance. Because hybrids are capable of extraordinary yields, the soil must be sufficiently fertile to attain the desired increase in size or quantity. A common problem with watermelon hybrids, for example, is that the center of the fruit can become hollow when grown in unsuitable soil or with an imbalance of nutrients or moisture.

Hybrids have one major drawback: The seeds saved from them may be sterile or may not grow true to their original variety.

It is important to understand that hybrid seed is not the same as genetically modified seed (commonly called GMO seed; the GMO stands for Genetically Modified Organism). Genetic engineering takes desirable genes from an animal, plant, bacteria, or virus and transfers them into another organism (in this case, a plant or seed) to achieve any number of desirable characteristics (in a plant or seed, these could be disease resistance or cold tolerance). GMO seed causes concern to many people in the organic and gardening communities (some of whom refer to feed seed as Frankenfood), because the long-term effects of GMOs to human health are not known— especially of varieties that have insecticidal properties.

Patented Seed

In recent years, the government has granted patents to unique open-pollinated varieties as an incentive to their breeders. Rather like an author collecting royalties on sales of a book, the breeder of a unique open-pollinated (nonhybrid) variety can now collect royalties on sales of his or her seed. You can save seed from patented varieties and plant them for your own use, but it is unlawful to sell the seed or the product of it without payment of a royalty to the breeder.

A hybrid, on the other hand, cannot be patented. That is because only the breeder knows the lineage that produced the result, and so hybrids offer their own built-in protection for the breeder. However, when a cross is extremely successful—for example, in the case of 'Burpee's Hybrid' cantaloupe—other breeders will make a guess at the parents and try to achieve the same or a similar result.

I asked a breeder of some patented open-pollinated varieties why he would even bother breeding hybrids, since their production was so much more expensive, and he could make as much money breeding open-pollinated varieties. He replied that there would always be a demand for hybrids: because of their superior performance, because quality is remembered long after price is forgotten, and because few open-pollinated varieties could yield as much as a hybrid.

HARDINESS ZONES

Hardiness zones are like climate predictions for how plants will perform in your garden. The USDA has published a hardiness zone map showing North America divided into 11 hardiness zones. Zone 1 includes Alaska, and Zone 11 includes Key West, Florida. The color-coded map shows the first and last frost dates for your area, so you can calculate how many frost-free days to expect during a growing season. While the overall map is highly researched, its zones are not very useful to the home gardener on a specific site. They don't, and can't, take into account the fact that a property can have a microclimate: A large body of water like a river or lake, or a big hill or mountain, for example, can create warmer or cooler conditions than the general zone map can predict. Within a garden or landscape, there also can be several warm spots, such as the south-facing wall along a house foundation or a sheltered courtyard. To determine which plants may do best in your hardiness zone, it is best to consult with your local Cooperative Extension Service or to visit a local garden center or nursery, to ask qualified personnel to guide you to seeds and plants that work in your particular climate or microclimate.

Even when you've chosen plants that work well in your zone and climate, you'll need to pay attention to the weather forecast in spring and fall. For example, when you've passed your average last frost date in spring and planted out some tender plants, you may need to cover susceptible crops if the temperature dips. Similarly, in fall, you may need to gather all your tender dahlias, gladioli, peppers, and tomatoes for taking indoors in case of frost. In the case of summer-flowering bulbs like dahlias and gladioli, be aware that frost may kill the green topgrowth and flowers, but the bulbs themselves will remain safe until a hard freeze—so you can delay for a few more weeks lifting the bulbs for storage indoors.

METHODS OF PROPAGATION

When you make new plants from existing ones, you are practicing propagation. Most propagation methods used by home gardeners are easy and require only basic gardening tools. Propagation is an inexpensive way to fill your garden with new plants, rather than buying plants at nurseries or garden centers. (Planting a seed is also considered a method of propagation—usually the easiest one!) To propagate new plants, you can divide plants, take cuttings, and try layering.

Division

Frequently the best way to produce more perennial or woody plants is to divide a plant's roots. Most plant roots grow sideways, forming a clump that can be safely divided after the third year. Sometimes the mature rootball must be dug up and divided, using a spade or garden fork, to create new full-size plants that can be planted right back into the garden. Other times you can see clumps of divisions sprouting around the outer edges of the mother plant, and it's easier to simply take a spade and dig up one of the small divisions. A trumpet vine, for example, will often send up young sprouts several feet from the mother plant, each one capable of being dug to produce a new vine. Usually it's best to divide in the spring, but many plants can be divided in summer or fall, even after the topgrowth goes dormant.

Stem Cuttings

A cutting is a piece of leaf, stem, or root that is separated from the parent plant and used to create a new plant. Many plants reproduce from cuttings, especially woody plants and perennials; a few annuals, like tomatoes, can also be grown from cuttings. Some plants, like Swedish ivy, are so easy to grow from cuttings that you can just take any stem section with a leaf node and root it in a glass of plain water. Other plants, like vining geraniums, need a moist potting soil to root in, aided by a rooting hormone (available from garden centers).

There are three kinds of cuttings. *Softwood cuttings* are generally taken in spring at the stem tips where the new growth is green and pliable; if you bend the stem, it isn't likely to break. *Semi-hardwood cuttings* are taken in summer, lower down the stem where the wood has stiffened; if you bend the stem, it's pliable, but resists breaking. *A hardwood cutting* is usually taken in fall, when the stem section has hardened into wood and resists bending.

To successfully root cuttings, your potting soil pH (the measure of its acidity or alkalinity) can be important, since some cuttings (such as berry canes) root more successfully in an acidic soil and others (such as cacti and succulents) in an alkaline one. Rooting mediums, or soils, should be sterile. If you are using your own compost or garden topsoil, bake it in the oven in a disposable aluminum turkey roasting pan at 450°F for 40 minutes to kill all disease organisms. Or you can purchase a ready-made potting soil.

For a softwood cutting, vines are the easiest plants to try, using a peat-based potting soil. You'll generally need a 4- to 7-inch section for a cutting.

Cut just below a node and scrape the cut end of the bark for about 1 inch up the stem to aid rooting. Remove all leaves from the part of the stem that will go into the soil. I have found the best way to propagate cuttings is to use an 8-inch clay pot, and to place the cuttings 2 inches into the soil, positioned around the rim of the pot. For some reason, cuttings placed around the rim take more successfully than cuttings placed in the middle of the pot. If you are growing vines that originate in desert or seashore areas, use a sandy soil rather than a peaty one—and always use salt-free sand, not seashore sand (commercial sandy potting soils are salt free).

When propagating a semi-hardwood or hardwood cutting, you'll have greater success if a tiny portion of a side branch is included at the cut end. This is called a heel.

Position your cuttings in pots and place them in a coldframe if they were taken in fall, or in a brightly lit indoor location (but not direct sunlight) if they were taken in spring or summer. Cuttings are susceptible to sunscald, so they are best lightly shaded to get them off to a good start, even during winter and even if they are sun-loving plants in their mature state.

Softwood cuttings root faster than semi-hardwood or hardwood cuttings, but they are also more susceptible to wilt. They can take from 3 to 12 weeks to form a healthy root system.

To propagate semi-hardwood, take the cuttings in summer. For hardwood cuttings, take the cuttings in fall after frost has made the plant go dormant, and take numerous cuttings (at least a dozen) to ensure success. Make the cuttings all the same length (6 inches is ideal) and distinguish the top of the cutting from the bottom with a colored marker pen, or by using a straight cut for the top and slanted cut for the bottom. To save space, bundle a few cuttings together, then tie these bundles together and label them with the name of the plant. Bury the cuttings in a box of damp sawdust and store the box indoors in a cool dark cellar over winter, allowing the cut ends to form calluses—this usually takes 6 to 8 weeks.

As soon as the ground thaws in spring and a warming trend begins, you can bring the calloused cuttings outdoors and set the bottom ends in containers of potting soil. The best containers to use for starting cuttings are 8-inch terra-cotta pots or shallow wooden boxes used to pack citrus fruits. These containers hold adequate amounts of potting soil and are easily covered by a sheet of clear plastic to retain moisture and humidity. Space cuttings 6 to 8 inches apart in the containers. Depending on the plant, it may take 2 to 6 months for the cuttings to root and show healthy topgrowth. They can then be dug up and transferred to their permanent places in the garden.

Soil Layering

This is an easy method for propagating woody plants with long stems, such as blackberry and grape canes. Simply take a long stem, scrape away some bark tissue from the underside about 4 to 6 inches from the tip, arch it to the ground, and bury the scraped portion with about 1 to 2 inches of soil, making sure that the stem tip is poking up into the air. Then weight down the buried part of the stem with a stone or bent piece of wire. The scraped portion of the stem will develop roots. The time needed to develop roots depends on the plant. Blackberries and raspberries take a few weeks, but other plants like a kiwi vine might require a few months. When it has rooted, simply cut the new plant from its "umbilical cord," dig it up, and either place it in a pot for further development or transfer it directly into the garden.

Air Layering

Air layering is my favorite method of propagation, because it's the most fascinating. Many plants that can be soil layered can also be air layered. The traditional method of air layering is to choose a spot at least 6 inches from the tip of a stem, scrape away the bark there in at least a 1-inch-wide band around the stem, and enclose the wound in moistened sphagnum moss (available from garden centers). Then wrap that stem area and moss in a clear plastic bag and secure it with rubber bands, leaving the stem tip in the air. By looking at the wound through the clear plastic, it's possible to

There are two layering methods for propagating woody plants. Soil layering involves scraping the plant's bark, arching it to the ground, burying the scraped portion, and then anchoring the shoot to the soil so roots can form. With air layering, you scrape the bark, wrap the wound with a sponge or sphagnum moss, and enclose the area with clear plastic. Once roots develop, you cut below the root mass to release the cutting.

see when roots develop. This is especially successful with fig branches. Another trick is to wrap a moist household sponge instead of sphagnum moss around the wound, wrap the sponge in clear plastic, and secure it with a rubber band. New roots from the wound will grow into the sponge. Yet another method for air layering is to take a paper drinking cup, cut a hole in the bottom, and thread it along the stem until the cup covers the wound. Fill the cup with potting soil, close its open end with masking tape to retain the soil, and enclose the cup in clear plastic. The stem will grow roots into the soil in the cup. When you see a bundle of roots through the plastic, cut off the stem, remove the cup, and use the rooted cutting as a transplant.

Simple Lath Houses Protect New Plants

A lath house is a structure above a nursery bed that keeps seedlings and cuttings lightly shaded until they are large enough to be transplanted to their permanent positions. Even plants that like full sun when mature prefer to grow in a lightly shaded area when they are starting life. The shade prevents sunburn and also prevents the soil from drying out too quickly. The structure is called a lath house because it's traditionally built of lengths of house lath, spaced like snow fencing. Lath houses can be large or small, permanent or removable, with sides and a roof; if you haven't seen one in use, think of it as a large slatted box, some high enough that you can stand inside. It can be constructed of lath or wood slats, lengths of snow fencing, or wood lattice. The goal of the slatted design is to shade plants from harsh sun while still allowing dappled light and air circulation.

There are also commercial products called rooter pots for easy air layering. One type of rooter pot is specifically for tip cuttings. It uses a special gel with the right concentration of root hormones to encourage rooting inside a clear plastic pot. Just poke a hole through the foil seal and insert your stem tip. Another rooter pot for basic air layering is a hinged opaque plastic one that you pack with coco fiber or sphagnum moss. You then lay the stem wound onto the fiber or moss and close the pot lid; an opening in the pot lid prevents the stem from being crushed. When you see roots poke through the bottom of the pot, you cut off the rooted stem and transplant it directly into your garden.

BUYING AND TRANSPLANTING PLANTS

The majority of plants for home gardens are purchased from local nurseries, although a moderate and growing number of gardeners are buying plants by mail-order or through Internet Web sites. Buying plants from afar is a terrific way to enjoy specialty plants or find plants not available in your local nurseries. Plants shipped by mail or carrier need special attention when they arrive. They can be small, even bareroot (with the nursery soil washed off their roots), and in need of potting before ultimately transferring them to the garden. Plants supplied by mail can sometimes suffer damage, such as broken roots and stems, in transit. These broken parts should be pruned away immediately, and the entire root system should be soaked in a bucket of water overnight before planting, to allow the plant to rehydrate fully.

When buying plants from a local garden center, examine the stem area at the soil line for any signs of girdling by mice (such as chewed bark), and inspect the tender parts of the branches for any signs of insect pests like scale and aphids. If you can, slide the plant out of the container to see if it is well rooted. A well-rooted container plant will retain most of its soil when transplanted, whereas a plant that was newly potted at the garden center might lose much of its soil when it is transplanted and thus risk dehydration. After you've purchased plants and are ready to transport them home in your car or truck, either place them inside your vehicle or cover their exposed branches with a tarp or blanket to prevent windburn and leaf drop.

Once you're at your planting site, carefully slide the rootball out of the container. Take a trowel or hand fork and scrape away some of the soil from the roots, so that the root tips are exposed. This allows the roots to grow out more quickly and establish the plant in its new home. If your garden soil is good, dig a hole to accommodate the rootball. In good soil, I like to plant the rootball slightly below the indigenous soil line, leaving a ½- to 1-inch rim of soil to act as a water catchment. In poor soil (like hard clay or porous sand), dig a deeper and wider hole (a spade depth deeper and twice the width of the rootball) and backfill the bottom and sides with improved soil (preferably high in organic matter). In exposed areas where wind might rock the plant, add a sturdy stake for support.

Controlling Pests
and Diseases

8

Plants are like people: If they avoid stress, they can avoid disease. Tests worldwide, at places as diverse as the Rodale Institute in Pennsylvania, the Good Gardeners Association in the United Kingdom, and Lincoln University in New Zealand, have shown that garden plots using natural compost for nutrients were not affected as much by pests and diseases as were plots using chemical fertilizers.

For stress-free, healthy plants capable of resisting disease, you should start with good soil. Rich, friable soil allows plant roots to spread unencumbered and absorb nutrients from natural sources such as homemade compost. Mix compost into the planting bed at the start of the planting season, and then apply later side dressings of additional compost, a soil drench of compost tea, or a foliar feed using an organic foliar fertilizer.

When you start to garden vertically, you will find that insect, pest, and disease problems (such as slug damage) automatically become less serious, because your plants are up off the ground, away from where many pests and disease organisms originate. The lush growth of vigorous vines can also resist attacks by pests and disease. The use of organic pest and disease control methods—like pruning away stems infested with aphids or bean beetle larvae—is much easier in a vertical garden, because the plants are mostly growing up and allow you to more easily spot any signs of trouble.

During my many years of gardening, I have rarely used a commercial pesticide or disease control, whether organic or chemical. Like most other organic gardeners, if I spot an infestation of an insect pest (for example, black aphids invariably infect fava beans in my garden), I prune out the part of the plant that is hosting a colony of pests and destroy it. Or I dislodge the colony with a strong jet of water and then rub the stems with a cloth to remove any hard-to-see dormant eggs. If flea beetles attack my eggplants, I generally use a homemade "fiery" brew containing 1 cup each of minced garlic and hot peppers liquefied in a blender and added to 1 gallon of water. I also add 1 tablespoon of coconut oil as a sticking agent. I spritz the fiery brew on the eggplant leaves, and the flea beetles depart for a friendlier neighborhood. I have also found that a foliar feed of fish emulsion helps deter many potential insect pests. Fish emulsion is a liquid fertilizer made from by-products of the fish oil and fish meal industry. It is usually sold as a concentrate, so you should dilute it with water, then use a spray bottle to apply it to foliage. Pests simply do not like the strong fish odor. I have used milky spore powder to help control Japanese beetle larvae, sprinkling it over lawn and soil areas (about 5 ounces of powder for an area 25 feet × 25 feet) and watering it lightly so the spores soak into the soil. Milky spore is a naturally occurring bacterium that attacks Japanese beetle grubs. One application, at any time during the year when the ground is not frozen, will reduce Japanese beetle populations for up to 15 years.

Gardening can be enjoyed by everyone, whether you have a spare hour or two each weekend or you devote most of your week, like I do, to growing and enjoying a diverse landscape of plants. But, it's important for me to say that good pest and disease control takes some effort—mostly in spending time observing what's happening in your garden and then reacting quickly when you notice damaged plants or see an infestation of insect pests.

Most home gardeners do not grow their produce to sell, so they can tolerate imperfections. As an organic gardener who's devoted to keeping chemicals out of my garden, I simply discard the parts of leaves, roots, or fruit that have blemishes, and then use the good parts. Nothing goes to waste, because I put the discarded parts into a bucket to add to my compost pile.

When you garden vertically, you are often gently guiding plants to wind around structures and supports, and you are coming in close contact with flowers, fruit, and foliage, giving you a clearer view. You're bound to be more aware of insects (good bugs and bad bugs), and you'll need to determine which pose a serious threat to your thriving plants. If you do not have a good book on pest identification and can't identify the insect with online resources, your local garden center or your local Cooperative Extension Service probably will have a guide you can use as a reference. Here are a few basics to understand in order to reduce damage from insect pests and diseases.

BENEFICIAL INSECTS

First, learn to recognize beneficial insects, because they can do more to protect your garden than anything you can do yourself. Many beneficial insects arrive naturally in your garden, and they're especially attracted to gardens planted with flowering annuals. They pollinate flowering plants and dine on harmful bugs, helping to maintain a biological balance in your garden. Beneficial insects need a few basic amenities, so you'll need to provide food, water, and shelter in order to entice them into your yard. Try adding a small water source, even if it's just a refillable pan of water. Small-flowered plants provide perfect food sources, and certain herbs (such as dill, parsley, mint, hyssop, and lemon balm) can be intermingled with your flower or vegetable plants to attract beneficials where insect pests are a problem. Beneficials require a safe place to live and lay their eggs, so provide plenty of mulch, compost, straw, or leaves over bare soil and on garden beds.

Second, if you feel your garden needs a little assistance from beneficials that you can't seem to attract, you can purchase them from Internet and mail-order sources that specialize in shipping biological pest controls. Before you buy, though, it's important to accurately identify the pest you're trying to eradicate (consider ladybugs beneficial, for example, because they prey on aphids), and be sure to understand the process of storing and releasing the beneficials into your garden.

Assassin bugs are effective predators of aphids and beetles. The nymphs lie in wait of prey, feeding on whiteflies and other small insects.

Ground beetles are 1 inch long and black with a green iridescent sheen. The adults and larvae are predators of cutworms, slugs, and snails.

Hover flies average ½ inch long and look like small hovering house-flies. The females lay their eggs among aphid colonies, and the maggot larvae feed on the aphids.

Lacewing adults feed mostly on pollen and nectar, but their larvae are active predators of insect pests, using pincers to capture and devour them.

Lady beetles or ladybugs mostly eat aphids, and are so widespread that they're found from Canada to South America.

Parasitic wasps prey on the larvae of problem insects, such as moths and beetles, and target pests like cabbageworms, codling moths, and corn borers. There are both small and large types of parasitic wasps. The braconid wasp is small—usually less than ½ inch. The females inject their eggs into the bodies of aphids and other host insects, parasitizing and eventually killing them.

Praying mantises (also called preying mantids) resemble sticks, with their narrow streamlined bodies. They have prominent front claws and triangular heads, and capture all kinds of pests with their large forelegs. Their papery beige-colored egg clusters can be found attached to twigs around the garden, hatching in spring during warm, sunny weather.

Spiders prey on mites, aphids, and many other kinds of insect pests.

HOMEMADE INSECT REPELLENTS

Most of the remedies you find in home remedy books do not work or do not work to control large-scale issues. For example, I haven't found using stale beer for drowning slugs to be effective. It catches a few, but tests at Michigan

State University in a greenhouse filled with slugs confirmed my own experience—that this widely touted home remedy cannot be relied on as an effective slug control. I have both slugs and snails in my garden, and whenever I detect their presence (holes chewed through leaves or brown stains on the ribs of lettuce and rhubarb), I will rise from bed early in the morning and handpick as many as I can find, dropping them into a glass jar for disposal.

Commercially available insecticidal soaps or oils can be purchased in garden centers or from Internet and mail-order sources. They do a good job of controlling a wide range of mostly soft-bodied insects, including aphids, squash bug nymphs, leafhoppers, and thrips. However, since these commercial soaps or oils are very concentrated, it's easy to overdo it and kill the whole plant, or kill beneficial insects, too. Before using a product, read the label carefully.

Here are two general-purpose home remedies that I have found effective against the majority of insect pests: homemade insecticidal soap and insecticidal oil.

Recipe for homemade insecticidal soap: Choose any liquid dishwashing soap that does not contain a degreaser, and mix eight drops of soap with 1 gallon of water to use as a spray. This is usually sufficient to treat annuals and vegetables. For perennials, use 2 tablespoons of soap, and for woody plants, use 3 tablespoons of soap. Spray early or late in the day to avoid the sun's strongest rays, which can burn plant foliage.

Recipe for homemade insecticidal oil: Choose a light cooking oil, such as corn, soybean, peanut, or sunflower oil. Mix 1 teaspoon of oil with 1 gallon of water. Spray sparingly, because insecticidal oils can suffocate plants, and always test a small area first before applying oils to an entire planting; shake the solution frequently while spraying. Commercially, insecticidal oils are sold as horticultural oil, summer oil, or dormant oil (dormant oil should only be applied in winter or freezing weather). Apply early or late in the day when the sun isn't as bright, to avoid "burning" plant foliage. A few drops of insecticidal oil applied to the silks of corn will deter the corn earworm before it has the chance to make itself at home.

Here are a variety of ways to control insect pests and diseases.

Use a sterile soil mix. For a traditional horizontal garden, this can be expensive if you buy a commercial product. Some vendors of topsoil and mulches will sell a steam-sterilized soil in which insect larvae, disease organisms, and weed seeds have been killed. In contrast, when you garden vertically, remember you need less soil, so it may be possible for you to sterilize enough topsoil yourself by baking batches in a disposable aluminum turkey roasting pan in your kitchen oven. Simply bake at 450°F for 40 minutes.

Do a thorough winter cleanup in your garden. Delegate all garden debris to a compost pile or a burn pile. Properly made compost will heat up and kill most dormant insect eggs and disease organisms.

Practice crop rotation for vegetables. Do not grow the same family of plants in the same space 2 years in a row. Rather, split your plot up into quarters and rotate crops so they grow in the same space once every 5 years. The four major plant families are: tomatoes, peppers, potatoes, and eggplants (solanaceous crops); peas and beans (leguminous plants); cabbages (crucifers), turnips, and radishes; and other root crops like beets, parsnips, and carrots.

Use floating row covers. These are made of lightweight horticultural fabric that covers crops but admits plenty of light and water, acting as a barrier against insects and disease.

Apply seaweed concentrate or fish meal. Use fertilizer drenches of seaweed concentrate or fish meal; the odor has a repellent effect on many insects.

Avoid overhead watering. A soaker hose that applies water directly to the root zone will help to stave off fungus diseases.

Avoid using insect traps. I am not a believer in using insect traps, such as Japanese beetle traps or sticky traps or cards to trap aphids. Research shows that beetle traps can attract many additional beetles to your garden, while sticky traps can kill beneficial insects as well as harmful ones.

Apply garlic and pepper sprays. Mix up your own garlic/pepper spray by combining 1 cup each of hot peppers and garlic cloves in a blender; press the liquefy button until you have a paste. Add the paste to 1 gallon of water and use it as an insect repellent. Or purchase a ready-made concentrate of garlic/pepper spray. Add 1 tablespoon of coconut oil as a sticking agent.

Use diatomaceous earth. Diatomaceous earth (often called DE) is a white powder made from diatoms (sea creatures with hard shells that formed thick deposits in areas of the globe once covered by ocean). DE is mined and sold as an insecticide, since the sharp, powdery granules destroy the breathing systems of many insect pests. It is used to control many soft-bodied insects, including slugs. Dust DE on foliage and coat the soil around plants, especially around anthills or insect nests. Always wear a protective mask when spreading DE.

Try Bt control. Bt (*Bacillus thuringiensis*) bacteria are actually a group of bacteria that can infect insects. One Bt variation is *B.t.* var. *kurstaki*, and it's used to control caterpillars, especially when they're small. You may need to repeat applications. *B.t.* var. *tenebrionis* controls beetle larvae, such as Colorado potato beetles, and *B.t.* var. *israelensis* controls fungal gnats and mosquitoes.

Use insecticidal soaps. Insecticidal soaps act as deterrents to insects on susceptible plants. Brussels sprouts attract aphids, and eggplants attract flea beetles; insecticidal soap is effective against both of these pests.

Use insecticidal oils. Certified organic plant oils are ideal for killing eggs and immature stages of insects; they do so by blocking the insect's supply of oxygen, and may also act to poison or repel insects. While these oils break down quickly and may not harm beneficial insects as much as other control methods, be sure to test an oil on a small area, following label directions carefully, before applying it on a large scale. By choosing certified organic, you are avoiding petroleum-based oils.

Apply milky spore. Consider the use of milky spore, because this bacterial insecticide kills caterpillars and beetle larvae, such as cutworm grubs.

Try baking soda sprays. For protection from and treatment of fungal disease, mix 1 tablespoon of baking soda, 1 tablespoon of insecticidal oil, and a few drops of liquid dishwashing soap per 1 gallon of water. Apply to plants with a sprayer.

Turn to commercial pest-control products. When all else fails, you may decide to use a commercial organic pest control. However, even if a product is labeled organic, it does not mean it is completely harmless to soil, plants, or beneficial insects. For the control of many insect pests—especially mites, aphids, whiteflies, and scales—consider the use of neem oil, a concentrate made from the seeds of the neem tree, a tropical plant native to India. Neem poisons many insects, yet it is harmless to humans and pets. Neem is also effective for the control of fungal diseases, particularly black spot, mildews, rusts, and scab. Also consider the use of spinosad, a natural organic insecticide for the control of grubs and caterpillars on vegetables and fruit trees. Another organic pest control product to consider as a last resort is natural pyrethrins, made from the pyrethrum daisy, a plant that can poison many insects. Pyrethrins are somewhat toxic to mammals, but are highly toxic to bees and fish; do not apply pyrethrins where bees are active or near bodies of water. For protection against fungal disease, research and consider the use of a liquid copper fungicide. It's so concentrated that you need to mix only 2 tablespoons with 1 gallon of water to make an effective spray. (Note: Even though some copper formulations are approved for use in organic gardens, these fungicides are toxic to earthworms and soil organisms, and the copper can build up to crop-damaging levels.)

COMPANION PLANTING

I am *not* a believer in companion planting for insect and disease control. For example, I have not found that garlic will confuse insect pests like carrot flies and repel them from a row of closely planted carrots. Neither do I believe that certain plants don't like—or somehow like—each other's company. Vegetables are not like black walnut trees, which exude a poison from their roots that inhibits other plants from growing near them. In my experience, all vegetable plants planted with correct spacing get along fine together. Moreover, most repellent qualities in plants are released only when the plant is bruised.

I *am* a firm believer, however, in the ability of certain plants to ward off insects when the plants are rendered into a liquid spray. For my fiery pepper/garlic insect repellent recipe, see the beginning of this chapter.

Companion planting does play a role in aspects of gardening other than insect and disease control. I *am* a believer in growing two or more plants up the same vertical support to increase yields from that spot. For example, the Amish are famous for growing corn, pole beans, and vining winter squash in the same space. These crops are known as the three sisters. The corn can be harvested before the pole beans and winter squash mature, with the cornstalks providing support for the other crops even after the corncobs are harvested and the cornstalks have dried. Another of my favorite companion plantings is pole lima beans and vegetable spaghetti squash positioned so that they share the same support. The vegetable spaghetti squash grow low to the ground, and the lima beans climb higher up.

COMMON ANIMAL PESTS

Following is a ready reference for common pests.

Deer. At Cedaridge Farm in Bucks County, Pennsylvania, we have deer on our property every night. We are located next to a large state park where deer are protected and free to roam, so we could not have a garden without deer control. We use different products depending on whether we wish to protect ornamentals or edibles. Whether it's labeled organic or not, I don't spray deer repellent on my vegetables; my preferred method of deterring deer is to fence them out. If you are considering using a deer repellent on edibles, check the label to see if it's approved for edibles and how close to harvesttime the product can be applied.

Most experts and reference guides state that a deer fence must be 8 feet high, but I succeed with my vegetable garden fence at only 5 feet high. Maybe that's because the deer in my area are lazy and find it easier to graze elsewhere, especially during spring and summer, when there's plenty for them to eat in nearby meadows and hedgerows. When they're confronted by my modest 5-foot fence, they simply walk around the perimeter rather than jump over it.

Some types of fencing can be expensive, so consider using a reasonably priced poly tape electric fence system, available from agricultural supply centers. A 656-foot roll of the ½-inch-wide white tape, which is threaded with an electric wire, costs about $40. While it's mostly used to keep horses penned inside an enclosure, it is also effective to keep deer outside, too: If they touch the poly tape, they get zapped and soon learn to avoid it. In addition to the tape, you'll need special posts (about $3 each). If, for example, you wanted to enclose a vegetable garden that is 42 feet × 42 feet, you would need 28 posts spaced 6 feet apart (8 posts total on each side, including 2 "shared" corner posts) and three strands of poly tape at three heights on the posts. You'll need at least 168 feet of poly tape for each height on the post (42 feet each side × 4 sides), for a total of 504 feet (168 feet × 3 heights) of poly tape for the enclosure. You'll also need either a control box, at about $60, for connecting the fence to an energy source; or a solar charger, for about $150. So for about $200 to $280, you can protect your entire vegetable garden for many years, with just a little upkeep. The poly tape fencing is easy for anyone to install, and it's effective for small and large gardens where deer wander in. My neighbor uses this type of horse fencing to protect a large planting of strawberries, and it works well. When trying to deter deer, the most important point to remember is that deer are *neophobic*, meaning that they have a fear of anything new. Most deterrents (such as strongly scented soaps hanging from posts or branches, balls of hair, or coyote urine) work for a short amount of time when first introduced, but are useless over the long term. The deer tend to avoid them when they are first used, but eventually the animals learn they are harmless and ignore them.

The same is true with many plants that appear on deer-resistant plant lists. I have seen ivy, daylilies, and even tulips on deer-resistant lists, but these are all favorite foods of deer in my experience. When plants like ivy, daylilies, and tulips are newly introduced to a garden, deer may avoid them if they are unfamiliar with them, but suddenly one day—after years of ignoring them—pow, they eat the lot. They then do the same the next year and the next. I used to have a fine planting of Japanese butterbur that the deer ignored, and I thought it was a deer-resistant plant. But after 7 years, the deer learned to like it, and every year thereafter they kept nibbling the new growth until it was completely eradicated.

For ornamental plants, the best deer protection is Liquid Fence. I have been to Liquid Fence's manufacturing plant in the Pocono Mountains of Pennsylvania and have seen their fermentation process. The liquid is a combination of garlic concentrate, powdered rotten eggs, and a bacterium that completes its life cycle during the mixing process and adds a repellent odor. The finished product is available as a 3-gallon concentrate that you mix with water and spray onto ornamentals. You'll need to add a sticking agent (coconut oil, for example) as suggested by the manufacturer, so the repellent stays effective under 1 inch of rainfall. It should be applied every 3 weeks, rain or not. I have found this product so satisfactory that I wrote my compliments to the manufacturer—and they ended up making their television commercial at Cedaridge Farm! Although the repellent odor of Liquid Fence is noticeable at the time of application, it remains noticeable only to deer when it dries.

Other foraging animals. Groundhogs, rabbits, and raccoons are the principal spoilers in my garden. Groundhogs and rabbits are best fenced out of a garden plot with chicken wire. An effective chicken wire barrier extends 24 inches aboveground and is buried at least 18 inches belowground to keep groundhogs and rabbits from getting over or burrowing underneath—in most cases. Raccoons, however, are excellent climbers, and will climb up and over fencing, even tearing plastic netting apart with their sharp claws. The only answer I have found for raccoons is to set Havahart traps early in the season to remove them from the garden.

COMMON INSECT PESTS

Once you have gained a little gardening experience and talked to other more experienced gardeners in your area, it's possible to know what pests are most likely to invade your space. For example, many areas of the Northeast will experience an invasion of Japanese beetles, and some properties are more prone to slugs and snail damage than others. When you know your enemy, you can be prepared ahead of time and take precautions—like using milky spore powder to reduce populations of Japanese beetle grubs. Unfortunately, there's a wide array of insect pests waiting to dine on your garden. Here are the ones you're mostly likely to encounter in your vegetable and flower gardens.

Aphids. These colonies of small pear-shaped insects are prevalent on fava beans and brussels sprouts and other vegetables and flowers, especially rosebuds and nasturtiums. Generally they are black, green, or gray. The best organic control is to wipe them off with a wet cloth or blast them with repeated jets of water; the water jets damage their soft bodies. For serious infestations, try insecticidal soaps, pyrethrins, or neem. Encourage ladybugs and lacewings in your garden, because they are natural predators of aphids.

Borers. Resembling grubs or caterpillars, these are the larvae of a moth or beetle, depending on the host plant. Borers burrow into stems of squash vines and the trunks of stone-fruit trees like peaches and cherries, causing the plant to wilt and die. On a squash vine, all or part of the plant may be affected. It may be possible to see where the grub entered the vine by spotting a hole and a pile of frass (sawdustlike debris). If you can, cut out the infected part of the vine and destroy it. Dusting plants early with Bt bacterial control can kill the worm before it enters the stem. As a last resort, use organic pesticides with spinosad.

Colorado potato beetles. In their immature stage, these are pear-shaped soft-bodied grubs that then change into hard-shelled black-and-yellow striped beetles. Both stages destroy potatoes, eggplant, and tomatoes. I control them by spotting them early and picking them off leaves and stems. As a last resort, you can use an organic insecticide such as a neem/insecticidal soap combination.

Cutworms. These are the larvae (caterpillar) stage of a moth that overwinters in soil, emerging at night to eat seedlings, especially pole beans. The larvae are usually fat, gray or brown, and lie curled up during the day. They are exposed when you dig up clumps of soil. When you see them, put them on a hard surface and squash them with your foot. The best defense is to fit your transplants (especially pole bean seedlings, peppers, and tomatoes) with paper or plastic collars using common disposable drinking cups. To make a cup collar, slit the cup up one side and cut out the cup's bottom, then push the collar into the soil up to the rim to ring the transplant.

Fall webworms. Webworms are caterpillars that are prevalent on peach, plum, and cherry trees. They form colonies within a protective web, venturing out at night to eat foliage. The silky web can be high or low on the tree. Use a long stick to dislodge the web and then crush the colony with your foot.

Flea beetles. These are tiny, about the size of pinheads, and mostly black or dark brown. One form has a pair of yellow stripes that can only be seen under a microscope. These beetles colonize the leaves of eggplants (their favorite food), but also attack potatoes and members of the cabbage family, like turnips and radishes. They reveal themselves by chewing myriad holes, so the leaves look like they've been peppered with buckshot. Floating row covers are effective and practical barriers on rows of eggplants, Irish potatoes, and sweet potatoes. Flea beetles are very difficult to control once there's an outbreak; you can try a broad-spectrum organic insecticide like neem or a pyrethrin concentrate.

Japanese beetles. These beetles are most conspicuous in summer, when the adults hatch from grubs that overwinter in soil and begin to voraciously eat a wide range of fruits, vegetables, and flowers. The beetles are particularly destructive of grape leaves, roses, pole snap beans, and raspberries, skeletonizing their leaves. The biological control milky spore can be administered to the soil in spring to kill the grubs, but it may take a year before you see a decrease in Japanese beetle populations. Hand picking is very effective, especially if done by young children paid by the jarful. Have them pick off beetles in the early morning or in the evening, when the bugs are less active, and drop them into jars of soapy water. Floating row covers are also effective. I've never been impressed with Japanese beetle bag traps, though; they seem to draw in beetles from neighboring properties and never seem to catch enough to make much of a difference. Neem and pyrethrins are organic pesticides you might resort to if infestations threaten entire plants or whole crops.

Leafhoppers. Resembling miniature green crickets that jump like grasshoppers, leafhoppers do not do significant damage by their chewing, but they are carriers of disease organisms and should be controlled. This is difficult without resorting to organic insecticides like insecticidal soap, a garlic/pepper spray, or neem.

Scale insects. Particular scale species attack particular plants; for example, euonymus scale attacks euonymus vines. Scale insects are sucking insects that look like scabs on woody plants. You can take a fingernail and pry these loose if there are just a few. Sometimes the scale insects are well camouflaged and hard to spot. Others—like oyster shell scale—are lightly colored and easy to recognize. They may be evident on only a few stems; in that case, they can be pruned away and burned, or you can take a toothbrush dipped in rubbing alcohol and scrub them off the stems. As a last resort, a combination neem/insecticidal soap concentrate is an effective control. If they have completely colonized a plant, it is best to destroy it by burning.

Slugs and snails. A slug is simply a snail without a shell. They are slimy creatures and when they feed on produce, they leave bitter-tasting scars and slimy trails that are also distasteful. (In the Pacific Northwest, a beast called a banana slug can grow to the size of a banana and destroy a *lot* of lettuce.) Hand picking in the early morning is my personal favorite remedy, especially after rainfall. I have never found the practice of drowning slugs and snails in dishes of beer very effective, and tests at Michigan State University have reached the same conclusion—the beer attracts a few slugs, but not nearly enough to be an effective remedy. Slugs and snails overwinter under debris, such as boards and loose stones, so a thorough garden cleanup will leave them with fewer places to hide. They also seem to like hiding under grapefruit rinds, so put out a couple of rinds in the evening and dispose of the slugs in the morning. Toads are terrific predators of slugs, so encourage toads by placing overturned clay pots (with a gap under the rim) in the garden; toads will hide under the cool clay pot during the day and devour slugs at night. Songbirds such as robins will also eat slugs. When sprinkled around seedlings, diatomaceous earth powder is effective against slugs, as are wood ashes, since their raspiness makes slugs uncomfortable.

Spider mites. These tiny spidery insects are often hard to detect until the infestation is so bad that the only course of action is to destroy the entire plant by burning it. Prevention is certainly better than trying to rid an established colony. You may be able to control spider mites by washing plants with water to remove them, or misting plants daily to raise humidity levels and help suppress mite reproduction. The first signs of their presence will be a lackluster appearance of some plant branches and the sight of fine webs. Place a white paper under the webs and shake the branches. If tiny spiderlike specks fall and crawl about, it's a sure sign of spider mite infestation. Control them by using an insecticidal soap or a combination soap/neem concentrate.

Tent caterpillars. These are similar to the fall webworm except they build their silklike webs in spring rather than fall. Take a long stick and destroy the web, crushing as many of the caterpillars as possible in the process. Tent caterpillars tend to colonize apple and pear trees.

Thrips. Thrips are hard to see because they are tiny—$\frac{1}{25}$ inch and smaller. They look like earwigs with featherlike wings, and they damage plants by sucking juices from them. You may notice malformed fruit, speckled leaves, and a lackluster plant appearance. Favorite target crops include cabbage, cucumbers, onions, and tree fruit. Control them by using insecticidal soap.

Tomato hornworms. These large green caterpillars are the larvae stage of a moth. They can measure up to 4 inches long, with a spike on their tail. I have never seen them in plague populations sufficient to do much damage to a tomato crop, but they will eat the leaves of eggplants, peppers, and potatoes. The bacterial control Bt will kill the caterpillar stage. The parasitic braconid wasp will inject its eggs into the caterpillar's body, and the emergent young will literally eat the creature from the inside out.

Whiteflies. These tiny white flies are colonizers, crowding around tender plant stems and sucking the life out of them. These flies can be a problem pest on cucumbers, melons, peppers, squash, tomatoes, and numerous ornamentals like nasturtiums. They secrete a black sticky substance called honeydew that can harbor fungus diseases. The most effective control is to catch whiteflies early: Wipe the colonies clean with a rag dipped in rubbing alcohol or blast them with a strong jet of water. Garlic/hot pepper spray and insecticidal soap are also effective controls. Use pyrethrins or neem as a last resort.

COMMON DISEASES

Plant diseases can take many forms—some as fungus diseases like powdery mildew, and others as nutritional deficiencies like chlorosis. The following are the most common plant diseases you are likely to encounter. Learning how to recognize and deal with them will help your garden thrive.

Anthracnose. This fungus disease appears as a leaf blight with leaf spots that enlarge and merge into each other, eventually defoliating the plant. Anthracnose is common among climbing roses. The disease has many manifestations and is difficult to control using organic remedies. The best prevention is to create healthy garden conditions and practice good garden culture, like removing weakened stems and plants and cleaning up garden litter after the growing season.

Bacterial wilt. You'll find bacterial wilt on members of the cucumber family, especially in the northeastern United States; this wilt exists but is less common in southern states and the West. The disease first affects the vine tips. Overnight, new leaves will wilt, curl, and show gray patches that turn brown, and the entire plant will become infected. The bacteria are spread by cucumber beetles. Pull up infected plants and burn them. Reduce cucumber beetle populations using safe organic controls like garlic/pepper sprays and insecticidal soaps. It's also possible to plant disease-resistant cucumber varieties.

Black spot. This spotty fungus is most prevalent on roses, starting as dark brown or black spots. The infected leaves will yellow, turn brown, and drop. The fungus spores overwinter in debris around the plant and on old canes. There are resistant rose varieties, although there are many strains of black spot; some resistant roses will succumb late in the season. Liquid copper fungicide and sulfur fungicides can be used as a last resort, but research your choices carefully because of environmental concerns. Be aware that there are also bacterial leaf spots that resemble black spot, and that these organic fungicides will not necessarily treat them.

Blights. The most troublesome blight is early blight, a fungus that will attack tomatoes and potatoes after periods of long rainy spells. The spores overwinter in garden debris. Destroy infected plants by burning them.

Blossom end rot. Blossom end rot is common on tomatoes and peppers, causing a fruit to develop a black sunken patch on its underside. This rot is caused by an imbalance of fertilizer in the soil (especially a lack of calcium), too high or too low soil acidity, and by irregular watering. Small-fruited varieties like cherry tomatoes are least likely to be affected.

Botrytis. This fungal disease is prevalent in summer and can disfigure flowers as well as foliage, turning the blossoms mushy. Botrytis is prevalent on ivy-leaf geraniums. It is best prevented by avoiding overhead watering and by deadheading faded flowers.

Cankers. These woody swellings along stems and trunks indicate that the plant has been damaged and bacteria have entered. Prune off affected shoots.

Chlorosis. This is simply a nutrient deficiency, evident when green leaves turn yellow, often leaving the leaf veins green. In acid-loving plants, it is usually a sign of iron deficiency. To remedy the problem, feed plants with an organic fertilizer containing trace elements, including iron and calcium.

Downy mildew. This disease is evident when leaves become covered with a downy white or gray covering. The fungus spores overwinter in crop residue and can be spread by wind or rain. The disease infects numerous vegetable crops, including the cabbage family, the cucumber family, peas, beans, and strawberries. Remove and burn infected plants. Look for and plant resistant varieties.

Fire blight. Fire blight is a serious disease that mostly affects berried plants like pyracantha and fruit trees, especially pears. The edges of leaves appear to be scorched as if by fire, and the berries or fruit become blackened. There is little you can do to prevent fire blight aside from planting resistant varieties. Prune away blight-infected stems and limit its spread by dipping your pruning shears in disinfectant between pruning cuts.

Leaf spots. These can be caused by a multitude of disease organisms, including bacteria, viruses, and fungi. Avoid overhead watering, and choose resistant plant varieties.

Mosaic. This viral disease mostly affects beans, but also damages cucumber family crops, tomato family crops, peas, and others. It starts as a yellow or brown mottling on leaves that curl down. The virus is transmitted by insects, such as aphids and cucumber beetles, but also can be carried on infected seed. The best prevention is to plant mosaic-resistant varieties. Once infected, there are no organic controls; remove and destroy infected plants.

Powdery mildew. This fungal disease is similar to downy mildew, but the gray or white discoloration is more powdery. It is a problem when growing peas for a fall crop, so look for resistant varieties. Indeed, many other plants susceptible to powdery mildew—such as grapes—have some resistant varieties available. Some gardeners find that the organic fungicides including *Bacillus subtilis*, potassium bicarbonate, or a 0.5 percent solution of baking soda (1 teaspoon baking soda in 1 quart water) may be applied effectively as preventives or to help control the disease. Spray infected plants thoroughly.

Root rot. This is difficult to control, because the disease organisms (there are several kinds) are hidden and protected by soil particles. Phytophthora rot is a particularly destructive disease that attacks mostly woody plants, causing the entire plant to suddenly turn brown and die. Or a portion of the plant may be infected, in which case the dead tissue can be pruned away, leaving living tissue to continue growing. Ensure good drainage for the best prevention.

Sooty mold. This is a black coating that covers the tops of leaves and is caused by a fungus. It is especially prevalent on fruit trees, such as apples and pears, with the black coating also covering the fruit. The fungus does not injure plants, although it can interfere with photosynthesis. Use a damp sponge or cloth to wipe the blemishes off leaves and fruit.

Sunscald. Sunscald is caused by extreme exposure to sun. Even vegetable varieties that relish sunlight can be susceptible to sunscald, especially tomatoes, eggplant, and peppers. It can happen when there is insufficient foliage cover, and following a long period of hot, humid weather with little or no cloud cover. During extreme periods of heat, you can protect plants with a canopy of floating row cover material.

Wilts. Wilts can be caused by fungi or bacteria, and also by physiological conditions, such as lack of water. The most prevalent fungus wilt is fusarium wilt, which causes the leaves of plants to suddenly turn brown and die. It is a problem with many vegetable crops including tomatoes, the cabbage family, cucumbers, and even root crops like beets. You should maintain healthy soil conditions, but the disease is difficult to prevent. Since there are no organic treatments, you may need to remove and destroy infected plants.

Controlling Weeds, Watering, Fertilizing, and Pruning

CHAPTER

9

The best investments I have ever made for my vertical garden beds are a soaker hose system—for watering with just a turn of a faucet—and black plastic for weed control in my vegetable plantings.

CONTROLLING WEEDS IN A VERTICAL GARDEN

Weed control for a vertical garden can be summed up in one word: mulch.

Mulch is simply a covering over the soil that creates a weed barrier. For me, the best kind of organic mulch for cool season crops is shredded leaves—they look so natural, decompose to add nutrients to the soil, and keep the soil cool. For warm season crops, I use black plastic; it transmits the sun's heat, retains soil moisture, and prevents weed growth.

Basically there are two kinds of weeds: surface-rooted weeds and deep-rooted weeds. Surface-rooted weeds like chickweed, crabgrass, and purslane are easily pulled, especially when the soil is wet. Usually, the entire root system will come up with a steady pull, and the weed can be discarded onto a compost pile. Deep-rooted weeds like dandelion, thistles, and dock are more difficult to eradicate once they're established. If you try to remove them by hand, you'll inevitably break off only a top portion, allowing the root to regenerate a new set of leaves. In many cases, even a small piece of root left in the soil can regenerate. In order to eradicate a deep-rooted weed, it is essential to use a forked metal weeding tool or a hand trowel for prying up

Eliminate deep-rooted weeds like dandelion with a hand trowel or pronged weeding tool. For the shallow-rooted weeds like crabgrass that pop up in a foundation bed, use a hoe or a hand fork.

the stubborn root. It is extremely important to eliminate weeds before they have a chance to set seed; once their seed is scattered, they can be very difficult to control the next season. Most weeds disperse their seeds in fall, so be sure to go through the garden frequently, yank them out, heap them onto a wheelbarrow, and delegate them to a compost pile.

The best weed protection is mulch. Mulched garden beds are healthier, more weed free, less prone to drought issues, and more attractive than unmulched gardens. There are two types of mulches: organic mulches and inorganic mulches. Organic mulches include compost, grass clippings, leaves, newspaper, peat, pine needles, sawdust, shredded bark, straw, and wood chips. I've had success with many of these mulches, because they decompose slowly and release nutrients into the soil, prevent weeds from germinating, and encourage earthworms that improve soil tilth (its physical structure). Organic mulches are generally loose and airy, so they must be applied in a thick enough layer to deter weeds. They start to decompose as soon as they're applied to soil, and therefore may need topping off before the end of the season.

Inorganic mulches include black and white plastic, shredded tires, and landscape fabric. I've used plastic for many years and am happy with the results. White plastic—which reflects heat—is an effective barrier for protecting cool season crops. Warm season crops like tomatoes, peppers, and eggplant prefer to be mulched with black plastic, since it absorbs heat and promotes early yields.

Mulching has other benefits besides weed control. Mulch maintains a stable soil temperature, allowing direct-sown seeds to germinate at a steady temperature whether it's cool or warm. Sugar snap peas will germinate in relatively cool soil (50°F), whereas lima bean and melon seeds need a soil temperature of 70°F and higher to germinate; these particular seeds benefit most from mulch, because it moderates daily high and low soil temperatures. Mulch is great for seedlings, too. Melons, for example, hate to have their roots subjected to alternate cooling and heating during spring and early summer, so mulch provides an even soil temperature for optimum growth. Mulching also conserves moisture by inhibiting evaporation and keeps maturing fruits from touching the soil and contracting disease.

Following is a list of common mulches and their benefits.

Mulches That Keep Soil Cool

These mulches keep the soil cool and moist in summer, reducing the need to water.

- Grass clippings are readily available, especially if you have a bag attached to your mower for collecting them. Apply to a depth of at least 4 inches. Some gardeners believe that as grass clippings decompose, they deplete the soil of nitrogen; but since nitrogen is such an unstable nutrient well provided for in compost and organic fertilizers, I don't hesitate to use grass clippings as a mulch.

- Newspapers are an effective weed barrier when several pages are overlapped and an organic mulch or topsoil is placed over them. Shredded newspapers are too lightweight, but are good to add to a compost pile. The newspaper industry claims that inks used in newspapers are not toxic. I believe it, since my earthworms thrive on shredded newspapers.

- Peat is good-looking and sterile but very lightweight until it's wet. Avoid applying it on a windy day. Peat needs to be applied to a depth of at least 4 inches to be effective. Peat supplies are said to be dwindling, and some gardeners forgo using it because it's not considered a sustainable resource.

- Pine needles are attractive (and are my second favorite mulch for aesthetic appeal after shredded leaves). Pine needles need to be applied to a depth of at least 4 inches. Some gardeners caution against using pine needles because they may make the soil overly acidic, but I have not found this to be true. A pile of pine needles I turned into compost tested neutral in a soil test.

- Straw retains its golden color for most of the season; by season's end, it turns a dull gray-green color. Straw needs to be applied to a depth of at least 6 inches to be an effective weed barrier. When using bales, you can peel off compacted slices and scatter a thinner layer (such as 2 to 3 inches).

- Shredded leaves add a rich look to beds and are my favorite organic mulch. Small leaves like willow and cutleaf Japanese maples generally do not need shredding, but oak and maple leaves do. Simply run over a pile of leaves with a lawn mower before using them as mulch. Better still, pile them into a corner of your garden and allow them to decompose into leaf mold for a double benefit—an effective mulch and a nutritious soil amendment.

- White plastic reflects heat and therefore benefits cool season crops like lettuce and cabbage. Purchase rolls of white plastic (choose plastic at least 4 feet wide) from a garden center, roll it out over rows before planting, anchor the edges with soil so the wind does not blow it away, and cut openings for your seeds or seedlings.

Mulches That Heat Soil

There are two inorganic mulches that heat the soil and are ideal for warm season crops.

- Black plastic absorbs heat and encourages early yields with warm season crops like tomatoes and melons. Purchase 4-foot-wide rolls from a garden center, roll out over your rows, anchor the edges with soil so the wind does not blow it away, and cut openings for seeds and seedlings.

- Landscape fabrics (also called geotextiles) allow water to pass through them. Usually black or red (red has been shown to increase tomato yields), they absorb the sun's heat and keep soil warm. They are an effective weed barrier and reduce the spread of soilborne diseases, because they eliminate splashing while you're watering or during rainfall. Although I don't use them at Cedaridge Farm, you may find that landscape fabrics are easier to work with than plastic, but note that they do degrade rapidly from UV rays.

WATERING A VERTICAL GARDEN

Vertical gardens are great if you're concerned about water conservation (and all of us should be!) or if you deal with low or irregular rainfall. Compared with a horizontal plot with its typical long rows, sprawling vines, and adjacent pathways, vertical gardens use less water, because the plants are more densely concentrated in a smaller area or footprint. When you water a vertical garden, you water directly at the root zone, especially if a soaker hose is used; there's no need to water unused soil in a wide row, spaces between plantings, or pathway edges. Of course, if you have a relatively small vertical garden—perhaps 4 to 8 feet of garden netting—watering by hand, either with a watering can or a watering wand, is easy. When watering small garden spaces, I use a 2-gallon capacity metal watering can; it's easy to lift and yet it delivers a good amount of water at one application.

Many gardeners like to water their traditional gardens with a lawn sprinkler placed between beds, but this can be wasteful, since the sprinkler head applies water in a broad swath, dousing some areas while missing others or applying water where it's not needed. I find soaker hoses and drip irrigation units much more efficient.

Soaker hoses are usually made of recycled rubber and have pores all along their length so that they can "sweat" moisture at a slow, steady rate. The goal is an evenly moist bed that absorbs water slowly so it holds moisture for your plants' roots. When a soaker hose delivers water directly to the root zone of a plant, less water is wasted through evaporation or runoff;

the slow drips also mean that nutrients aren't flushed downward with heavy watering away from plant roots. Even though these benefits are terrific, there's an additional one—targeted watering means the area along the edges of a vertical gardening bed remains drier, which discourages weeds from sprouting. All soaker hoses are not created equal, though; you may need to evaluate a few different brands of soaker hose until you find the one that works with your home's water pressure and your vertical garden plantings. Some soaker hoses can even work by gravity feed from a raised rain barrel, and some can be buried out of sight.

I have tested numerous irrigation systems for vertical gardens, and the one I like for efficiency and reasonable cost is manufactured by Irrigro. This company sells a starter kit suitable for small garden spaces, and it's available at irrigro.com. Drip systems are in use in many gardens and are often the choice of gardeners who use greenhouses or container plantings. Drip systems usually have emitters, which are small openings that release water by drops right to plant roots. Personally, I don't favor emitters, because they can become clogged and the spaghetti-like emitter connectors can become tangled, but they are favored by gardeners with a lot of containers to water.

FERTILIZING A VERTICAL GARDEN

While many organic gardeners rely entirely on homemade compost to feed plants, others (like me) will provide a fertilizer boost by using an organic fertilizer. The problem with a lot of nonorganic fertilizers is that they are formulated from chemicals that, over time, can produce a toxic buildup of salt in the soil. In contrast, organic fertilizers not only provide the essential plant nutrients in natural form, but they supply organic tilth that acts as roughage and conditions your soil rather than creates a salt buildup.

The three major plant nutrients—nitrogen, phosphorus, and potassium—are given as percentages on a fertilizer package, such as 10-20-10, meaning 10 percent nitrogen, 20 percent phosphorus, and 10 percent potassium. When you compare a commercial chemical fertilizer with an organic formulation, you will often find that the analysis for the organic fertilizer is lower (for example, 3-6-3) than a similar size chemical fertilizer package. While it seems like the organic product is less nutritious, organic fertilizers are, in fact, more efficient at feeding plants and do so over a long period.

Both chemical and organic fertilizers can be granular or liquid, and either slow acting or fast acting. Most organic liquid fertilizers can be applied as a soil drench or sprayed on the upper and underside of leaves as a foliar feed, since plants are capable of absorbing nutrients through stomata (pores) on leaf surfaces. Phosphorus (responsible for flower and root development) and potassium (responsible for disease resistance and overall vigor) can remain in the soil for long periods, but nitrogen (responsible for healthy leaves) is notorious for leaching away quickly after rainfall. Leafy crops like cabbage and lettuce especially need nitrogen.

Generally speaking, vegetables, berry bushes, and fruit trees require more regular feeding than flowering plants like annuals and perennials. With flowering plants, one application at the start of the growing season is usually sufficient, but vegetables can be greedy feeders, especially fruiting vegetables like tomatoes, peppers, melons, and squash. If you are relying on compost to feed these plants, be sure to make several applications around the roots during the growing season. Also be sure that the compost is rich in phosphorus, since lack of phosphorus is often the cause of late ripening of tomatoes and melons or poor yields. The addition of bonemeal to compost will significantly improve its phosphorus content and effectiveness.

PRUNING A VERTICAL GARDEN

In a vertical garden, pruning is mostly reserved for vining plants and woody plants. Proper pruning keeps plants healthy and within bounds. Pruning is used to remove diseased or dead parts, to encourage branching or bushy growth, to encourage a plant to grow in a particular direction or shape, to eliminate crowded branches or foliage, to reduce the overall size of the plant, to improve air circulation, and to increase flowering.

I use three types of pruning tools for my vines: First, a hand pruner allows me to prune stems of up to ½ inch in diameter. Second, a two-handled lopping pruner allows me to prune thicker stems up to 1 inch. Third, a folding pruning saw allows me to prune the thickest stems and branches. When using a pruning saw on thick, woody stems, it is generally best to make three cuts to prevent tearing bark below the cut. First, make an upward cut from underneath the branch, 1 or 2 inches out from the trunk for thinner branches and up to 1 foot out from the trunk for thicker ones. Cut halfway through the branch from the bottom. Second, make a downward slanting cut to meet the first cut and remove the branch. Third, remove the branch stub by cutting along, but never into, the branch collar at the trunk.

How you prune a vine depends on the effect you wish to achieve and whether you seek to rejuvenate an overgrown plant, shape it, or restrict its growth. Generally, the best time to prune a flowering plant is immediately after flowering, since this gives the remaining stems time to develop new flower buds. However, most vines have such abundant growth that pruning to shape the vine or keep it within bounds can be done at any time. Be aware that hidden among tangled stems of many flowering vines may be a hornet's nest and at their base may be a ground wasp's nest.

Annual vines, such as morning glories or scarlet runner beans, generally don't need much pruning, as their stems are lightweight and their growth is restricted to one flowering season. Usually, to rejuvenate perennial vines or woody vines, such as clematis and trumpet creeper, you can prune the entire vine back to within 12 inches of the soil line. This forces new growth. When you do this, you may lose a season's flowering or fruiting, depending on whether flowers are formed on new wood or old. If flowers are formed on old wood, as with wisteria, climbing hydrangea, and climbing roses, rather than cutting the entire vine to the ground, it is better to thin the stems, allowing up to five main stems to support flowers and force new growth for succeeding years.

Some vines grow in beautiful sinuous lines, like grapevines and kiwi vines. You may want to prune away all the lower stems and leave a topknot of old wood as a canopy; this is especially effective with clematis and silver fleece vine. You may also wish to prune a vine to a single trunk, so that it forms a topknot and resembles a tree form; this is a popular practice with wisteria and trumpet creeper.

You may wish to prune for a special shape. For example, apples, pears, and other fruit trees with pliable branches can be shaped (or espaliered) to create parallel laterals (or horizontal branches) or a fan arrangement against a wall. Pruning certain vigorous vines like kiwi and grape to two main leaders (or trunks) will encourage larger fruit and larger fruit clusters. See Chapter 11 for more information about espalier pruning of fruits.

After winter and as plants start to leaf out, you should inspect vines, especially flowering roses and clematis, for signs of winterkill. This occurs when part of a plant is killed by cold and turns brittle; you'll need to remove these damaged or dead stems.

Some vines may be grafted (when one living plant has been attached to a second living plant), so you may see unusual growth below the graft at the base of the trunk that you want to remove by pruning. For example, many climbing roses are grafted onto a hardy root stock, and many fruit trees are grafted onto special root stocks to make them hardier or to create a desired shape. You may notice the graft union just above the soil line; it shows itself as a swollen part of the stem. Any stems that sprout below the graft union will be inferior and should be pruned away; these undesirable shoots are called suckers. If suckers are left to mature, they will drain the plant of energy. Another type of sucker grows on tree branches above bud unions. These occur mostly on fruit trees and are called water sprouts. They grow upright, often by the dozen, on an angled or horizontal branch. They make the tree look unattractive, especially when the leaves drop, and they generally produce inferior flowers or fruit. Simply remove them with hand pruners when they are young.

For most vertical gardening situations, the objective is to train a vine to grow up as a column rather than to spread out—unless, of course, you are growing the vine to cover a wide expanse, such as a chain-link fence or a fan trellis. To encourage a tight vertical column, prune the lower side branches so the plant's energy is directed into the lead shoot, and then prune the plant at the top when it has reached the desired height.

Vegetables for
Vertical Gardens

CHAPTER

10

A survey recently conducted by the Garden Writers Association about gardening trends revealed that beginner vegetable gardeners are most interested in *achieving high yields* and *saving space*. That's understandable, because high yields are the reward we expect after investing our time and money growing plants; and we equate saving space with saving labor, since the smaller the space we cultivate, the less work is involved. Vertical gardening fulfills both of these criteria: By growing tall vines instead of short, bushy plants, we increase yields dramatically (up to tenfold in the case of pole beans), and by shrinking the space our food crops need (reducing the area a vining cucumber plant occupies from 4 square feet to 1 square foot, for example), we reduce our workload correspondingly.

Forget the idea of a large garden with sprawling vines and fruit rotting on wet mulch or bare soil. Instead, embrace the idea of plants raised up off the ground, the fruits of your labor visible and within easy reach, the plants less susceptible to pests and diseases, and the roots easily accessible to efficient watering, weeding, and fertilizing.

VEGETABLES FOR VERTICAL GARDENS

With just a narrow strip of soil, using homemade or store-bought trellis or garden netting, successful vertical gardens can be created that are free-standing or placed against a wall where reflected heat can encourage earlier yields and protect from late frost.

Moreover, the planting strip can be a mere 12 inches wide, allowing you to grow an attractive curtain of climbing vegetables, fruits, or flowers. Then you can add more compact plants, like lettuces and peppers, as foundation or "footprint" plants, or you can grow them in tower pots. Also consider using tall plants, such as sweet corn and okra, as support plants for beans and vining squash. The Amish (as Native Americans did before them) use these "three sisters" of the vegetable world as a space-saving system in their gardens.

I've reaped the benefits of vertical gardening over the past 20 years, because I've used my Pennsylvania property, Cedaridge Farm, as an experimental station, where thousands of visitors have seen and admired my results during summer visits.

There simply isn't an easier, more productive way to garden than vertical gardening. It really works, and I want you to share the pleasures of vertical gardening, too.

You may be surprised to learn that there are climbing varieties for most major vegetable families, even climbing zucchini and climbing spinach. And there are terrific vegetables that you don't always associate with climbing—like climbing yams. In the following pages, I identify these climbers with a trellis logo. Vegetables that do not climb—like lettuce, peppers, and cabbage—but that can be grown vertically in tower pots to save space or used as foundation plants are identified with a container or a raised-bed logo. Support plants like sweet corn and okra are shown with a logo showing a row of stalks.

The vegetables that are most suited to vertical gardening have a vining habit or a long stem that can be trained to climb. The main vegetables used in a vertical garden climb or clamber up supports, while others act like understudies, filling in at ground level. Many of the climbers (like cucumbers) have tendrils that will grasp a pole or trelliswork for support, or they may have stems (like pole beans) whose lead shoots twine and pull themselves free of the ground in an upward spiraling movement. Other vegetables with long stems (like tomatoes) climb with assistance; the most common way to help them climb is to use twist ties to secure their stems to an upright pole or trellis.

This chapter's list of plants features the best performers for the four types of plants (see pages 16 and 17) used in a vertical garden—climber, foundation, container and tower pot, and support—and includes some unusual plants, too. In many cases, these are heirloom varieties that have been brought back into cultivation in recent years as a result of the public's interest in old-fashioned varieties. Visit your local garden center or specialty nursery to find a wide array of seeds and plants. With so much interest in vegetable gardening for health reasons—and with the development of new varieties—the selection increases each new season. When seed and plant shopping early in the season, do an Internet search on the varieties I mention below to find the best sources.

BEANS, POLE

No class of vegetable is better adapted to vertical gardening than pole beans. The lead shoot grows skyward in a rapid twining movement that allows it to wrap around poles and coil through trellis or garden netting for support. In seed catalogs you will often find pole beans classified according to their area of popularity or origin. Asian beans, for example, are a group that relish warm, sunny days and tend to be more disease resistant than the regular snap beans that have been popular throughout Europe and North America for centuries. Large-seeded lima beans originate from South America, and although they grow well in most areas of the United States with warm summers, the vines have difficulty in maritime climates such as those of coastal Maine and the United Kingdom. The popular snap bean used to be called a string bean because of a fibrous suture running the length of the pod, but plant breeders have succeeded in breeding out the strings so that modern pole snap beans are virtually stringless.

A single planting of pole beans will remain productive the entire growing season, provided that the pods are picked regularly to force new flowering and pod formation. Beans grown up poles also tend to be more flavorful than their bushy counterparts, because the extra vine coverage is able to collect more chlorophyll and ensure a more robust product.

Naturally, a vine that produces up to 10 times more pods than a bush variety requires a more fertile soil and more moisture. With both bush and pole varieties, the pods are best harvested when they are young and firm, and the seeds inside the pod are small. Left on the vine, pods eventually turn brittle and dry. At this stage, they can be shelled and the seeds used as dried beans.

Earliest yields are possible by planting through black plastic mulch, which helps warm the soil. Although transplanting 4-week-old seedlings is recommended for earliness, pole beans generally resent any kind of root disturbance, so be sure their rootballs remain intact. Be aware that when direct-seeded, pole beans can rot easily during cool, wet conditions. This is especially true of pole lima beans. A simple way to avoid bean seed rot is to pre-germinate seeds on a moist paper towel and plant the germinated seeds as soon as they show a root and the first pair of leaves (called cotyledons).

When bean vines are killed by frost, gather and delegate them to a compost pile or burn them so that any insect larvae or disease organisms are killed.

Plant breeders have worked on many of the popular bean varieties and dwarfed them to produce bushy varieties no more than 18 to 20 inches tall. These bush varieties require no staking and are suitable for mechanical harvesting. While this is laborsaving, the bush varieties produce a fraction of the yield of a pole variety in the same space, and their productive life is short—often a matter of only 2 or 3 weeks. For a continuous yield, succession planting is necessary for bush varieties—every 3 weeks up to the beginning of August in most areas of the United States.

Asian Winged Beans

These frost-sensitive pole beans are similar in climbing habit to pole snap beans, except the flowers are a beautiful sky blue, and the pods are a strange color and shape— bright green with four ruffled raised membranes or "wings" that extend from opposite sides. In addition to the pods, other parts of the plant are edible—the leaves as a

The unusual Asian winged bean climbs just like a traditional pole bean; slice it crossways and use it in stir-fries.

substitute for spinach and the roots for chewing raw or for sautéing, with a nutty flavor. I grew them one year and found them as easy to grow as any other pole bean. They are a staple in Asian and Thai cooking, but their flavor is quite different from that of traditional beans. Personally, I did not care for the flavor of the cooked beans as much as that of pole snap beans or pole Romanos, but the interesting wings on the bean pods are a real novelty.

Plant seeds 1 inch deep at least 12 inches apart alongside strong poles, garden netting, or a trellis for support. Plants grow quickly to 10 feet high and bear hundreds of pods that are best eaten young and tender in stir-fries. Ultimately, the pods will grow to 6 inches long, when they can be sliced for cooking—either as a stir-fry or by steaming. After the pods dry, the seeds can be removed, dried, and stored in jars.

A similar vining vegetable, known as the asparagus pea, is grown for its winged pods. It grows to 4 feet high and features brown flowers. The pods are similar in appearance to the winged bean, although they are not as large; the pods are best steamed or used in stir-fries.

KEY CHARACTERISTICS

Origins: Obscure for both Asian winged bean and asparagus pea, but probably the Mediterranean region

Zones: 5–11 as a warm season vegetable

Propagation: By direct-sown seed, or start indoors 4 weeks before outdoor planting (recommended for short season areas). Allow 85 days from seed to harvest for Asian winged beans, 75 days for asparagus peas.

Pests and Diseases: Root rot in poorly drained soil, and Japanese beetles

Height: 10 feet for Asian winged beans, 4 feet for asparagus peas

Supports: Strong poles such as bamboo canes, trellises, or heavy-gauge reach-through garden netting

Asparagus Beans (aka Yard-Long Beans)

I like the flavor of asparagus beans; they're a little like thin asparagus spears. I generally grow them every year at Cedaridge Farm, saving seed from one year to the next, as none are hybrids (seeds saved from hybrids, in contrast, produce inferior results). They grow quickly, and one plant can produce an impressive yield. Don't wait until the pods have reached full maturity to harvest, though, because at that stage they can become flavorless and stringy. The pods of asparagus beans can grow to 3 feet long, but they are at their most tender when young, before they reach 6 to 8 inches long. The vigorous vines need strong poles, garden netting, or a trellis for support. Both green-podded and purple-podded varieties are available. Plant seeds 1 inch deep and at least 12 inches apart. Provide full sun and a fertile soil with good drainage. Asparagus beans are best sliced into small pieces 2 to 3 inches long and stir-fried or steamed. When the pods turn brittle, the dried seeds can be stored in jars and used as shell beans, and used as seed for growing the next season's crop. The following two varieties are novelties, either because of pod color or seed color.

'Chinese Red Noodle' (80 days) has gleaming red pods up to 18 inches long and small red seeds.

'Thai Black Seeded' (80 days) has light green pods with small black seeds. Beans grow to 3 feet—the ultimate "yard-long bean"—and are my personal favorite.

KEY CHARACTERISTICS

Origins: Obscure, but probably the Mediterranean region

Zones: 5–11 as a warm season annual

Propagation: By direct-sown seed after frost danger has passed, or started 4 weeks before outdoor planting. Although many seed catalogs specify 80 days from seed to harvest, I pick young pods at 70 days.

Pests and Diseases: Japanese beetles and bean beetles

Height: Up to 15 feet

Supports: Strong poles such as bamboo canes, trellises, or heavy-gauge reach-through garden netting

---

Lima Beans

At Cedaridge Farm, I would never be without my pole lima beans. Their tall, vigorous vines cloaked in large, dark green, leathery spear-shaped leaves seem to be a symbol of garden health and productivity. They are best grown up strong poles in teepee fashion for support.

Most areas of the United States with long, hot summers offer perfect conditions for growing pole lima beans. They relish the heat, and provided that they are watered regularly during dry periods, the pole limas are far superior to bush lima beans in size and flavor. The vines are heavy: One year I had an entire 15-foot row topple over, because the vines were so heavily laden with beans and foliage. The white flowers are formed in clusters, so up to a dozen pods can form on a single flower stem. The seed is highly susceptible to rotting in the soil under cold, wet conditions, so delay planting until several weeks after the last expected frost date. Provide full sun and a fertile, well-drained soil. Growing through black plastic mulch will enhance yields and earliness.

The most popular pole lima variety is the heirloom 'King of the Garden'. The leathery pods are not edible, but can contain up to five large beans, often called butterbeans. These are usually pale green at maturity, but change to pure white when dry. Feel the pod before picking to ensure that the beans have swollen inside the pod; the pods can be deceptive and give the appearance of being fully mature, but may actually require another week for the beans to fatten. Cook by boiling or steaming. Also store the dried beans in glass jars for adding to soups and stews.

Other good pole lima bean varieties include:

'Big Mama' (80 days) grows vines up to 10 feet high and pods up to 8 inches long, and the pods are packed with up to six unusually large beans (even bigger than 'King of the Garden'). For maximum yields, start seed 4 weeks before outdoor planting to produce healthy transplants, and plant through black plastic mulch to keep the soil warm.

'Christmas Lima' (75 days) is an heirloom variety that produces large, maroon speckled beans up to 1 inch wide. Unlike that of most other colored beans, the color is retained after cooking. The beans are meaty and make a satisfying side dish to mashed potatoes or corn.

KEY CHARACTERISTICS

Origins: Native to South America

Zones: 5–11 as a warm season annual

Propagation: By direct-sown seed after frost danger has passed, or started indoors 4 weeks before outdoor planting. Allow 75 to 80 days from seed to harvest.

Pests and Diseases: Mostly rot from planting seed too early; also Japanese beetles and powdery mildew

Height: Up to 20 feet

Supports: Strong poles such as bamboo canes, trellises, or heavy-gauge reach-through garden netting

Romano Beans

These flat-podded pole beans have a melt-in-your-mouth quality when lightly steamed and come in green, yellow, and purple varieties. Generally, to save space, I will plant three colors in a circle around a tripod support.

The vines of pole Romanos are vigorous, so they require strong poles, garden netting, or a trellis to grow tall. Once they start bearing, the vines continue nonstop until fall frost, when the pods will become dry and brittle. The tender pods are wide, flat, and up to 8 inches long. Plant seeds 1 inch deep and space plants at least 6 inches apart. Provide full sun and a fertile, well-drained soil. The white flowers are self-fertile and formed in clusters, yielding groups of bean pods for easy picking. The more the beans are harvested, the more flowers are produced to yield a continuous harvest. The pods themselves are best sliced into 1- to 2-inch segments and boiled or steamed for a few minutes until tender. Pods left on the vines to dry will yield shell beans that can be stored in jars for adding to soups and stews and for growing next season's crop, as none are hybrids.

A good heirloom golden-yellow Romano is 'Gold of Bacau' (65 days). A productive, low bushy type to use as a footprint plant beneath pole varieties is 'Jumbo', with wide, flat pods up to 10 inches long, but they are best when harvested at 7 inches.

KEY CHARACTERISTICS

Origins: Obscure, but probably the Mediterranean region

Zones: 4–11 as a warm season crop

Propagation: By direct-sown seed after frost danger has passed, or started indoors 4 weeks before outdoor planting. Allow 70 days from seed to harvest.

Pests and Diseases: Mostly cutworms, Japanese beetles, and powdery mildew

Height: Up to 10 feet

Supports: Strong poles such as bamboo canes, trellises, or heavy-gauge reach-through garden netting

Runner Beans

The pole runner bean is a popular vegetable in the British Isles and other parts of Europe with a maritime climate or cool summers; most areas of the United States have poor conditions for growing runner beans, because the beans resent high heat and humidity. Coastal areas such as the Pacific Northwest and Maine can grow delicious runner beans, but gardeners in other parts can be disappointed by the tough, inedible quality of the pods. The vines climb by twining, producing heart-shaped leaves in threes, and clusters of mostly red flowers, followed by flat, dark green pods that can be up to 12 inches long. The pods are best cut into 1- or 2-inch sections and steamed or boiled to make them tender. The dried pods can be shelled and the seeds stored in glass jars. Seed colors can be brown, black, or white, depending on variety. Plant seeds at least 1 inch deep and 6 inches apart in full sun and fertile, well-drained soil. Use tripods or garden netting for support. In addition to those with scarlet flowers, there are also white and bicolored pink and scarlet flowering varieties. The vines flower continuously, so many gardeners like to grow them for ornamental value and to attract hummingbirds.

If you have tasted runner beans in Europe and would like to give them a try, grow them as a fall crop, planting seed in mid-August so plants mature during cool conditions.

KEY CHARACTERISTICS

Origins: Native to South America

Zones: 3–9 as a cool season annual

Propagation: By direct-sown seed after frost danger has passed, or started indoors 4 weeks before outdoor planting. Allow 75 days from seed to harvest.

Pests and Diseases: Mostly Japanese beetles and powdery mildew

Height: Up to 15 feet

Supports: Strong poles such as bamboo canes, trellises, or heavy-gauge reach-through garden netting

Shell Beans

A very large number of pole bean varieties are grown for their seeds rather than for their pods, which can be fibrous and unsuitable for eating. There is considerable color variation among these beans, including white, black, red, orange, brown, beige, and speckled. Provide plants with full sun and a well-drained, fertile soil. Grow up tripods or garden netting for support. Plant seeds 1 inch deep and at least 6 inches apart, and allow the vines to intermingle. I rarely grow shell bean varieties, because my snap pole beans and lima beans generally provide sufficient pods to dry on the vine for harvesting as shell beans. However, here are some recommended shell bean varieties, either because of their ornamental pods or colorful seed.

'Brockton Horticultural' (85 days) has highly decorative pods that are green with red stripes. The oblong beans are pink with red spots, and meaty and delicious added to soups and stews.

'Good Mother Stallard' (85 days) is an almost round, white bean with heavy maroon mottling. It has a rich, meaty flavor that's valued for soups.

'Speckled Cranberry' (65 days) was introduced into the United States from England in about 1825 and has earned a reputation as the best of the pole shell beans. The oval beans are beige with maroon speckles, and have a long shelf life when dried and stored in jars.

KEY CHARACTERISTICS

Origins: Obscure, but possibly the Mediterranean area

Zones: Mostly 4–11 as a warm season annual

Propagation: By either direct-sown seed after frost danger has passed, or started indoors 4 weeks before outdoor planting. Maturity dates vary according to variety; usually 85 days for dry pods.

Pests and Diseases: Mostly Japanese beetles and powdery mildew

Height: Up to 15 feet

Supports: Strong poles such as bamboo canes, trellises, or heavy-gauge reach-through garden netting

Snap Beans

Green-podded snap beans are America's favorite homegrown vegetable. Like I do with pole Romanos, at Cedaridge Farm I like to plant three colors of pole snap beans in a circle around a tripod support—a green-podded variety, a yellow-podded variety, and a purple-podded variety (and even speckled kinds). At farmers' markets, I have noticed the green-podded snap beans far outsell the yellow, purple, or speckled. To my taste, the greens do taste best, but I like looking at an assortment of colors in my garden. There are numerous bush varieties of snap beans, but the pole varieties are heavier yielding and will bear from early summer to fall frost. The shelled beans can be stored for years in jars and are variously colored, including white, brown, black, and speckled. The fast-growing vines climb by twining and require strong poles or a trellis for support. Plant seeds 1 inch deep and at least 6 inches apart in full sun and fertile soil with good drainage. Pick most pole snap beans *before* the beans swell the pods. Keep the pods picked to ensure a continuous harvest.

The heirloom variety 'Kentucky Wonder' is popular, but tends to turn fibrous quickly. 'Blue Lake' is a much tastier, more recent introduction and is more productive. The white flowers are borne in clusters with sometimes six or more pods maturing to a cluster. Cut the pods into 1- to 2-inch segments and stir-fry or steam for best flavor. Boiling is also satisfactory. The young pods are excellent for pickles and for five-bean salad, which combines five

The famous 'Lazy Wife' pole bean, with its ribbed pods, has all but disappeared from seed catalogs, but it was the first stringless pole bean, and it's still the best for flavor.

colors of both pickled pods and cooked shelled beans. Use the shelled beans in soups and stews and to make delicious baked beans. The following are additional recommended pole snap varieties.

'**Cherokee Trail of Tears**' (85 days) is the bean that the Cherokees took to Oklahoma when the US Government forced the tribe to relocate from its ancestral home in the Great Smoky Mountains in 1839. That forced march is known as the Trail of Tears, because an estimated 4,000 people perished during the journey. The 6-inch edible green pods contain jet-black beans suitable for black bean soup when dried.

'**Lazy Wife**' (80 days) is an heirloom pole snap bean that was introduced by Burpee Seeds in its 1888 garden seed catalog. Discovered in Bucks County, Pennsylvania, among German immigrant farmers, it was the very first stringless pole bean. This accounts for its uncharitable name, since housewives generally had the responsibility of tediously de-stringing snap beans. In my opinion, it is the very best pole bean for flavor, requiring just a few minutes of cooking to render the 5- to 6-inch green pods tender and so delicious they seem to melt in your mouth. The almost round, white seeds are shiny and look like marbles. After the pods have dried and the beans are shelled, they make the best baked beans I have ever tasted. Stored in a glass jar, the seeds will keep for years.

Shortly after World War II, the 'Lazy Wife' bean disappeared from catalogs, as earlier-maturing and more disease-resistant varieties were introduced by breeders. I acquired a shoebox full of seeds from a local Bucks County farmer named Bill Byrd, who had been saving his own seed ever since Burpee stopped selling it. After he passed away, his wife Esther presented me with his stock seed for the following season, hoping I would perpetuate it. That was in 1964, and I have been saving the seed ever since.

A word of caution concerning this heirloom variety, however: In the 1980s, a mail-order seed house offered 'Lazy Wife' beans in its catalog, but when the initial supply was sold out, the company substituted another variety—a bean that produces white, crescent-shaped beans. Several seed companies began raising their own seed crops using the substituted seed, so that the bean sold as 'Lazy Wife' today is unlikely to be the true variety. From my own tests, each of these substituted beans has not proven to be the original 'Lazy Wife' variety. I am hoping that the real 'Lazy Wife' bean becomes available to the public again, either through a seed-saving organization or through a commercial reintroduction. It will surely be worth the effort.

'**Purple Pod**' (68 days) has 6-inch-long edible pods that are slightly flattened and purple, though they turn green when cooked.

'**Rattlesnake**' (70 days) has edible green pods that are speckled with purple. When the seed dries, it turns a speckled brown.

KEY CHARACTERISTICS

Origins: Obscure, but probably the Mediterranean

Zones: 4–11 as a warm season annual

Propagation: By direct-sown seed after frost danger has passed, or started indoors 4 weeks before outdoor planting. Allow 70 days from seed to harvest.

Pests and Diseases: Mostly cutworms, Japanese beetles, and powdery mildew

Height: Most up to 15 feet

Supports: Strong poles or bamboo canes, trellises, or heavy-gauge reach-through garden netting

BEETS

Beets are a cool-season root crop suitable for growing in tower pots or as a foundation planting in front of climbing plants. Beets resent transplanting and must be direct-seeded. The plants are hardy and can be sown outdoors several weeks before the last frost date. Plant seeds at least 2 inches apart and ½ inch deep. Most seed packets contain beet seed joined together in clusters (though they may look like single seeds), and so even with careful spacing, several seedlings are likely to sprout from the same planting hole. Thinning is essential to allow the beets to develop to edible size. Start to harvest beets when they're the size of a golf ball. In addition to the familiar red beets, also consider 'Chioggia' for its red-orange skin color and interior striping, and 'Burpee's Golden' beet for its appetizing orange-yellow color and extra tender tops. These tops make a fine substitute for spinach.

KEY CHARACTERISTICS

Origins: Native to Europe

Zones: 3–11 as a cool season vegetable

Propagation: By direct seeding. Maturity averages 50 days.

Pests and Diseases: Slugs and wireworms

Height: Up to 2 feet

Uses: Grow in tower pots with several beets to a pot, or as a foundation plant in front of climbing plants.

CABBAGES

This is a cool season vegetable suitable for growing in tower pots, usually one per pot, or as a foundation planting in front of climbing plants. You'll have the best results by choosing compact varieties such as 'Stonehead' and 'Gonzales'. In addition to plain green cabbage, there also are Savoy cabbages with dark green crinkled leaves around a heart of gold, or red leaves. Also consider compact varieties of Chinese cabbage such as bok choy and Michihili. Cabbage can be direct-seeded, but seeds are best started indoors, planted ¼ inch deep. When hardened off, space transplants at least 12 inches apart. They will tolerate mild frosts.

KEY CHARACTERISTICS

Origins: Native to coastal Europe, especially France

Zones: 3–11 as a cool season vegetable

Propagation: By direct seeding, or starting seed indoors 5 weeks before outdoor planting. For early varieties, expect 60 days to maturity; for late varieties, 100 days to maturity.

Pests and Diseases: Slugs, cabbage loopers, and black rot are the main problems.

Height: Up to 18 inches

Uses: Grow in tower pots with one plant per pot, or as a foundation plant in front of climbing plants.

CARROTS

Carrots are a cool-season root crop suitable for growing in tower pots or as a foundation planting in front of climbing plants. The shape and length of the carrot "root" varies according to the variety and ranges from round like a radish to 8 inches long like an icicle. In addition to orange, there are scarlet, maroon, white, and yellow carrots, usually sold as a mixture. The seed is tiny and will blow away if you even breathe on it. Always direct-seed, since seedlings' roots resent transplanting. Plant with just enough soil to anchor the seed, no more than ¼ inch deep, and thin to at least 1 inch apart. A stump-rooted carrot like 'Royal Chantenay' or 'Nantes' is preferred for tower pot culture.

KEY CHARACTERISTICS

Origins: Native to Europe

Zones: 3–11 as a cool season vegetable

Propagation: By direct seeding. Maturity of early varieties takes 65 days.

Pests and Diseases: Mainly carrot fly and wireworms

Height: Up to 18 inches

Uses: Grow in tower pots with six plants to a pot, or as a foundation plant in front of climbing plants.

CHARD, SWISS

Also known as silverbeet or perpetual spinach, Swiss chard is not a climber, but it is suitable for growing in tower pots or as foundation plants in front of climbing plants. Valued as a heat-tolerant substitute for spinach, the variety 'Bright Lights' won an All-America Selection award. Developed by a New Zealand home gardener, it has 11 colors of edible midribs including white and various shades of red, pink, yellow, orange, purple, cream, and lemon. The bumpy, glossy green leaves are tender enough to use raw in a salad when picked young, and delicious steamed for just a few minutes for a flavor like collard greens. Moreover, the more you pick the stalks (which can be cut into 1-inch sections and braised like celery), the more new leaves form in the middle.

In addition to being heat resistant, Swiss chard is tolerant of light frosts and will remain in the garden even until the ground freezes in winter. Some seedsmen sell individual colors, including the white, red, and gold varieties. Seed can be direct-sown, covered with half an inch of soil, even before the last frost date in spring. But if you start the seed indoors, you will be able to see what colors are in your mixture and choose the best ones for transplanting. 'Bright Lights' is so decorative it is used as an ornamental in container plantings, especially as a central accent. In mild winter areas, Swiss chard will survive the winter and go to seed the following year, as it is a biennial.

In my experience, both 'Rainbow' and 'Five Color Chard' are inferior varieties without the color range of 'Bright Lights'. Nor do they have leaves as tender as 'Bright Lights' when cooked as a spinach substitute.

KEY CHARACTERISTICS

Origins: Native to Europe

Zones: All, as an annual

Propagation: By direct-sown seed, or started indoors 6 weeks before outdoor planting

Pests and Diseases: Mostly slugs and foraging animals like groundhogs and deer

Height: Up to 3 feet

Uses: Grow in tower pots with one to three plants per pot, or as a foundation plant in front of climbing plants.

CHAYOTE

Pronounced *chay-ho-tay,* this is a type of tender gourd that produces green pear-shaped fruit on a vigorous vine. It requires a strong trellis for

support, since the rampant vine produces heavy stems and foliage. The fruit is solid all the way through, with a texture like a potato but a flavor more like water chestnuts. The fruit can be eaten raw, but it is best sliced and steamed, stir-fried, or boiled until tender (usually 10 to 15 minutes). Harvest chayote when it's the size of a mature Bartlett pear, before the fruit drops. When mature, the fruit drops from the vine and buries its broad base in the ground, splitting and sending up a sprout to make a new vine. The fruit can be stored for a month or more in the crisper section of a refrigerator.

The vines need 6 to 9 months of warm, frost-free weather to produce a decent harvest, so chayote is more often grown in areas like southern Florida and southern California than in short-season areas like the Northeast. To grow, obtain a fruit from a grocery store and plant almost entirely, with the narrow end projecting 1 to 2 inches above the soil. A single vine is capable of producing 100 fruit, each averaging a pound apiece. Because of its aggressive nature, the vine is best grown over an arbor like a grapevine. Varieties are variable in the size of their fruit. 'Perlita', from Guatemala, grows to the size of a large lemon.

KEY CHARACTERISTICS

Origins: Native to Mexico

Zones: 6–11 as an annual

Propagation: By direct planting of the tuberous fruit after frost danger has passed, or started indoors 6 weeks before outdoor planting. Allow 190 or more days to harvest.

Pests and Diseases: Cucumber beetles

Height: Up to 25 feet

Supports: Use strong poles such as bamboo canes, trellises, or heavy-gauge garden netting. Also consider growing chayote over an arch or arbor.

Although sweet corn does not climb, its strong, tall stems make it an excellent support for annual vines that grow vertically, especially pole beans and winter squash such as butternut. By planting an early-maturing sweet corn variety (70 to 80 days), the cobs can be harvested before the pole beans and the winter squash vines compete for production. Indeed, among Amish growers, sweet corn, pole beans, and winter squash are known as the "three sisters."

Space sweet corn plants at least 9 inches apart in rows 2½ feet apart, direct seeding 1 inch deep after frost danger has passed. The height of corn plants depends on variety, but most grow 6 to 8 feet tall, producing cobs filled with delicious kernels that can be white, yellow, or bicolored. I particularly like to grow "Super Sweet" hybrids because in addition to enhanced sugary flavor, the conversion from sugar to starch after picking is much slower (up to 10 days when stored in the crisper section of your refrigerator) than that of standard sweet corns, which can start to lose their sweetness within hours of picking.

To ensure that cobs are filled to the top with kernels, be sure to plant seeds in garden blocks of at least three rows, since pollen from the tassels must fall onto the silks to pollinate them and ensure kernel development and plump ears of corn. As soon as you see the silks appear, be sure to water the plants regularly until harvest, as watering in the early and final stages of cob development produces even rows of plump kernels and good flavor.

The sweet corn pages of catalogs can contain dozens of varieties. The white variety 'Silver Queen' (91 days) is almost always listed, but it is rather late maturing, so I don't recommend it for a "three sisters" planting. Here are my favorites for growing as support plants in a vertical garden.

'Early Xtra-Sweet' (71 days) is a super-sweet corn hybrid with golden yellow kernels that are honey sweet and ears that are 9 inches long.

'Golden Bantam' (80 days) is an open-pollinated heirloom introduced in 1902; the ears are shorter than most other sweet corns' (up to 6 inches), but the yellow kernels are delicious and the seed can be saved from one generation to the next.

KEY CHARACTERISTICS

Origins: South America

Zones: 5–11

Propagation: By direct seeding after frost danger has passed. Some varieties are more prone to rot from cool conditions than others, so check catalog descriptions. Also suitable for transplanting when seedlings are small

Pests and Diseases: Mostly corn earworm and corn smut, a black sooty growth on the cobs that is used in Mexican dishes for its mushroomlike flavoring

Height: 6 to 8 feet

Uses: Can grow in tower pots with one plant per pot, but best used as a support for climbing plants like pole beans and winter squash

CUCUMBERS

Cukes were intended by nature to climb, since the vines have tendrils that allow them to grasp thin poles, garden netting, or a trellis for support. The two most common cucumber types grown in home gardens are slicing cucumbers *(Cucumis sativus)* and pickling cucumbers (*C. anguria*), although slicers can be used for pickles and pickle cucumbers for slicing. There are also a number of gourds commonly called cucumbers, such as the snake cucumber, and in fact cucumbers and gourds are closely related. Although cucumbers are grown mostly to be eaten raw, fresh off the vine, many cookbooks feature them in recipes for soup, frying, and stewing.

Cucumbers are a warm season crop that's sensitive to frost damage. Either direct-sow seeds 1 inch deep and 18 inches apart, or start seed indoors 4 weeks before outdoor planting for healthy transplants. Harden off transplants in a coldframe before placing them in their permanent outdoor positions. Allow the vines to knit together to form a dense mass of foliage.

Since the fruits of slicing cucumbers can be heavy, a good way to grow them is up bamboo canes that lean into each other to form a tent. This allows the fruit to hang down freely for easy harvesting and perfect straightness. Although there are bush cucumbers with short vines, these are not generally long lived and produce only small numbers of fruit compared to the vining kinds. Raising cucumbers off the ground also improves air circulation and reduces the risk of disease.

Metal teepee support for cucumber vines. The variety 'County Fair' is self-pollinating and extra-high yielding.

Normally, a cucumber vine has male and female flowers—the females with immature embryos beneath them. These female flowers require cross-pollination from a male flower, generally achieved by bees. However, plant breeders have made some improvements over standard cucumber varieties to ensure higher yields by developing all-female vines. Some all-females produce almost 100 percent female flowers, requiring a standard variety to be grown nearby for pollination, but others are self-pollinating, requiring no male flowers to set fruit. If a seed packet or catalog description says "seed of a pollinator included," that means the female plants are incapable of pollinating themselves. The male pollinator can be a slicer or pickle variety.

All-female cucumbers are generally classified according to size: standard (such as 'Tiffany'), intermediate (such as 'Byblos'), and mini (such as 'Cucino'). My choice for extra-large yields is any standard all-female variety that sets only female flowers and is self-fertile, requiring no cross-pollination. This is known as a *parthenocarpic* cucumber. Most parthenocarpic cucumbers are bred for greenhouse use only: They are seedless, and if pollinated outdoors by bees, seeds develop inside the cucumbers, making them gourd-like and of poor quality. Other varieties of parthenocarpic cucumbers are bred for outdoors, but should also be isolated from cross-pollination. Seed packet or catalog descriptions generally differentiate between the different kinds. My favorite varieties are listed below.

Both slicing and pickling cucumbers can have tiny black or white spines that are easily rubbed off. It's a matter of personal preference if you peel cucumbers prior to eating them fresh in salads. Peeling is generally a good policy with standard varieties, as poorly grown standard cucumbers can develop a bitterness in their skin. Bitterness in cucumbers is caused by a compound called *cucurbitacin* that accumulates under the skin near the stem end following a period of stress such as drought. But most Japanese and European cucumbers have exceedingly tender, non-bitter skins and are called burpless cucumbers; the skin on burpless cucumbers can be eaten, because it's digested more easily.

Soil for cucumbers should be well drained and rich in organic matter. Choose a sunny location, and grow the plants through black plastic mulch for extra earliness. The plastic heats up the soil and will accelerate maturity by up to 2 weeks. If you use organic mulches like straw or shredded leaves, allow the soil to heat up thoroughly before applying them. Prevent cucumber beetles from damaging the vines and fruit by using floating row covers over the supports or an organic insecticide like an insecticidal soap or garlic/pepper spray.

Harvest cucumbers when they're a glossy, dark green color. For continuous harvests and to promote longevity of the vine, pick cucumbers every 2 or 3 days. Cucumbers left on the vine will turn yellow, indicating over-ripeness, and will drain the plant of energy. The fruit will store for 10 to 14 days in the crisper section of your refrigerator.

In addition to the foregoing all-female cucumbers, here are some specific cucumber recommendations.

'County Fair' (48 days) is a high-yielding hybrid pickle cucumber developed by the USDA. The first seedless cucumber for outdoors, it is self-fertile and highly productive.

Horned cucumber, also known as jelly melon (120 days), has shown up in the fresh fruit section of supermarkets for many years, ever since New Zealand growers began to grow it commercially and market it as an exotic fruit. Botanically known as *Cucumis metulifer*, the horned cucumber requires a long growing season and may not ripen in northern gardens, but it is an interesting novelty for vertical growing. The orange, oval fruits are the size of goose eggs; the green interior has numerous white seeds surrounded by a jellylike pulp with a sweet-and-sour flavor reminiscent of lime. Grow through black plastic mulch to encourage earliness.

'Lemon' (65 days) is one of a number of cucumber oddities worth growing vertically. Its fruit are yellow-skinned and similar in shape and size to softballs. 'Crystal Wax' is similar in appearance but with a white skin instead of a yellow one. 'Crystal Wax' is also the name of a cucumber sold mostly in Europe and Australia/New Zealand. It is similar in appearance to 'Lemon' but with a white skin instead of a yellow one.

'Marketmore 76' (58 days) is a development of Cornell University. It is a good standard slicing cucumber variety with excellent disease resistance. This is probably the most popular cucumber grown by home gardeners.

'Orient Express Burpless Hybrid' (64 days) is a burpless cucumber with fruits that are generally long and bumpy, with a tender green skin. 'Orient Express' is a popular high-yielding Japanese-type non-bitter cucumber ideal for vertical gardening.

'Parisian Pickling' (50 days) is a pickle cucumber—commonly called a cornichon—and is a familiar sight on the supermarket shelf. You'll find them as the small, sausage-shaped pickles crammed into jars and often offered as a salad ingredient at the salad bar. Although the fruits are generally harvested small, they can be left on the vine to grow to the size of a regular cucumber for slicing.

'Poona Kheera' (60 days) is a familiar sight in Indian markets. This true cucumber produces large oval fruit up to a pound each and with brown skin when ripe. The flavor is sweet and mild, and the plants are disease resistant.

'West Indian Gherkin' (62 days) has fruit that measure just 2 inches long. A single vine can grow 50 or more small, spiny, oval fruit prized for pickles, but they are bitter tasting if eaten raw. Another good vining miniature cucumber suitable for pickles is the Mexican sour gherkin (60 days), with fruit of similar size but resembling tiny watermelons. 'Miniature White' (50 days) has a tender skin, sweet mild flavor, and a pleasant, clean crunch when eaten raw and sliced into salads.

KEY CHARACTERISTICS

Origins: Native to India

Zones: 5–11 as an annual

Propagation: By direct-sown seed after frost danger has passed, or started indoors 4 weeks before outdoor planting. Maturity depends on variety.

Pests and Diseases: Mostly cucumber beetles and powdery mildew

Height: Up to 10 feet, depending on variety

Supports: A low, slatted A-frame structure (4 feet long × 3 feet wide × 3 feet high); or a bamboo scaffold, trellis, or heavy-gauge reach-through garden netting

EGGPLANTS

Also known as aubergines, eggplants are a warm season vegetable suitable for tower pot culture, especially a medium-size variety like 'Dusky Hybrid' planted one to a pot. Eggplants can also be used as foundation plants in front of climbing plants. Seed should be started indoors ½ inch deep at least 6 weeks before outdoor planting when frost danger has passed. Although black is the most common, there are white, green, pink, purple, and striped bicolored varieties. Related to tomatoes and peppers, eggplants demand fertile soil in full sun and good drainage. Although they are generally considered to be self-supporting, their stems are brittle and heavy fruit or winds can damage the plants. Therefore, a stake or short trellis is recommended to keep the plants erect and bushy.

KEY CHARACTERISTICS

Origins: Native to India

Zones: Suitable for 5–10 as a warm season vegetable

Propagation: By seed; allow 70 days to harvest.

Pests and Diseases: Flea beetles and sunscald

Height: Up to 2 feet

Uses: Grow in tower pots with one plant per pot, or as a foundation plant in front of climbing plants, keeping each plant erect with a 2- to 3-foot stake.

GOURDS

Most gourds are edible when young and their outer skin is soft. This includes the Chinese loofah gourd (also known as Chinese okra, sponge gourd, and angled gourd). The long, dark green, sausage-shaped gourds have ribs running along their length. When young, the fruit can be sliced and used in stir-fries. At maturity, the skin hardens, and the interior becomes extremely fibrous. By fall, these fruits can be harvested, the skin removed, and the stringy interior used as a scouring pad or a bathing sponge.

Start seed indoors 4 weeks before outdoor planting and transfer to the garden after frost danger has passed. Plant the seed 1 inch deep and space the vines at least 12 inches apart. The vines need full sun, a fertile soil, and good drainage. Although they can be grown up strong bamboo canes for support, consider using them to cover arbors, arches, and chain-link fencing. The large yellow flowers are extremely decorative. Encourage earliness by growing through black plastic mulch.

Many gourds are grown for Thanksgiving decorations, including the red, cream, and green–striped 'Turk's Turban' gourd.

Other useful edible gourds include the following:

Armenian cucumber (70 days) is not really a cucumber, but an edible gourd with a pale green tender skin and slender, ribbed, cucumber-shaped fruits up to 3 feet long. An heirloom from Armenia, the fruits are best picked when they are 16 inches long and tender. The flavor is mild and similar to zucchini. Prepare the harvested fruits in the same way you would use zucchini.

Bitter gourd, also known as bitter melon and balsam pear, (75 days) has vigorous vines with tendrils that allow it to climb unaided. Known botanically as *Momordica charantia,* this plant has decorative, dark green, ivylike leaves that form a dense screen and produce pear-shaped fruit up to 8 inches long. Colored pale green, they have a bumpy skin and are valued for stir-fries in Asia. A smaller version—known as the balsam apple—has fruit up to 3 inches long and pointed at both ends. Best eaten thinly sliced at the green stage and stir-fried, the fruits turn orange at full maturity. They then split open to reveal bright red seeds.

Snake gourd, 'Cuccuzi' (75 days) features long, green-and-white striped fruits that can measure up to an incredible 4 feet long when grown on a trellis that allows the fruit to hang straight down. They are most tender when harvested young and used in stir-fries. Very popular in Asian markets, snake gourds are also useful as a Thanksgiving decoration.

KEY CHARACTERISTICS

Origins: Native mostly to Africa and India

Zones: 5–11 as an annual

Propagation: By direct-sown seed after frost danger has passed, or started indoors 4 weeks before outdoor planting. Allow 75 days to harvest.

Pests and Diseases: Mostly borers and powdery mildew

Height: Up to 10 feet

Supports: Use strong poles such as bamboo canes, trellises, or heavy-gauge reach-through garden netting. Best of all, grow them over trellised arches, so that the decorative fruits can hang down through the foliage.

HERBS

A large number of herbs can be grown in tower pots, such as basil, chives, oregano, parsley, sage, and sweetleaf stevia, mostly planted one or two to a pot. Or they can be used as foundation plants in front of climbing plants. A few can be grown as vining plants: These include hop (used as a flavoring in beer), vining scented-leaf geraniums, and climbing roses with highly scented petals used for potpourris. Many herbs originate in hot, dry, inhospitable regions and have developed their spicy flavors to ward off foraging animals and insect pests. They demand full sun and soil with good drainage. Most common herbs are grown from seed that can be direct-sown, but they are better started indoors 6 weeks before being trans-

Grow herbs like scented leaf geranium vertically in space-saving tower pots. This metal tower pot system has a central post and up to a dozen hoops at various heights, all in the space occupied by one regular container.

planted outdoors. I find that many herb gardens need some vertical accents for aesthetic appeal, and in my own herb garden I have divided the space into quadrants, with a metal or rustic wooden teepee at the center of each.

KEY CHARACTERISTICS

Origins: Mostly native to the Mediterranean

Zones: 4–11 grown as warm season annuals

Propagation: By seed, spacing plants 6 to 12 inches apart, depending on variety

Pests and Diseases: Mostly root rot from overwatering

Height: Up to 2 feet

Uses and Supports: Grow compact bushy herbs like parsley in tower pots with one or two plants per pot. Grow vining herbs like hops up trellises, heavy-gauge garden netting, wooden or metal teepees, arches, and arbors.

LETTUCES

No, to my knowledge, there is not a climbing lettuce or even a good climbing lettuce substitute, but lettuce and other salad greens like endive, radicchio, spinach, and mesclun mixes can be grown in tower pots, planted one to a pot. Or they can be used as foundation plants in front of climbing plants. Lettuces are cool season crops that can be direct-seeded or started indoors to gain healthy transplants 4 weeks before outdoor planting. Most lettuce varieties can be classified as loose-leaf lettuce, which forms a rosette of loose leaves; head lettuce, which forms a tight, crunchy head; or cos lettuce (commonly known as romaine), which grows an erect head of leaves with a crunchy heart. Loose-leaf lettuce will take crowding, but head lettuce and cos lettuce are best transplanted correctly spaced at 12 inches to help them develop their crisp, crunchy heads. (Head lettuce simply resents crowding.) Lettuce is also good to grow as an edging at the base of vining plants like pole beans.

Another class of lettuce, known as 'Batavia', is semiheading (which features a loosely folded head). My favorite is 'Sierra' because it stays edible when other lettuce varieties have bolted to seed.

'Buttercrunch' (45 days) is a sensational head lettuce, sometimes sold as 'Kentucky Limestone'. Developed by Cornell University plant scientists, it won an All-America Selection award for its crisp, crunchy, buttery-yellow heads. It's my favorite for growing in tower pots for its tight, compact habit.

KEY CHARACTERISTICS

Origins: Native to Europe

Zones: 3–11 as a cool season crop. Tolerant of mild frosts.

Propagation: By direct seeding, planted ¼ inch deep

Pests and Diseases: Mostly slugs and aphids

Height: Up to 6 inches for head and leaf lettuce; 12 inches for cos

Uses: Grow in tower pots one to a pot, or as a foundation planting in front of climbing plants.

MELONS

The most popular melons grown in North America are cantaloupes, also known as muskmelons. Some—like 'Burpee's Hybrid' cantaloupe (82 days)—weigh up to 6 pounds each and require slings to support their weight on the vine. Smaller varieties such as 'Minnesota Midget' (74 days) weigh 2 pounds and will hang from the vine without support. Two other excellent small melons that require no support when grown vertically are 'Ha'Ogen' (80 days), a sweet green-fleshed Israeli melon, and 'Charentais' (80 days), a sweet, perfumed, orange-fleshed Mediterranean melon. Both mature as one-serving-size fruit.

Melons require full sun and a well-drained, fertile soil, preferably on the sandy side. Seed can be direct-sown 1 inch deep with the vines spaced 2 feet apart so they knit into each other. Alternately, start seed indoors 4 weeks before outdoor planting after frost danger has passed in spring. Melons stop growing when the soil temperature drops below 70°F; so to encourage earliness, plant transplants in slits or holes cut in black plastic mulch, as this warms up the soil and keeps it warm during cool nights. Harvest cantaloupes when the ribs are still green and the rind is yellow; the stem should separate from the melon with a gentle tug.

Other good melons to consider for vertical gardening are:

'Burpee's Ambrosia Hybrid' (86 days) is proof that hybrid melons can be far sweeter than heirloom nonhybrid kinds. 'Ambrosia' has such a superb flavor that many melon growers keep its name a secret so you will keep going back to them for more, or they will invent a name of their own to keep you from growing your own from seed. The netted fruits grow to 4 pounds and have a small seed cavity. Combined with a thin rind, this is the perfect home garden melon.

'Burpee's Early Hybrid Crenshaw' (90 days) is the first and best early-ripening Crenshaw melon. Although individual fruits will weigh up to 14 pounds, they can be supported on erect vines with a cloth or net sling. The fruits show perfect ripeness when the dark green skin turns yellow.

Considered by many to be the best flavored of all dessert melons, the pinkish-orange flesh is sweet and juicy, delectable when served with a slice of prosciutto ham. 'Early Sugarshaw Hybrid' is a similar variety offered by some seed houses.

'**Emerald Gem**' (85 days) was discovered in Michigan and introduced in 1886. Its name and the publicity surrounding its release helped make it the most popular melon of its day. Individual fruits weigh up to 2 pounds and have a dark green skin with prominent pale green ribs and orange flesh that's sweet and juicy. The almost-spherical fruits are small enough to hang from the vines without slings for support.

'**Jenny Lind**' (80 days), a small melon shaped like a turban, was named for a popular singer of the 1940s. Its fruits have dark green skin and glistening, light green, sweet flesh. Individual fruits weigh up to 2 pounds each and don't need slings for support when grown vertically.

'**Tigger**' (85 days) has small fruits with a powerful pleasant perfume and sweet white flesh that is flavored like Asian pears, in my opinion. Also called 'Tiger', its yellow fruits with orange mottled stripes are the size of Valencia oranges. It's similar in appearance to another ornamental but bland melon, the 'Queen Anne's Pocket Melon', which was carried by Victorian ladies in their pockets and purses. I'm looking forward to the day when some enterprising plant breeder crosses the single-serving-size 'Tigger' with a larger sweet melon to produce an even sweeter flavor.

For information on Watermelons, see the entry later in this chapter.

KEY CHARACTERISTICS

Origins: Native mostly to Persia

Zones: 5–11 as an annual

Propagation: By direct-sown seed after frost danger has passed, or started indoors 4 weeks before outdoor planting. Maturity varies; usually 80 days.

Pests and Diseases: Bacterial wilt spread by cucumber beetles. Cover supports with horticultural fleece. Sprinkle diatomaceous earth around plants at seedling stage to control slugs.

Height: Up to 6 feet

Supports: Best grown up trellises or heavy-gauge reach-through garden netting

OKRA

Often called gumbo or lady's fingers, the dwarf variety of okra, 'Annie Oakley', is suitable for growing in tower pots, two or three plants to a pot. Taller varieties of okra like 'Clemson Spineless' can be used as supports for vining crops such as pole beans and squash. Okra is a warm season vegetable that takes high heat and humidity. Provide a fertile soil in full sun and good drainage. Okra is a type of hibiscus and produces white hibiscus-like flowers that last a day, immediately followed by green pointed pods that are tender when harvested young (3 inches or shorter). Left to mature to full size, the pods become fibrous (they make attractive dried flower arrangements). The round white seeds are tender when young, then turn black and develop a bullet-hard coat. Before sowing, soak seeds in lukewarm water overnight. The seed can be direct-seeded, but I prefer to start seed indoors 4 weeks before outdoor planting. Plants grow quickly and within 60 days will start to yield pods. Keep the plants picked, so that production continues all season until fall frost. Mulching with black plastic promotes earliness.

KEY CHARACTERISTICS

Origins: Native to India

Zones: 5–11 as a warm season vegetable

Propagation: By direct-sown seed after frost danger has passed, or started indoors, planted ½ inch deep

Pests and Diseases: Aphids

Height: Up to 2 feet

Uses and Supports: Grow dwarf varieties in tower pots. Use tall varieties as supports for vining plants like pole beans.

ONIONS

Although onions are not suitable for climbing, they can be grown in tower pots or grown as foundation plants in front of climbing plants. Onion relatives like shallots, garlic, and leeks are also suitable for growing in tower

pots. Onion sizes vary greatly—from tiny pearl onions the size of marbles to giant slicing onions such as 'Ailsa Craig', 'Walla Walla', and 'Robinson's Mammoth', an English selection almost the size of a soccer ball. There are onions for specific regions—some like short days of sunlight, others prefer long days, and a third kind such as 'Walla Walla' can grow virtually anywhere. Provide onions with a fertile, high phosphorus, well-drained soil in full sun, and irrigate during dry spells for the biggest bulbs. Onions grown from seed, rather than 1-year-old sets, actually produce the biggest bulbs, because onions are biennials. They go to seed the second season, and expend a lot of energy in seed production. Maturity for the big onions averages 85 days, and up to 100 days for leeks. Harvest onions and garlic when the tops bend over and the leaves start to dry out.

KEY CHARACTERISTICS

Origins: Native to Egypt

Zones: 4–11 as an annual

Propagation: By sets or seeds, either direct-sown or started 6 weeks before outdoor plantings. Young transplants will tolerate mild frosts.

Pests and Diseases: Onion maggots may burrow into the bulbs and cause rot.

Height: Up to 12 inches

Uses: Grow in tower pots with three or four plants per pot depending on variety, or as a foundation plant in front of climbing plants.

PEAS, ENGLISH

Shell peas, edible-pod snow peas, and edible-pod sugar snap peas are all cool season crops that can be direct-seeded into the garden several weeks before the last frost date. Before planting, peas generally benefit from a dusting of a black powder called an inoculant that helps form nitrogen nodules among the roots for maximum yields. These types of peas are distinctly different from Southern crowder peas and black-eyed peas, which are really beans and prefer hot summer days. English peas are available as short vine types that require no staking or tall vine types that can grow to 6 feet high.

Shell peas—such as 'Green Arrow', with up to 11 peas to a pod—can be eaten raw fresh off the vine, popped out of their inedible pods, or cooked to make them more tender and sweet. Edible-pod peas—such as 'Oregon Giant'—commonly known as snow peas, are best harvested *before* the peas swell the pod. After they swell the pod, the peas are still edible, but the pods dry out and turn tough and fibrous, lacking flavor. Snow peas are popular in Asian stir-fries. Another edible-pod pea—the sugar snap pea—is best eaten when the mature peas swell the pod. The pod walls do not become fibrous until they dry out; rather, they produce a crisp, crunchy taste treat when eaten raw. They are delicious eaten fresh off the vine or steamed for just a few minutes. The original sugar snap pea—'Sugar Snap'—requires 70 days to harvest and still has the best eating quality, in my opinion. Earlier varieties such as 'Super Sugar Snap' are mildew resistant and suitable for growing as a fall crop when mildew-prone varieties fail. You can pick sugar snap peas either young or mature (I prefer them at the mature stage). Generally, sugar snaps have a suture running along their pod length; this is best removed by pinching off the stem end to pull away the suture.

Pea vines are much lighter in weight than pole beans and do not require such strong support. A makeshift trellis of crisscrossed bamboo canes is sufficient to support a row of English peas, planted on both sides. The trellis can be flat or tent shaped. The seeds should be planted 1 to 1½ inches deep in fertile, well-drained soil in full sun. The vines tolerate crowding, so the seeds can be spaced 4 inches apart. The vines have tendrils that allow them to climb unaided. Since peas are subject to rot if the soil is too cool and wet, instead of direct seeding, you may prefer to soak the seeds on a moist paper towel until the seed coats split and roots emerge. These pre-germinated seeds will have a higher rate of success when planted in the garden.

Other novelty vining peas that can be grown vertically include:

'Blue Podded' (80 days) is a shelling pea that has violet-purple pods and pink flowers. Plants grow to 6 feet high, and the shelled green peas are mostly used in soups and stews.

'Golden Sweet' (65 days) was discovered in India, and the pods are the color of yellow wax beans. The edible-pod peas are best eaten before the peas swell the pods, just like Chinese snow peas. The flowers are pink, and the round seeds are beige with purple flecks. Plants grow to 6 feet high. When the pods dry, the mature peas can be shelled and used in soups and stews.

KEY CHARACTERISTICS

Origins: Native to Europe and North Africa

Zones: 4–10 as a cool season annual

Propagation: By direct-sown seed, or started 4 weeks before outdoor planting. Allow 60 days for early varieties.

Pests and Diseases: Mostly aphids and powdery mildew (especially in a fall planting)

Height: Up to 6 feet

Supports: Grow up twiggy branches pushed into the soil to stand erect; up bamboo canes that create a scaffold; or on trellises, garden netting, and chain-link fencing.

PEPPERS

Peppers will not climb, but they are suitable for growing vertically in tower pots or as foundation plants in front of climbing plants. Indeed, pepper plants are like eggplants—their stems are brittle and break easily from wind and mishandling. It's advisable, therefore, to give them a bamboo stake or to plant them inside a short wire cylinder to help support the weight of their fruit. There are sweet bell peppers that mostly ripen from green to red, but can also be cream, yellow, orange, purple, or black, depending on the variety. Hot peppers can present a rainbow of all these colors on the same plant. Both kinds like a fertile, well-drained soil in full sun, and spacing at least 18 inches apart. Start seed indoors at least 6 weeks before outdoor planting when frost danger has passed. Growing through black plastic mulch promotes earliness and high yields. When picking peppers, harvest by cutting the fruit with hand pruners, leaving some neck attached. Because the stems are brittle, pulling or tugging to remove fruit can cause whole branches to break off.

My personal favorite sweet variety is 'Gypsy Hybrid', because it is the most cold-tolerant sweet pepper, ensuring a harvest of yellow, orange, or red peppers. Hot peppers have different degrees of heat. The icicle-shaped cayenne is one of the hottest and most prolific, with one plant capable of producing more than a hundred red peppers. 'Green Anaheim' is one of the mildest, suitable for stuffing with chopped meat, cheese, and minced onions and serving with salsa for a Mexican treat.

KEY CHARACTERISTICS

Origins: Native to South America

Zones: 5–11 as a warm season annual

Propagation: By seed started 6 to 8 weeks before planting outdoors when frost danger has passed

Pests and Diseases: Slugs and sunscald

Height: Up to 2 feet

Uses: Grow in tower pots with one plant to a pot, supported by a 2- to 3-foot bamboo cane, or as a foundation plant in front of climbing plants.

POTATOES, SWEET

The sweet potato forms edible tubers underground, but also produces long vines that can be trained to climb up or allowed to cascade down from a window box planter to create a curtain of decorative leaves. Sweet potatoes are tender, warm season vegetables. They are grown from slips, which are sprouts that form on the tuber when it is soaked in water or planted in soil. Simply obtain a sweet potato from a garden center or produce counter and suspend it over a glass of water, allowing the tuber to touch the water, or plant it in soil with the top of the tuber exposed. Within days, the tuber will sprout dozens of green shoots that develop roots. These can be separated from the tuber and planted, with the roots in the soil and the green part above. Plant the slips at least 12 inches apart and provide a 6-foot trellis or garden netting for the vines to climb.

Provide full sun and a fertile, well-drained soil. Harvesting can occur within 100 days. Choose the disease-resistant variety 'Beauregard' for high yields. The orange-fleshed tubers can weigh a pound each and are delicious as a cooked vegetable. There are also ornamental sweet potatoes with yellow and bronze leaves, suitable for hanging baskets and window box planters and commonly sold in the annuals section at local garden centers. These produce edible tubers, though not as many as a culinary variety like 'Beauregard'.

KEY CHARACTERISTICS

Origins: Native to South America

Zones: Suitable for 5–11

Propagation: By tuberous offshoots, transplanting after frost danger has passed. For early varieties, allow 90 days to harvest.

Pests and Diseases: Slugs and rot from cool weather

Height: Up to 6 feet

Uses and Supports: Suitable for tower pots so the vines trail down like a curtain, or grown as a climbing plant up trellises and garden netting

PUMPKINS

Related to gourds, pumpkins are a symbol of fall harvest and Thanksgiving celebrations. Their pale yellow interior makes delicious pie filling. The fruits come in all shapes and sizes, from miniatures no bigger than a tennis ball to giants like 'Prizewinner' (120 days), capable of growing to 100 pounds and much larger (the world record is more than 1,500 pounds, grown in Ohio). Mini pumpkins such as 'Jack-be-Little' are mostly decorative, and will hang from their vines without slings. Any pumpkin heavier than 6 pounds, such as a New England pie pumpkin (115 days), may need support. In addition to orange pumpkins, there are white varieties. The vines can be extremely vigorous and can take over a small space, but wayward vines can be controlled by pruning the lead shoot after it has reached the desired height. Supports must be strong, such as a wooden trellis and nylon garden netting.

Also consider growing plants over arches, so the fruits hang down below the vines and foliage.

Direct-sow seeds into a fertile, well-drained soil in full sun, or start seed for transplants 4 weeks before outdoor planting when frost danger has passed. Pumpkin vines relish high heat and warm soil. Planting through black plastic mulch will promote earliness. The fruit can be stored well for months in a cool, frost-free place, provided that the stems remain hard and intact. Soft-stemmed pumpkins or fruits with stems missing soon perish from rot.

KEY CHARACTERISTICS

Origins: Native to North and South America

Zones: 5–11 as an annual

Propagation: By direct-sown seed after frost danger has passed, or started indoors 4 weeks before outdoor planting. Allow 90 to 100 days for early varieties.

Pests and Diseases: Mostly powdery mildew and borers

Height: Up to 15 feet

Supports: Use a strong wooden trellis or builder's wire, or heavy-gauge reach-through garden netting. Consider growing on chain-link fencing, such as a dog pen or swimming pool enclosure, or on arches like pergolas, where the vines can climb up and over the structure, allowing the fruit to hang below the foliage.

SPINACH, CLIMBING

Also known as Malabar spinach, this fast-growing vine produces dark green, succulent, heart-shaped leaves that are heat resistant and an excellent substitute for regular spinach that cannot tolerate heat. Plants will grow to 10 feet high and allow harvests within 50 days of direct seeding in spring after frost danger has passed. Sow the seeds ½ inch deep in a sunny, well-drained soil. The stems of climbing spinach are red, and the pink flowers highly decorative. The more the leaves are picked for summer salads or cooking, the more new leaves are produced. Harvest the most tender, topmost whorls of leaves. Malabar spinach is sometimes confused with the equally heat-resistant New Zealand spinach, which is a shorter vining type that grows up to 4 feet tall.

KEY CHARACTERISTICS

Origins: Native to Asia

Zones: 4–11 as an annual

Propagation: By direct-sown seed after frost danger has passed, or started 4 weeks before outdoor planting. Although catalogs often say 90 days to harvest, you can start to harvest after 50 days.

Pests and Diseases: Mostly slugs

Height: Up to 10 feet

Supports: Strong trellises, heavy-gauge small or wide-spaced garden netting, arches, and arbors

SQUASHES, SUMMER

Most summer squash—such as green zucchini squash and yellow crookneck—have been bred to be dwarf varieties, so that they produce their fruit on bushy plants unsuitable for growing vertically. However, there are several summer squash varieties that are eminently suitable for growing up a strong trellis.

Climbing 'Black Forest' zucchini is a unique type of summer squash, because it produces a vine up to 5 feet tall, with clusters of cylindrical dark green fruits best eaten when they are 6 inches long. This squash matures in 65 days, and the plants bear all summer if the fruits are picked regularly. It's easily supported by a single bamboo stake (use twist ties to keep the vine erect), or by planting it inside a wire cylinder.

Climbing 'Trombone' zucchini, also known as 'Zucchino Rampicante' (60 to 85 days), is an Italian heirloom that produces vigorous vines with tendrils, allowing it to climb unaided. The fruit is shaped like a trombone, with a long, curled neck and a bulbous base. There are two stages when the fruit can be harvested—soon after the fruit is pollinated and still pale green in color (starting in 60 days), or later in summer (starting in 85 days) when the skin turns beige or brown. This zucchini is so long that in its green

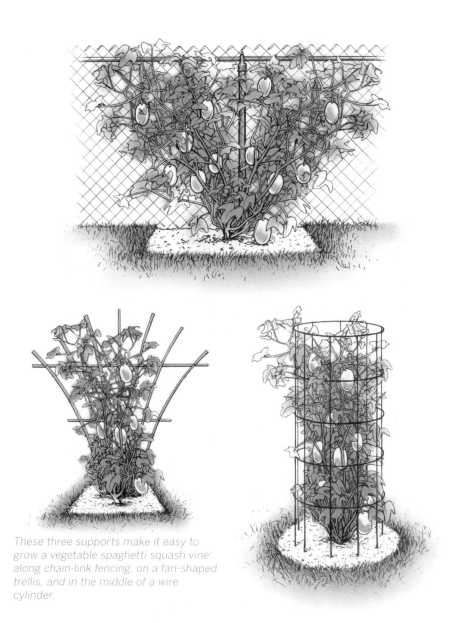

These three supports make it easy to grow a vegetable spaghetti squash vine: along chain-link fencing, on a fan-shaped trellis, and in the middle of a wire cylinder.

immature stage, I have been able to cut 300 slices from its neck section—all seedless, since the seeds are concentrated in the bulbous base. The flavor is tender and mild, just like that of a zucchini squash, especially when steamed. At the mature brown stage, the flesh tastes more like a winter squash. The mature fruit can be stored for months in a cool, dark, frost-free place. Keep the vine picked, and up to 50 fruits are possible from a single plant.

'**Vegetable Spaghetti**' (80 days) grows a vigorous vine similar to that of 'Trombone' zucchini, but the fruits are shaped like an oblong melon, with either creamy white, yellow, or orange skin, depending on variety. Up to a dozen fruit is possible from a single plant. At maturity, the fruits have a hard shell like a winter squash and similarly can be stored in a cool, dark place for long periods. But the interior is like no other squash: Cooked, it fluffs up into long cream-colored strands just like pasta spaghetti, but without the calories. The strands will soak up the flavor of whatever sauce you want to serve on it, whether marinara sauce, clam sauce, or parsley butter. Some catalogs classify it as a winter squash, but since it matures in summer weeks ahead of winter squash, other seedsmen list it as a summer squash.

I rate vegetable spaghetti as one of the easiest vegetables to grow vertically from seed. And one of the most profitable, as well, since the fruits can weigh 5 pounds each. I have seen them on the produce counter at many supermarkets for $2.50 a pound. Since a 5-pound vegetable spaghetti will total $12.50 at the market, and a vine can produce a dozen fruits, that's a potential value of $150 per vine—all for about 15 cents per seed!

Vegetable spaghetti was discovered in China by the Sakata Seed Company (now headquartered in Yokohama, Japan), although all squash are believed to be from the Americas. No one can explain how the squash reached China, but when Mr. Sakata put it in his seed catalog in 1934, he called it spaghetti squash, and it did not sell. He believes it was difficult for seedsmen and their customers to imagine a squash tasting like spaghetti, so he removed it from commerce. But later, in 1960, he reintroduced it as vegetable spaghetti. That small change—calling it vegetable spaghetti instead of spaghetti squash—made all the difference, especially when he promoted it as a low-calorie substitute for spaghetti.

The vegetable spaghetti that Mr. Sakata introduced has a pale yellow skin and is still available. But since then, other plant breeders have introduced new varieties with an orange skin and even one with a yellow-and-orange mottled skin. The interior flesh is still a creamy white, irrespective of the skin color, and I still prefer the Sakata original for its impressive size and yield.

What few people realize is that vegetable spaghetti is a climbing vine, with tendrils that allow it to be self-supporting. It will grasp any kind of trellis, and it especially likes to climb a chain-link fence. In 1982, I collaborated with herbalist Phyllis Shaudys on a book titled *The Vegetable Spaghetti Cookbook*. I wrote the plant's growing instructions, and Phyllis tested 100 recipes. In the introduction to the book, she explained that her first experience with vegetable spaghetti was when she and her daughter Kim decided to lose weight. They each lost 40 pounds on a vegetable spaghetti diet, not only using it as a substitute for pasta, but also using it in bread, salads, relish, and desserts. There are only 29 calories in a 3½-ounce serving (about one-third the calories in the same portion of pasta).

To cook a vegetable spaghetti squash, preheat the oven to 450°F, and pierce the shell of the squash so it does not burst. Place it right on the rack and bake for 45 minutes, turning it over halfway through baking. Remove from the oven and slice the fruit in half with a sharp, serrated knife. Scrape out the seeds. Then remove the spaghetti strands with a fork, fluff them, top with sauce, and enjoy!

These remarkable climbing squashes can be direct-seeded by planting the seeds 2 inches deep after frost danger has passed in spring. They require full sun, a fertile soil, and good drainage. Plant at least 2 feet apart, and allow the vines to knit together. The use of black plastic as a mulch will ensure earliness.

KEY CHARACTERISTICS

Origins: Native to North and South America

Zones: 5–11 as an annual

Propagation: By direct-sown seed after frost danger has passed, or started indoors 4 weeks before outdoor planting. Maturity varies according to variety. Early varieties yield in 45 days.

Pests and Diseases: Mostly borers and powdery mildew

Height: Up to 8 feet

Supports: Grow up strong trellises, heavy-gauge reach-through garden netting, or chain-link fencing, such as a dog pen or swimming pool enclosure.

Winter squash require a longer growing season than summer squash. Some have been dwarfed to produce fruit on a bush plant, but the most productive and best flavored grow long vines suitable for growing vertically. Following are recommended winter squash varieties with reasonably small fruit, most of which do not require slings for support.

'**Buttercup**' (95 days) is a small, round, flattened winter squash with a dark green skin and gray "button" at the blossom end. The orange flesh is delicious when baked, tasting like a sweet potato. Individual fruits weigh 3 pounds each, enough to serve two people. The fruit stores for months after harvest in a cool, dry, frost-free place.

'**Delicata**' (100 days) is a small-fruited oval winter squash with a white green-flecked skin and green stripes along its ribs. Developed by Cornell University, the plants produce short, mildew-resistant vines up to 4 feet long. Winner of an All-America Selection award, the fruits average seven per plant and weigh up to 2 pounds, allowing them to mature on the vine without slings for support. The pale orange flesh is especially tasty when baked and eaten with a spoonful of maple syrup, or with a ground beef mixture stuffed into the seed cavity. As the fruit ages, the white parts of the skin turn yellow. Two other winter squashes similar in appearance to 'Delicata' are the smaller-fruited 'Sweet Dumpling' that displays heart-shaped fruits, and 'Carnival', similar in appearance to an acorn squash but with white, yellow, and green mottling. These squash vines will need assistance to climb, so use twist ties to attach the stems to a trellis or netting. All like to be grown through black plastic mulch for earliness and high yields.

Kabocha (95 days) describes a family of flattened, round, small-fruited winter squash that vary in color. The hybrid variety 'Sunshine' won an All-America Selection award for its deep orange, almost scarlet skin color and deep orange, flavorful flesh. Individual fruits average 4 pounds and therefore do not need slings for support when the vines are grown vertically. There are also gray and green Kabocha squashes.

'Table Ace' (85 days) is a hybrid acorn squash whose fruits are dark green (almost black), shaped like a heart, with prominent ribs. The fruits are sufficiently small (3 pounds) and hang down the sides of the plant without support. The sweet orange flesh is delicious, tasting like a sweet potato. Bake in halves and add a tablespoon of maple syrup in the seed cavity to create a memorable taste treat during fall. White- and orange-skinned versions of 'Table Ace' are also available.

'Waltham Butternut' (105 days) fruits can weigh up to 5 pounds and therefore should be supported on the vine by slings when grown vertically. The cylindrical fruits have a bulbous base. Beige in color on the outside, they have deep orange flesh with a flavor similar to an acorn squash when baked.

KEY CHARACTERISTICS

Origins: Native to North and South America

Zones: 5–11 as an annual

Propagation: By direct-sown seed after frost danger has passed, or started indoors 6 weeks before outdoor planting. Maturity varies according to variety. Early varieties require 85 days to harvest.

Pests and Diseases: Mostly borers and powdery mildew

Height: Up to 10 feet

Supports: Use strong trellis or builder's wire between posts, or use heavy-gauge reach-through garden netting. Long vining types like butternut can be grown over arches so the fruit can hang down below the foliage, or grown along stretches of chain-link fencing.

TOMATOES

The world record height for a tomato vine is 25 feet, using the variety 'Better Boy' hybrid. This was grown by an Arkansas farmer who produced more than 300 fruits on a single plant. Another extremely vigorous climbing tomato is 'Trip-L-Crop' (also known as 'The Tree'). When you see tree tomatoes advertised, this is usually the variety used. Both 'Better Boy' and 'The Tree' tomato produce large fruits, up to 1 pound each.

The terms *determinate* and *indeterminate* are used to differentiate between tomato plants that remain bushy (like the determinate variety 'Patio') and those that continue to grow a long vine (like the indeterminate 'Better Boy'). Although many indeterminate tomatoes have exceedingly long vines suitable for growing vertically, they need assistance in order to stand erect. A disadvantage of determinate (bushy) tomato varieties is that once the plant has set a crop, it generally stops growing and ripens its fruit all at one time, then dies before the tomato growing season is finished.

This 'Better Boy' hybrid tomato is supported by parallel strands of string to hold up the incredible yield from this variety.

For an indeterminate (vining) tomato to climb, it needs a strong pole such as a bamboo cane, with twist ties used to secure the tomato's main stem in several places, so the vine stands tall. Alternatively, the plant can be grown in the middle of a wire cylinder with a mesh wide enough for the tomato to poke its side branches through and become virtually self-supporting. Tomato plants will also grow up a trellis and garden netting attached to a sunny wall.

Some seed sources classify tomatoes according to their period of ripening: early, midseason, and late. Many small-fruited tomato varieties are early, whereas most medium-size and large-fruiting varieties are either midseason or late. To determine whether a tomato is early, midseason, or late, check the number of days to maturity on the seed packet or catalog description. A variety that ripens in 60 to 70 days is considered early, 70 to 80 days midseason, and 80 to 90 days or more late. These figures are not the number of days from seed to harvest, but from *transplanting* to harvest.

Transplants should be 6 weeks old, stocky and dark green, preferably with no flowers yet formed (or else with only a few tight bud clusters showing) in order to reduce transplant shock. Avoid plants that have had to stretch toward the light or whose top growth is excessive compared to the rootball, and always choose plants that have been hardened off in a cold-frame for a week to help them endure cold nights. Since tomatoes are susceptible to frost damage, delay planting until after the last expected frost date, and cover at night if the weather forecast predicts the likelihood of an unexpected frost. The covering can be overturned bushel baskets, glass cloches, or anything to hold in heat, such as newspapers, a bedsheet, or plastic garbage bags. A stressed tomato plant can take a long time to recover. Planting the rootball deep encourages extra roots to develop along the lower stem, and encourages lateral roots that can spread out in all directions close to the soil surface for extra feeding capability and stability.

The color range of tomatoes today is extraordinary. Many small-fruited varieties such as cherry and pear tomatoes are available in all shades of red, plus pink, yellow, orange, green, cream, purple, maroon, chocolate, and almost black, along with striped bicolors. A collection of these in a basket can look like a bowl of jelly beans.

It is amazing how much misinformation surrounds the setting of fruit. The fertilizing of tomato fruits is greatly misunderstood. Since tomato plants are self-pollinating, it is *not* necessary to take an artist's paintbrush and dab pollen from one flower to another to improve pollination and fruit set. All that's necessary for the flowers to set fruit is a slight movement of the flower cluster to mix up the pollen. Even a gentle breeze can achieve this, but you can also shake the flower trusses to help ensure pollination. Pollination is inhibited during cold weather and hot, humid conditions.

It is interesting to note that different ethnic groups like different kinds of tomatoes. For example, American gardeners prefer them round and red; the Japanese prefer their tomatoes red with green shoulders; and Russians prefer them to be maroon. Whatever color they are, a mature green tomato can be picked and ripened indoors at room temperature, since the ripening process is not stopped by picking. Pick ripe fruit often to encourage continuous flower formation, and pick cherry tomatoes the moment they turn red, prior to cracking.

It is estimated that there are more than 5,000 varieties of tomatoes, with dozens more introduced each year, as both professional breeders and

Troubleshooting Tomatoes

Although tomatoes are among the easiest vegetables to grow vertically, certain problems can impair their harvest. Here are the most common.

Anthracnose is a fungus disease that normally occurs late in the season. Perfectly healthy tomatoes can suddenly show discoloration from round black sunken patches. These are caused by a fungus that can be present on contaminated seed and also on garden debris. In addition to a good garden cleanup in winter and burning or composting dried tomato stems, you can choose resistant varieties.

Blossom-end rot is a blackening of the skin at the blossom end of the fruit. It can be caused by irregular watering and by lack of calcium in the soil. This problem mostly occurs on medium and large-size fruits. If the blackening occurs on the sides of the fruit, it is more likely to be anthracnose.

Cat face is a corky disfiguration that occurs on mostly large-fruited tomatoes, and some varieties are more prone than others (in my experience, 'Supersteak' is one of the least prone). The disfiguration may look unsightly, but the blemish is normally only skin deep and is easily cut away. If the corky disfiguration occurs as a stripe down one side of the fruit, it is usually caused by imperfect pollination. Again, the corky streak is easily cut away.

Cracking affects some varieties more than others. For example, many cherry tomatoes will automatically crack when they have passed perfect ripeness. 'Sun Gold' and 'Sweet 100' are examples. Pick the fruit often and before the overripe stage.

keen amateurs make crosses and offer their introductions over the Internet. Following are some tomato varieties specially suited for vertical gardening, widely available through seed catalogs.

'**Aunt Ruby's German Green**' (85 days) is one of several large-fruited tomatoes that remain green when fully ripe. Test for ripeness by feel—ripe

Late ripening or poor fruit set is mostly caused by too low or too high a temperature, or infertile soil. For tomato plants to set high yields, they need an organic fertilizer high in phosphorus. Also, if tomatoes are fed with animal manure high in nitrogen, this can cause more leafy growth than fruit formation. To improve earliness, cover the soil with black plastic mulch. This warms the soil early, keeps the soil warm during cool nights, and will advance ripening by 2 weeks or more. If you use an organic mulch such as shredded leaves or straw, be aware that this will keep the soil cool, so apply it after the soil has had a chance to warm up.

Nematodes are microscopic worms that live mostly in sandy soil and present a big problem in Southern states, attacking the roots of tomato plants and causing them to wilt. Nematodes do not like soils with a high organic content, so enrich yours with compost. Nematodes travel through soil, so another remedy is to grow your tomatoes in sunken pots using a sterile commercial potting soil from a garden center. Or you can sterilize batches of garden topsoil yourself by baking it in an oven for 40 minutes at 450°F, using a disposable aluminum turkey roasting pan.

Sunscald is caused by overexposure to the sun, causing fruit to form a pale sunken white or yellow patch. I have never seen cherry tomatoes suffer sunscald, but it is a common ailment on medium-size and large-fruited varieties during long, sunny, cloudless periods of hot, humid weather. It is also common on vines that are heavily pruned, eliminating foliage cover.

fruit turns pale green, but fruits can be eaten at any stage as fried green tomatoes or in a bruschetta. The 'Beefsteak'-size fruits can weigh 1 pound or more.

'**Better Boy Hybrid**' (75 days) is a derivative of the famous 'Big Boy' hybrid, but with improved disease resistance. The large, smooth, flavorful, meaty fruits can weigh up to 1 pound, produced on vigorous vines that generally stay below 10 feet tall, but can exceed 25 feet.

'**Big Rainbow**' (80 days) has many other names, including 'Striped German', 'Pineapple', 'Flame', and 'Virginia Sweets'. An heirloom variety with a sweet flavor, the golden yellow fruits with red streaks will easily grow to 2 pounds each. This is one of my favorites for flavor and attractiveness.

'**Black Krim**', also known as '**Black Russian**' (82 days), is one of many large-fruited maroon tomatoes from Russia that is almost black on the outside and a mixture of maroon and red on the inside. It has good meaty flavor and is especially attractive when sliced. Its globe-shaped fruits measure up to 5 inches across.

'**Brandywine**' (80 days) is the *original* Brandywine, introduced in 1889. After 100 years, it still produces deep red fruits up to 1 pound each, with a smooth, round shape and a meaty and delicious flavor. Several other Brandywines have been introduced, including pink (known as 'Sudduth's Strain'). There is also a yellow and a black Brandywine, and all four colors are sold as a mixture by some seed companies.

'**Costaluto Genovese**' (78 days) is sometimes sold under the name "Ugly Tomato," because of its outer appearance. Most gardeners prefer large-fruited tomatoes to be round and smooth skinned, but this Italian "cushion" (or corrugated) heirloom variety has deeply ridged fruits. They're a deep red color, juicy, and attractive when sliced into a scalloped or star pattern.

'**Early Cascade**' (57 days) is the perfect mid-size tomato, ripening its round, red, billiard-ball-size fruits in clusters of six to eight. The vines are vigorous and have stamina to crop continuously from July 4th to fall frosts. Other early-ripening mid-size and large-size tomatoes tend to lack good flavor, but not 'Early Cascade'. And in my experience, it's earlier and more productive than 'Early Girl'—another mid-size hybrid.

(continued on page 229)

VERTICAL GARDENING

WHAT IS A VERTICAL GARDEN?

Create simple bamboo scaffolds to support climbing Malabar spinach; with a vertical support like this, you can grow an abundance of spinach in a very small space.

Vertical gardening enables you to combine climbing plants with foundation, or low-growing, plants. These pole beans make good companions for a row of cabbage.

Seize opportunities to create a wall of color by combining climbing plants, such as 'Heavenly Blue' morning glory, with bedding plants like wax begonias.

An expandable wooden trellis can be used to support pole snap beans.

Freshly dug from the soil, this is the harvest from a single 'Beauregard' sweet potato vine. The long vines can be trained to climb or allowed to cascade over a container.

'Yellow Baby' watermelon is an ice-box-size variety that is cold tolerant, almost seedless, and perfect for growing up a trellis or netting.

Place a hydroponic tower pot system on your patio to ensure fresh basil within a few steps of your kitchen.

The ingredients in a typical sterile potting mix for use in containers and raised beds include (from top to bottom) slow-release fertilizer pellets, vermiculite, perlite, urea (nitrogen), and black peat.

Most vertical garden structures like this pole bean lean-to use only a narrow bed of prepared soil, saving you time and energy compared with digging traditional garden plots.

183

The shade-tolerant clematis 'Carnaby' is a beautiful vine for a garden pergola.

CHAPTER
3

ARBORS, ARCHES, PERGOLAS, AND TRELLISES

When grapevine leaves turn golden yellow in fall, this large pergola glows with color.

184

Black bamboo is decorative but not reliably hardy for gardens north of Washington, DC.

Yellow-groove bamboo has interesting yellow-and-green striped canes and makes a sturdy trellis, but it does need to be contained because it spreads by runners.

Allow flowering clematis and climbing rose to entwine and intermingle on a wooden arbor, and your bench will become a favorite garden hideaway.

Vining ivy-leaf geraniums climb a store-bought trellis to frame a window in this serene garden.

'Blaze' climbing rose covers a small arbor with one plant positioned on each side of the support and the canes trained up by twist ties.

This homemade wooden arbor is covered in builder's wire to support an assortment of squash and cucumber vines.

186

If you have limited space, try growing edibles like 'Buttercrunch' lettuce in a Hydro Harvest Farms hydroponic system. Plants grow in tower pots in a soilless growing medium of vermiculite and perlite fed with a liquid fertilizer.

Crisscross pairs of bamboo poles with a single cane running along the top, then add garden twine to support climbing pea vines.

These three-tier tower planters help grow an assortment of plants on a paved surface at Cedaridge Farm.

The no-dig Skyscraper Garden is perfectly suited for flowering vines, such as two colors of morning glories, vining nasturtiums, and sweet peas. This type of planting is highly attractive to hummingbirds.

The Skyscraper Garden shows off its results—vigorous climbing 'Trombone' zucchini, 'Early Cascade' tomatoes, and 'Orient Express' climbing cucumbers. I've harvested as many as 20 zucchini, 500 tomatoes, and 50 cucumbers from this unit.

This arrangement of tower pots at Cedaridge Farm is displayed on two quarter-round tiered metal plant stands, creating a semicircle. The terra-cotta-colored pots with watering trays are planted with an assortment of edible plants and ornamental vines.

Three bamboo canes secured with a long twist tie is a simple-to-make support for tomato vines.

Many garden centers and catalogs offer attractive obelisks that support climbing vines like mandevilla.

Pansies flourish in a simple plastic pouch planter. These cylindrical pouches are filled with potting soil and have planting holes perfect for growing pansies, petunias, impatiens, or strawberries.

A maypole bean support features strands of string radiating out from the top of a sturdy pole and held taut to the ground by pegs.

Use privet twigs arranged in a circle to support tall-growing delphinium stems. Similar supports work well for sweet peas.

CONTAINERS AND HANGING PLANTERS

Flowering annuals create curtains of color, mostly growing in window box planters and terra-cotta pots held aloft by hangers. Foliar feeding with a backpack sprayer stimulates flowering.

Decorative metal wall planters can create a vertical presentation of foliage and flowers in a small patio setting.

Mandevilla x amoena 'Alice du Pont' is perfect for growing up a trellis in a Versailles planter box.

Mix pots of annuals, such as impatiens and petunias, on shelves and pedestals to design a memorable vertical garden.

'Buttercup' English ivy is trained so it completely cloaks an ornamental urn. A similar cloaking technique can be used to decorate tree trunks.

Metal hangers help to create a vertical column of pots and surround this sunny window with annuals such as petunias, impatiens, and geraniums.

Whiskey half-barrels can be used to grow runner beans on a brick patio. Let the vines climb strands of string hung from a wooden frame.

Ruby Swiss chard forms a pillar of crimson stalks in a strawberry barrel; a single barrel holds as much as a standard 15-foot row of chard.

In hanging basket planters at different heights, 'Whirlybird' nasturtiums form a wall of hot colors.

Ivy-leaf geraniums in hanging baskets create a nonstop flower- and foliage-covered privacy wall.

Tiers of window boxes and hanging basket planters present a riot of color from annuals along the sunny side of this home.

Recycle a plastic container to start a batch of seedlings.

This pregerminated pea seedling has a healthy root system. Use only robust seedlings; if any appear weak or yellow, don't move them to your garden bed.

This quart-size juice container is filled with potting soil to allow the plant to develop a deep, vigorous root system. At transplant time, the cardboard is easily peeled away and the plant can be placed in a garden bed with minimal root disturbance.

Many vegetables and fruits, including grapes, can be damaged by late spring and early fall frosts; whenever possible, protect vegetables with floating row covers.

Clematis can suffer from chlorosis, a nutrient deficiency that yellows a portion of the leaf but leaves the veins green.

Black rot can affect all parts of the grape plant; the grapes will rot, shrivel, and harden.

Black spot leaves tell-tale black blotches on rose leaves that will eventually drop off.

This geranium flower has been disfigured by Botrytis blight, which initially shows up as water-soaked spots and fuzzy gray or whitish growth.

The fungus anthracnose starts as small spots, but they'll quickly merge and leaves will turn brown and die.

Bacterial wilt on a cucumber vine causes it to wilt and collapse suddenly. Remove and destroy infected plants as soon as you see the problem occurring.

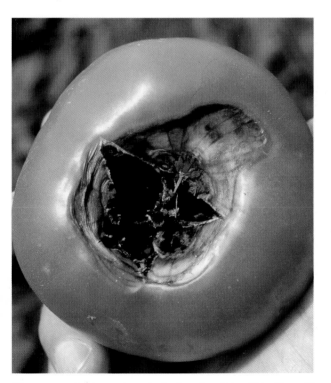

Blossom-end rot on a tomato fruit makes it inedible. You will notice a dark, sunken area on the blossom end of the fruit.

CONTROLLING WEEDS, WATERING,
FERTILIZING, AND PRUNING

Unless the stem tops are controlled by pruning, many vines will produce top-heavy foliage and sparse growth along the lower part of the vine.

A mulch of shredded leaves helps control weeds, looks natural, and adds humus to the soil as it breaks down.

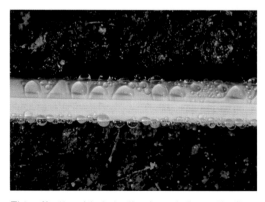

This effective drip irrigation hose is "sweating" moisture from pores all along its length.

With sugar peas supported by a trellis above, a drip irrigation line runs the length of the bed.

The cucumber 'Tall Telegraph' grows perfectly formed fruit when grown up a wooden fence.

Asparagus beans, or yard-long beans as they're often called, can't be missed when they're grown vertically on garden netting.

Pumpkins can grow vertically! 'Baby Bear' pumpkin is an ideal small size for growing on a strong trellis or heavy-gauge garden netting.

Pole beans come in many colors. This harvest includes a purple-podded variety, yellow wax beans, and a mottled bean.

199

You'll be successful with almost any tomato variety, if you offer it support. These yellow plum tomato vines are supported with parallel strands of string stretched between posts.

The pole snap bean 'Blue Lake' is noted for superb flavor; offer it a tripod and watch it produce an amazing yield.

The heirloom 'King of the Garden' pole lima bean needs a strong support like a teepee with rope strings; there are often a dozen pods to a cluster.

Unlike regular spinach, climbing Malabar spinach is heat resistant and everbearing; grow it on a support like this maypole with radiating strings.

Here's the famous tomato/potato combination plant, produced by grafting a tomato onto a potato so that potatoes grow among the roots and tomatoes among the foliage.

The asparagus pea, also known as the winged pea, is actually a legume. Some people find that the pods, often steamed or used in stir-fries, are more flavorful than snow peas.

A simple net sling supports the weight of a ripe melon when it's grown vertically. Slings can be used to support small pumpkins, winter squash, and vegetable spaghetti in a vertical garden. Small, single-serving-size melons generally do not require slings.

Melon 'Ha'Ogen' resembles a super-sweet 'Charentais' melon, but with green flesh. It's a single-serving-size melon with a delicious flavor, and it's ideal for growing up a trellis or garden netting.

Use pruned tree branches as strong tripods for a bumper crop of scarlet runner beans. The beans' red flower clusters look decorative in a vegetable bed.

The vines of pole Romano beans are vigorous, so you'll need to give them plenty of strong support, like a bamboo or branch tripod.

'Delicata' winter squash is not only delicious, but it is also amazingly productive. This is the harvest from a single vine grown vertically—with no support slings needed!

Purple-podded peas, also known as blue peas, are an heirloom variety that produces purple pods and green peas and readily climbs garden netting.

No summer squash I have ever grown can outyield 'Trombone' climbing zucchini. This vigorous variety, capable of producing on a single plant 50 fruits with long curved necks and bulbous blossom ends, climbs unaided up a strong support.

CHAPTER

11

FRUITS FOR
VERTICAL GARDENS

Train blackberry canes along double wires strung between posts, using crossbars to affix parallel strands.

Anyone who likes tree-ripened peaches should try growing some on a short section of freestanding espalier. Even in a home garden, it's easy to espalier peach trees, here in a diamond pattern against a fence.

This espaliered pear tree is on a southwest-facing wall at Chanticleer Garden in Wayne, Pennsylvania. where the wall provides privacy for a swimming pool. Pears tolerate shade better than any other fruit trees, including apples and peaches.

This espaliered apple tree forms a heart shape—and makes a heartfelt statement in this garden. It's a good example of how pliable the branches of fruit trees like apples, pears, and peaches can be.

If you have a long expanse of wall, consider adding a trellis for an espaliered fig tree. The trellis is affixed to the wall, yet it allows for air circulation and maximum fruit set.

A single grapevine can be trained to grow up and around an entrance. Here it creates a gorgeous sight, its fall foliage contrasting with the stone wall of a barn.

Modern day-neutral strawberries with long runners can be trained to grow up a trellis to produce abundant fruit.

Muscadine grapes, like these bronze- and green-skinned varieties, are especially suitable for Southern gardens.

Crabapples provide bounty when espaliered against the side of a garage. You'll only need nails and string or twist ties to secure the pliable branches in a horizontal branching pattern.

A mix of tall climbing 'Galaxy' sweet peas offers a rich color assortment.

Vining ivy-leaf geraniums trail long stems to create a curtain of color from a window box.

The flowers of the Mexican flame vine look like a shower of sparks from a flamethrower; the fiery spikes will be in continuous bloom from early summer to first fall frost.

The fast-growing black-eyed Susan vine climbs almost any support. Used here to decorate a shade house over nursery beds, the vine features thousands of trumpet-shaped flowers.

Climbing nasturtiums scramble up the side of a shed, with a bit of garden netting for support. You can direct-seed nasturtiums in your garden after your last frost in spring.

'Grandpa Otts' morning glory is a beautiful blue-flowering vine, the flowers a deeper blue than the popular 'Heavenly Blue'. The flowers of 'Grandpa Otts' also have purple markings at the base of each petal.

Though the flowers of these 'Million Bells' mini petunias are one-quarter the size of regular petunias, the sheer quantity of blooms provides dramatic visual impact when cascading from hanging baskets and planters.

The variegated form of evergreen wintercreeper climbs a trellis to create a curtain of decorative foliage. Variegated wintercreeper is more refined and easier to control than English ivy.

Perennial sweet peas can climb to 8 feet high in a single season. They are smaller-flowered than annual sweet peas and lack fragrance but are just as beautiful.

Virginia creeper is often a favored vine for covering stone cottages, walls, and historic structures. Though not evergreen, it develops brilliant red color in fall.

211

You can expect this type of growth from flame nasturtium if you live where summers are cool, such as in the Pacific Northwest and coastal Maine.

Potted Star jasmine (Trachelospermum jasminoides) can grow as tall as a person in a single season.

Clematis terniflora, the sweet autumn clematis, decorates an ornate metal fence with a waterfall of foamy and fragrant flowers.

Fiery red bougainvillea climbs a house wall to create a vertical garden above a generous selection of container plants.

In a small-space courtyard garden, the long, spreading stems of Boston ivy frame a window displaying a cascade of ivy-leaf geraniums.

213

*'Henryi' clematis
decorates a lamppost
magnificently,
climbing a cone frame
made of chicken wire.*

Boston ivy (Parthenocissus tricuspidata) decorates a wall in fall foliage colors. Although not evergreen like English ivy, its leaves turn beautiful pink and red in fall.

The yellow form of trumpet honeysuckle makes a beautiful patio accent and is highly attractive to hummingbirds zooming by.

Cross vine needs a strong support, such as builder's wire or a pergola, but you'll be rewarded with a curtain of trumpet blooms in spring.

The stunning orange blossoms of Campsis x tagliabuana 'Mme. Galen' attract hoards of hummingbirds. Train this vigorous trumpet creeper up any rough surface, such as a brick wall or split-rail fence.

Simple trellises can offer good support for climbing roses and other vines.

'Diamond', a mini-leaf form of English ivy, features variegated green and white foliage that gives it a silvery appearance.

The flowers of climbing hydrangea can be the size of dessert plates and can reach 30 feet in height climbing up a strong structure.

Clematis 'Ernest Markham' growing up a single strand of wire beside a garage door is a welcoming site for gardeners and guests.

At Bodnant Garden, North Wales, in June, you'll see the famous golden chain tree tunnel with the pliable branches of Laburnum trained over a metal arch.

Clematis 'Madame Edouard Andre' climbs an arch in Monet's Garden in Giverny, France.

This massive and abundantly blooming 'Wedding Day' climbing rose almost reaches the roof of a two-story house.

Bignonia capreolata, also known as cross vine, grows up the side of the house at historic Bartram's Garden in Philadelphia.

Coral pea is a tender tropical vine that can be grown in a container to climb up and cover an arbor. When the season ends, it can be cut way back and overwintered indoors.

Blue sky vine is a tender perennial that must be grown in a pot and taken indoors during periods of frost.

To tame the thorny branches of Pyracantha coccinea 'Mohave', espalier parallel branches against a stone wall or fence.

A single vine of 'Lady Banks' rose covers an arbor with its glorious yellow blooms.

If Southern gardeners want to cover an arch with a stunning blue flower, they can plant the tender vine Plumbago capensis 'Monet'.

Purple 'Jackmanii' clematis and pink 'Cornelia' rose make perfect companions growing up a trellis.

Wintercreeper, including the variegated forms, is often the top pick for cloaking walls, stumps, and trellises; here it frames a front doorway.

221

14

DESIGNING WITH ORNAMENTAL VINES

Using wire netting for support, Clematis montana *in white, light pink, and deep pink drapes over an entire cliffside—vertical gardening on a grand scale.*

Clematis montana *cascades in curtains of white star-shaped flowers from the branches of a eucalyptus tree.*

White wisteria flowers drape from a pergola, framing a secluded bench in a small backyard inner-city garden designed by New Zealand garden writer Robyn Kilty.

Beautiful 'Avalanche' climbing roses cover an arch and the top of a privacy fence, helping to create a quiet sanctuary for reading and contemplation.

A weeping spruce planted above a rock wall creates a beautiful soothing textural quality as it drapes its branches down around a stone bench.

A "green wall" designed by French garden designer Patrick Blanc decorates the wall of a glass-roofed courtyard at the Hotel Pershing in Paris. Tropical vines are planted in a special felt curtain that a fertilizer-and-water solution drips through.

English ivy cloaks a locust tree to soften the entrance to a small yard. Virginia creeper, trumpet creeper, and wintercreeper are other good vines to cloak mature tree trunks.

The entrance to the guest cottage at Cedaridge Farm is laden with vines and foliage, both to cool the cottage and to lend an air of coziness and privacy for guests.

A high waterfall with boulders is softened by English ivy and the cascading branches of a weeping blue spruce in a dramatic backyard water garden.

English ivy can take many forms; this threadleaf variety is one of the most decorative and well suited for climbing walls and fences.

This guest cottage is covered with climbing roses, trumpet creeper, and clematis, and is screened by small trees to produce an informal, decorative effect.

Climbing Virginia creeper blankets the roof of this rustic gazebo and provides a cooling respite on a hot day.

Imagine how pleasant it is to relax on this patio with lush grapevines creating a shady canopy!

Though this looks like a vine-covered wall, it's actually a Benjamin fig tightly pruned to create a vertical wall of foliage. Creeping fig (Ficus pumila) can create a similar effect growing on a wall.

'Nelly Moser' clematis twines its pink-striped blooms through the flowering branches of its support plant, an Exbury hybrid azalea. The lightweight clematis vine creates an attractive plant partnership with the azalea shrub.

At master French Impressionist Claude Monet's garden in Giverny, France, roses are trained into tree forms, with their top canes spread out over the spokes of a metal umbrella for support.

The vertical garden designed by Brazilian landscape architect Roberto Burle Marx at Longwood Gardens in Kennett Square, Pennsylvania, features a waterfall of "silver threads" with accents of bromeliads and ferns planted in rock crevices. A vining philodendron (right) creeps up a stone wall.

The staked 'Early Cascade' tomato shows how appropriate its name really is; this variety produces medium-size fruit from early summer to fall frost.

'Jubilee' (70 days) produces large orange fruits that average 12 ounces, with a sweet, mild flavor. The vines are highly productive. For smaller orange fruit, see 'Sun Gold Hybrid', and for an orange tomato with extra high vitamin content, grow 'Caro-Rich' (72 days).

'Striped Cavern' (80 days) is similar in shape and appearance to a sweet bell pepper, and the thick-walled fruits are hollow and useful for stuffing. The fruits weigh up to 8 ounces and have red skin with yellow stripes. Why grow a tomato instead of a bell pepper? Because the 'Striped Cavern' vines produce several times more fruit than a bell pepper plant in the same space when grown vertically. An all-red variety, 'Burgess Stuffing', is also sold by seed companies, identical in shape and size.

'Sun Gold Hybrid' (55 days) bears cherry-size fruit in long clusters, draped down the sides of the plant like chains of beads. The flavor is so sugar-sweet, it's like eating sugar candy—so sweet, in fact, I have eaten them as a dessert with ice cream.

'Super Marzano' (70 days) is an Italian paste tomato with good disease resistance. The plants produce large plum-shaped fruits up to 5 inches long and high in pectin. This tomato produces sauce with a naturally thick consistency. Most Italian paste tomatoes have short vines (determinate), but 'Super Marzano' grows a tall vine.

'Supersteak Hybrid' (80 days) is bigger than Beefsteaks, and the fruits are also more smooth, rounded, meaty, and delicious. Individual fruits are as big as a grapefruit.

'Sweet 100' (56 days) is a popular red cherry-size tomato, producing fruit in generous clusters—as many as 100 fruit on a single stem—hanging down the plant like a beaded curtain.

Tomato/Potato (55 or more days depending on the graft). Did you know it's possible to graft a tomato plant onto a potato plant, in order to produce tomatoes on the vine above and potatoes in the soil among the roots? It's quite simple: Take a potato tuber such as 'Yukon Gold' or 'Red Pontiac' and core it lengthwise all the way through with a potato peeler so you can see daylight through the hole. Then take a small tomato transplant with soil around its roots and gently poke the top of its stem through the potato hole as far as it will go. The potato tuber should act like a collar, forming a graft at the base of the tomato plant, with the tomato's rootball protruding from underneath. Plant the pair in the garden, with the potato 1 to 2 inches below the soil surface. The two will grow together, allowing you to ripen tomatoes aboveground and then, at the end of tomato season, to pull up the entire plant to reveal full-size potatoes among the roots.

'White Beauty' (85 days) is an ivory white, mild, sweet-flavored fruit averaging 8 ounces, with few seeds. For larger fruit (Beefsteak size), grow 'Snow White'.

KEY CHARACTERISTICS

Origins: Native to South America, mostly Chile and Peru

Zones: 5–11 as a warm season annual

Propagation: By seed started 6 weeks before outdoor planting when frost danger has passed. Seed packets always calculate days to harvest from transplanting a 6-week-old seedling. Allow 55 days for earliest varieties, 90 for late varieties.

Pests and Diseases: Mostly blossom-end rot and sunscald. See "Troubleshooting Tomatoes" on page 178 for other potential symptoms and solutions.

Height: Usually up to 10 feet, but varies according to variety

Supports: My preference is a wire mesh cylinder up to 6 feet tall with the tomato plant positioned in the middle, so it can grow up and spread its side branches through the mesh to be self-supporting. However, tomato vines can be grown up single poles (like bamboo canes), trellises, and heavy-gauge reach-through garden netting. Twist ties are generally needed to keep the vines erect.

TURNIPS

This fast-growing cool-season root crop does not climb, but it is suitable for growing in tower pots or as foundation plants in front of climbing plants. In addition to yielding sweet edible round roots, it produces edible tops that can be cooked like collard greens. Provide fertile soil with good drainage in full sun. Direct-sow seed even before the last frost of spring, as the seedlings tolerate light frost. Sow seed ½ inch deep and thin to stand 2 inches apart in broad rows. 'Purple Top White Globe' is the most popular home garden variety, requiring 45 days to maturity, but 'Tokyo Cross', an All-America Selection award winner, will produce golf-ball-size sweet turnips in just 30 days.

> ### KEY CHARACTERISTICS
>
> **Origins:** Native to Europe, and a member of the cabbage family
>
> **Zones:** 3–11 as a cool season annual
>
> **Propagation:** By direct-sown seed even before the last spring frost date
>
> **Pests and Diseases:** Mostly wireworms that burrow into the roots, causing blemishes
>
> **Height:** Up to 18 inches
>
> **Uses:** Grow in tower pots with three plants to a pot, or as a foundation plant in front of climbing plants.

WATERMELONS

Many watermelons are too big and heavy to be considered for a vertical garden. This includes heavyweights like 'Crimson Sweet' and 'Klondike', and of course monsters such as 'Charleston Grey', 'Carolina Cross', and 'Jubilee'. Some of these giant-size watermelons will grow to more than 100 pounds. In contrast, the smaller "icebox"-size watermelons and even smaller "personal size" are a perfect choice for vertical gardening. These will mature on vertical vines, especially if the fruits are supported by slings of light fabric (such as cheesecloth).

Of all vegetables commonly grown in North America, I have found watermelons to be the most challenging. They need a fertile, well-drained soil, and when grown vertically or horizontally, they require plenty of space for the vines to spread in order to set fruit and ripen. The plants relish hot weather and need watering during dry spells in order to avoid hollow centers. Birds such as crows and rodents such as rats and mice can damage the fruit before it's completely ripe and cause it to rot.

To grow watermelons vertically, provide a strong support, such as a bamboo trellis, and guide the lead shoot up it with twist ties, so that it can climb with the aid of tendrils. As fruits set, use twist ties to secure the stem above each fruit directly to the support, so the fruits do not drag down the stems and vines with their increasing weight. When direct seeding, wait until the soil has warmed up (since cool nights will hinder growth) and space at least 3 feet apart. Watermelons can also be cradled in cloth slings to keep the fruit from dragging down the vine. Tie the ends of the cloth to garden trellis or netting.

Watermelons respond well to sandy soils, good drainage, and plenty of compost. To encourage early ripening, start seed 4 weeks before outdoor planting and plant through black plastic mulch. Harvest watermelons when the tendril closest to the fruit turns brown.

A question often asked about watermelons is: "How can you make seed for a seedless watermelon?" It's rather like crossing a jackass (or male donkey) and a mare (female horse) to produce a mule. The jackass provides the seed for the mare to get pregnant and give birth to a mule, which is sterile (cannot reproduce itself). Similarly, the mother plant of a seedless watermelon needs to be pollinated by a regular watermelon grown nearby in order for her to produce seedless fruit. A great advantage to seedless watermelons, besides making them easier to eat, is the fact that seedless watermelons tend to be sweeter, since they can put all their energy into fruit—rather than seed—formation. However, be aware that seedless watermelons are more challenging to grow than seeded watermelons, not only because they need a regular watermelon to be grown nearby for pollination, but also because they can be susceptible to "hollow heart," in which their interior flesh may contain a large empty cavity. Various stressful physiological conditions can cause this, including cool weather, overfertilization, and high rainfall. Always grow seedless watermelons through black plastic mulch. This warms the soil early, stabilizes soil temperature, and conserves moisture, which help the fruit develop quickly.

Following are my personal favorites for vertical gardens.

'Mini Yellow Hybrid' (78 days) is a personal-size yellow-fleshed seedless watermelon ideal for vertical gardening, since the individual fruits weigh just 2 to 4 pounds. A regular watermelon, such as 'Sugar Baby', is needed nearby for pollination and fruit formation.

'Snack Pack' (75 days) is a variety of personal-size watermelon that is half the size of icebox types and suitable for serving a single person as a dessert. Individual fruits weigh just 3 to 4 pounds. The seedless fruit is the size of a medium-size cantaloupe, and like most seedless watermelons, its lack of seeds produces an exceedingly sweet flavor.

'Solitaire Hybrid' (75 days) is a personal-size watermelon with seeds, easier to grow than the seedless varieties. Fruits average 4 pounds and can be grown vertically with or without slings for support. The dark green skin has light green mottling and a thin rind, making it a perfect home garden variety.

'Sugar Baby' (75 days) has dark green round fruits and crimson flesh with black seeds. Developed by Sakata Seeds, the Yokohama, Japan, seed house, 'Sugar Baby' is the most popular seeded watermelon among home gardeners. It's classified as an

The icebox-size watermelon 'Crimson Sweet' produces vigorous vines that are ideal for training up supports.

icebox watermelon, because it can fit into the crisper section of most standard-size refrigerators.

'Yellow Baby' (70 days) won an All-America Selection award for its earliness and sweet flavor. This yellow-fleshed icebox-size watermelon was developed at a high-altitude breeding facility in Taiwan, enabling it to ripen fruit under conditions too cool for most other watermelons. 'Yellow Baby' (known as 'Yellow Orchid' in China) has crisp, juicy, pineapple-yellow flesh and 50 percent fewer seeds than regular icebox watermelons. Although single fruits can weigh up to 12 pounds, they can be supported by slings to prevent them from pulling down the vine.

KEY CHARACTERISTICS

Origins: Native to the Kalahari Desert, Africa

Zones: 6–11 as a warm season annual

Propagation: By direct-sown seed after frost danger has passed, or started indoors 4 weeks before outdoor planting. Allow 75 days for early varieties.

Pests and Diseases: Mostly borers and powdery mildew

Height: Up to 6 feet

Supports: Use strong trellises, or heavy-gauge reach-through garden netting, or chain-link fencing.

YAMS, CHINESE CLIMBING

Chinese yams are hardy perennials that resemble morning glory vines with their heart-shaped leaves. They can grow to 10 feet high and more in a single season, producing round or sausage-shaped brown-skinned underground tubers that are bright green on the inside. They're delicious to eat steamed, boiled, or cut into slices and stir-fried. To grow vertically, simply provide a strong bamboo tripod for support. Plants are difficult to obtain through normal sources such as garden centers, so visit a store specializing in Chinese foods and purchase a yam for planting. Half-bury the fruit, smooth side down and knobbly side up. The yam will sprout and grow vines quickly. Full-size fruit require 150 days of frost-free weather to develop. Although the tops are sensitive to frost and will die back to the ground in winter, roots can remain dormant and spring back to life the following season.

Do not confuse the Chinese yam with the air potato (*Dioscorea bulbifera*)—a similar species that has escaped into the wild and become invasive in parts of southern Florida, Arizona, and California. The potato-like tubers of the air potato form on the vine and fall to the ground when ripe, but they are considered poisonous.

Chinese yam fills a wire cylinder support by the second season and produces underground edible tubers.

KEY CHARACTERISTICS

Origins: Native to China

Zones: 6–11 as a warm season annual

Propagation: By seed or by tubers planted after frost danger has passed. Allow 150 days to harvest.

Pests and Diseases: None serious

Height: Up to 15 feet

Supports: Use a strong trellis or heavy-gauge garden netting, or grow plants up chain-link fencing, wire cylinders, and over arbors.

Fruits for
Vertical Gardens

11

The advantages of growing fruit vertically are similar to growing vegetables vertically—high yields and space saving. Space saving is especially important for fruit trees, because a standard apple tree or a standard cherry tree can occupy a large area of garden or lawn. Indeed, I have an apple tree at Cedaridge Farm, planted as a lawn accent, that is now 30 feet high and 20 feet wide. Standard cherries can be even taller and wider. By choosing a dwarf apple variety or a sweet cherry that bears when young (like 'Stella'), it's possible to train fruit to grow vertically, either as a tight column, as a high hedge, or flat against a wall. Some fruit trees—like Colonnade apples and pears—have been specially bred to grow tall and narrow, capable of bearing a pillar of fruit.

Many of the world's most delicious fruits and berries will grow vertically. Grapes are the best example, extending their sinuous canes immense distances. At Cedaridge Farm, I have black 'Concord' grapes, planted in the 1940s by a previous owner, climbing up into the leaf canopy of a tall hedgerow, completely naturalized and untended, delivering huge quantities of juicy black grapes every season in late summer. In other parts of the garden, I have red 'Suffolk' and green 'Cayuga' grapes growing over arbors and arches. Every garden, no matter how small, has room for a grapevine.

Berry plants such as raspberries and blackberries have pliable canes that extend long distances. Tying these to a trellis for support or against a sunny wall, splayed out like a fan, is an excellent way to grow them to conserve space and avoid snagging yourself on the canes. Similarly, fruit trees like figs have pliable branches that can be splayed out against a trellis to produce fruit vertically. The practice of training berry bushes and fruit trees against a trellis is known as espalier (see "How to Espalier Berries and Fruit Trees in a Vertical Garden" on page 207). The following list includes both hardy and tender fruit crops that grow well vertically. By "hardy" I mean plants like apple and pear trees that can tolerate long periods of winter dormancy; by "tender" I mean plants that cannot tolerate a long period of cold or frozen soil.

BLACKBERRIES

Relatives of the rose family, blackberries grow wild over most areas of the United States, forming dense thickets of thorny canes that flaunt masses of pink or white flowers in spring, followed by sweet black fruit resembling large raspberries. The main difference between blackberries and raspberries is that the blackberry retains its soft white core when picked, while the raspberry's white core stays on the vine, leaving a hollow berry. Blackberries start off green and ripen in late summer, turning red and black when fully ripe. Be forewarned: Blackberries that resist being picked will invariably be sour. Tug a berry gently, and if it yields, then it is most likely to be sugary sweet. Eat the berries fresh off the vine or use as a pie filling and for making jam. For pie filling, blackberries and apples are an especially good combination.

Blackberry varieties are characterized by three main growing habits—trailing, erect, or semi-erect—which are all suitable for vertical gardening. 'Logan' and 'Boysenberry' are considered trailing blackberries, because their canes spread out almost horizontally. Erect blackberries, such as 'Cherokee', grow stiff, upright canes ideal for training up a sunny wall or fence. Semi-erect blackberries are the most widely grown in home gardens. They have arching canes that can be trained to grow horizontally or erect up a trellis or along wires. 'Chester Thornless' belongs to this group.

Most blackberries produce fruit on second-year canes, meaning they do not produce fruit on the new season's canes, although there are exceptions. All blackberries are perennial and produce new canes from their roots. After harvest, the 2-year-old canes (those bearing fruit) should be removed to allow new canes to reach full development. All blackberries are self-fruitful (meaning they pollinate themselves), so only one plant is needed for a generous harvest. Blackberries can remain productive for 15 to 20 years.

Cultivated blackberries are much different from the wayside kinds you'll find growing wild (or invasively, as they do in the Pacific Northwest); cultivated varieties are capable of yielding larger fruit and having canes that are free of thorns. To grow blackberries, choose a sunny location with fertile, well-drained soil. The planting bed need not be wide. Either maintain a strip of soil using an organic mulch or black plastic to keep down weeds, or make a raised bed 1 to 2 feet wide. You'll find blackberry canes in containers at local garden centers or 1-year-old bareroot stock from mail-order sources. For bareroot stock, plunge the roots in a bucket of tepid water overnight to give them a good drink. When planting trailing varieties that will be trained to grow vertically, space them 4 feet apart. Erect varieties can be spaced 2 feet apart, and semi-erect varieties 5 feet apart when planting in a straight line.

To multiply blackberries, use the tip layering technique: Simply take a long cane and bend it to the ground. Scrape away some bark tissue about 1 foot from the cane end, cover the scraped area with soil, and weight it with a stone, leaving the cane tip poking up into the air. In about 6 to 8 weeks, roots will develop at the scraped part, so you can cut off the new plant from the mother plant, dig it up, and plant it in a new position.

Two excellent thorn-free blackberry varieties are 'Darrow' with white flowers and 'Chester Thornless' with pink flowers. Both produce large, sweet thimble-size berries. Blackberries have also been crossed with other bramble fruits to create even larger fruits, including the loganberry and boysenberry, which are ideal for growing vertically.

For a small home garden, the most efficient way to grow a blackberry is splayed out in a fan shape against a sunny wall or fence. Simply take the canes and stretch them out straight from the main trunk in a semicircular pattern, like the spokes of a wheel. Attach the canes to the wall by using twist ties to secure the canes to nails, or use a fan trellis and use twist ties or string to hold the canes in place.

KEY CHARACTERISTICS

Origins: Native to Europe

Zones: 4–9

Propagation: By tip layering

Pests and Diseases: Aphids, Japanese beetles, anthracnose, and blight

Height: Up to 10 feet

Supports: Train up trellises, especially fan trellises, or along parallel wires between posts.

FIGS

Edible figs have long, pliable branches that allow them to be grown vertically and trained up to roof height. Figs usually produce multiple trunks that can be splayed out in a fan pattern against a wall or supported by a fan trellis placed in a container. Associated with a Mediterranean climate, some fig varieties are reasonably hardy, and even in areas where they have difficulty surviving severe winters, plants can be protected with mulch or uprooted and taken indoors. The hardiest varieties are 'Brown Turkey' and 'Chicago Hardy', although it is difficult to tell the two apart since they both bear dark brown fruit. These are self-fruitful and capable of producing two flushes of fruit each season—a small flush in spring and a larger crop in fall. The leaves are highly decorative, large, and deeply lobed.

South of Philadelphia on the East Coast and south of Vancouver on the

West Coast, along with most areas south of Memphis in the middle of the United States, figs can survive outdoors without protection. Farther north, figs can be grown in containers and moved indoors, or pruned to about 4 feet from the ground and wrapped in a wire cylinder filled with shredded leaves to protect them from the cold. Although the leaves will drop, the roots and stems will remain dormant and sprout new green growth at the onset of warmer temperatures. Water sparingly if you've taken the container indoors in winter—just enough to keep the soil from drying out completely. Increase watering when new green leaves appear, and start feeding with a granular or liquid organic fertilizer. 'Brown Turkey' and 'Chicago Hardy' bear small fruits with sweet, dark red interior flesh. To obtain the largest fruit, consider the 'Kadota' variety (a yellow fruit when ripe); the skin of this variety is tender and requires no peeling.

To grow figs vertically, plant against a fan trellis attached to a sunny wall, and splay out the pliable branches flat against the trellis, using twist ties to secure them. Figs also are suitable for growing in whiskey half barrels. Plants prefer a fertile, sandy soil or a loam soil with good drainage.

In areas with mild winters where the plants remain evergreen, figs will generally produce two harvests a season—one in late spring from fruit formed in early spring and another in fall from fruit formed in summer. If you have a sunroom or conservatory where the plants can remain evergreen during winter, it's often possible to harvest a first crop even before placing plants outdoors, or soon after outdoor planting.

KEY CHARACTERISTICS

Origins: Native to Persia

Zones: 7–10 (6 with protection)

Propagation: By air layering

Pests and Diseases: Mostly fig beetles prevalent in Southwestern states, and scale insects

Height: Up to 10 feet

Supports: Grow against a trellis (especially a fan trellis) or splay out against a wall in a fan shape.

GRANADILLA

The yellow pulp of this fruit is used to flavor the gourmet ice cream called passionfruit. It is a tender tropical climber that features large white flowers with blue bands and long blue filaments arranged like crowns. Round or oval fruit ripen in fall, turning purple and wrinkled. The brittle shell can be peeled to reveal a mass of black seeds surrounded by a sweet jelly, which is often mixed with mango and orange to create a delicious tropical mixed-fruit drink. A commercial crop in New Zealand, the granadilla is grown along wires like grapes. Plants require full sun, fertile soil, and good drainage.

KEY CHARACTERISTICS

Origins: Native to Brazil

Zones: 10–11

Propagation: By seed, softwood cuttings, and soil layering; hybrids by cuttings or layering

Pests and Diseases: Minor slug damage

Height: Up to 15 feet

Supports: Strong trellis, chain-link fences, and split rail fences; also arches and arbors

GRAPES, DESSERT AND WINE

If you have space for only one climbing vine on your property—like over an arbor or pergola or along a sunny wall—make it a dessert-quality grapevine (dessert grapes are also known as table grapes). A single vine of a modern variety like 'Cayuga' can produce a modest harvest the second season after planting and as much as 42 pounds of fruit in its fourth season.

If you decide to include grapes in your garden, you'll need to decide whether you prefer to grow dessert-quality grapes like 'Concord' or wine-quality grapes like 'Baco Noir' (or maybe you'll decide to grow both). Among dessert grapes there are slip-skin varieties that have a tough skin you discard when eating fresh off the vine or when making pies; there are

Prune grapevine to grow along a single-wire horizontal support. Select two leaders on the vine, and prune away all secondary shoots so all of the plant's energy is directed into the leaders. Bunches of grapes will form from the spurs.

tender-skin varieties that allow you to eat the skin; plus there are seedless grapes that have tender skins like 'Thompson's Seedless'.

Some grape varieties are adapted to a particular region, so consult with your local extension service before choosing which variety to grow. Most wine and dessert grape varieties grown in North America are classified as northern or southern. Northern grape varieties are hardy and can be black, white, or red. Many northern dessert grapes, such as 'Cayuga', also make good wine. For southern grape recommendations, see "Grapes, Muscadine" on page 246.

Grapes grow in a wide variety of soil types, from clay to sand, although grapes must have good drainage in a clay soil and need plenty of compost mixed into a sandy soil. Full sun is essential. Other factors in good grape

'Cayuga' is a dessert-quality white wine grape capable of producing high yields.

production are pruning and training; without proper pruning and training, your grape clusters are likely to be sparse and the grapes small. At Cedaridge Farm, I have 40-year-old 'Concord' grapevines growing in a hedgerow of tall maples and junipers, with the vines climbing up to 60 feet. These vines yield bushels of fruit each season of a fairly decent size, but the grapes would be larger if the vines were pampered a little by pruning out the weakest vines in spring. All grapes need support: You can choose to plant a grapevine to grow up a pole, flat against a sunny wall (called espalier), along a split-rail fence, or over arbors, arches, and pergolas. You can also train a plant or several plants like professional orchardists do along wires strung between posts. Whatever support you choose, be sure it is strong—grapevines loaded with foliage and fruit can be extremely heavy.

Irrespective of the support you choose, the main objective after planting your vine is to prune away all but the strongest shoot in order to encourage a vigorous root system. Guide the shoot upright by tying the stem to a bamboo cane or a taut string. Grapevines use tendrils to climb and will quickly grow upward to the top of your trellis; when the lead shoot reaches that topmost point, cut the shoot above a leaf node and prune away any other side shoots that form *except* the pair of shoots that grows opposite each other below your cut end. Train these side shoots sideways along a wire or along a fence rail, or angle them up and over an arbor. These shoots will form your fruiting canes. The biggest mistake home gardeners make is not pruning away enough wood when the vine is dormant (usually between December and March), so don't be shy about pruning.

In the second growing season, remove all new side shoots and cut back the two topmost side canes, leaving up to seven buds on each, making a total of 14 fruiting buds. After the second season ends, select a new pair of "arms," leaving up to seven buds on each to set new bunches of fruit. It may seem drastic to prune away 90 percent of the branching stems in order to keep two strong new canes, but the objective is to prevent the vine from overbearing and overburdening itself with fruit, because that will drain the plant of energy and result in small-size grapes and grape clusters. With grapevines, fruit is borne on the current season's shoots from buds set on the previous season's growth, so you must keep selecting new pairs of canes at the end of each growing season to make cropping continuous. Shoots arising from 2-year or older wood are usually not fruitful.

Surprisingly, grapevines don't require a lot of feeding: Just rake a general-purpose organic fertilizer into the upper soil surface in spring or use a foliar feed. Compost is also desirable at the start of the growing season, although organic mulches that cool the soil may delay ripening. To hasten fruit ripening, plant a grapevine through black plastic mulch. Do not allow weeds to grow up against the trunk. Variety recommendations are difficult to make, because your climate and microclimate must factor into your choice. At Cedaridge Farm, we favor 'Concord' for its large black fruits, 'Suffolk' for its large red fruits, and 'Cayuga' for its large green fruits. At Cedaridge South, my Sanibel Island property in Florida, these standard grapevines don't grow, so I have planted heat-resistant muscadine grapes.

In my experience, there is nothing quite so decorative as a tunnel of grapevines with heavy fruit clusters in different colors hanging beneath the foliage. Just plant and allow grapevines to grow up and over a pergola connecting two sunny garden spaces or connecting a back door of the house to the garden.

Origins: Native to Europe and North America. Most wine and table grapes are hybrids.

Zones: 5–8 (7–11 for muscadine)

Propagation: By cuttings and soil or air layering

Pests and Diseases: Mostly Japanese beetles, birds, wasps, phylloxera (an aphidlike insect that colonizes roots), bunch rot, and powdery mildew. 'Concord' is resistant to rot and powdery mildew.

Height: Up to 30 feet

Supports: For stability, plant against a strong trellis (especially one mounted against a south-facing wall), a chain-link fence, a split-rail fence, or along parallel wires between two posts. My favorite use for grapes is covering an arch, arbor, or pergola, especially one made of metal, since the dense knit of a grapevine's branches can quickly rot wooden structures.

GRAPES, MUSCADINE

In southern states, the extremely sweet bronze- or white-skinned muscadine grapes are popular for their productivity and heat resistance. Botanically known as *Vitis rotundifolia*, they can suffer damage whenever the temperature dips below freezing. The variety 'Magnolia' can survive cold winters, but invariably suffers winterkill north of Washington, DC. Native to southern states, muscadines tolerate a wide range of soils, providing they are in full sun in a well-drained spot. The variety 'Magnolia' and a number of other black or bronze varieties are self-pollinating, so only one plant is needed to set generous quantities of fruit. Other varieties, such as scuppernong, possess only female flowers and need another male-female plant for pollination. Purchase bareroot or potted year-old rooted cuttings for planting in spring after frost danger has passed. Set the plants at least 10 feet apart. For home gardens, the most desirable support is a strong pergola, arbor, or arch. Orchardists prefer a double-wire system whereby a wooden T crossbar is used to string a set of double parallel wires at the same height, spaced at least 4 feet apart.

After planting rooted cuttings, trim away all but one or two main shoots and use twist ties to help them to reach up the trellis. Remove all side shoots when the vine reaches the wire, then prune the tip of the single main stem to force buds on opposite sides of it to grow sideways along the wire. By the second season, the vine will be long enough to bear a good quantity of fruit. After the second season, prune back all side shoots, leaving three buds on each of them to set new bunches of fruit. After fruiting, these side shoots can be cut back to three buds each successive season to keep the vine bearing generously.

Keep the root zone (an area at least 2 feet in diameter) free of weeds, by shallow hoeing or by applying an organic mulch such as pine needles or wood chips. A mulch of black plastic is also suitable. Muscadine grapes are not nearly as demanding as northern grape varieties for insect and disease control. To prevent depredation from birds and wasps, cover the vines with horticultural fleece (a thin polypropylene fabric), sold at garden centers.

I honestly believe there is nothing quite so delicious in fruit flavors as a muscadine grape. I cannot think of any standard dessert grape that can match it for sweetness and uplifting aroma. I would rather feast on a bunch of muscadines than on a peach or a mango. If you have room for only one fruiting vine in your garden, I recommend you make it a muscadine. Even if you have no garden soil—maybe just a patio with a paved surface—you can grow a muscadine in a whiskey half barrel. The most ingenious umbrella-like support I've seen for a muscadine on a patio was made from a discarded, rusty, antique tractor wheel. The main trunk of the muscadine vine scrambled up a central support post and then fanned out along the spokes of the wheel to drape its fruit clusters above the patio.

KIWIFRUIT, ARCTIC

There are two kinds of kiwi vine grown in North America—the hardy Arctic or Siberian kiwi (*Actinidia arguta*), and the tender New Zealand kiwi (*A. deliciosa*). The Arctic kiwi produces much smaller fruit—about the size of a large oval grape—than the New Zealand kiwi does. Even though its individual smooth-skinned fruits are small, one Arctic kiwi vine is capable of producing 10 gallons of fruit per season. The fleshy interior is exceedingly sweet, especially when the fruit feels soft at harvest. The main variety grown commercially is 'Anna', the result of a Russian breeding program. For home gardens, the most popular variety is 'Issai', since it is self-pollinating (whereas other varieties of Arctic kiwifruit need a male to pollinate the all-female vines). Arctic kiwi orchardists in the United States mostly grow 'Ken's Red', an extremely sweet-flavored variety.

An ornamental Arctic kiwi, *A. kolomikta*, is also a tough winter-hardy species grown mostly for its white-and-pink variegated juvenile leaves. The fruits are smaller than regular arctic kiwis, but edible and sweet nevertheless. A primary reason for failure to survive the first year is the plant's susceptibility to root rot and trunk injury from alternate thawing and freezing. The trunk becomes more winter hardy with age. Here in Pennsylvania—and in the case of a few plantings I have seen in Ohio—all fruiting

Arctic kiwis are grown along sheltered, sunny walls with excellent drainage. The survival rate can be increased by growing the Arctic kiwi in a 5-gallon container for its first winter. Move the container to a sheltered area close to the house during winter to protect the roots from freezing, and transplant to its permanent position only in the second season.

For pruning, follow the advice given for grapes.

My Zone 6 Pennsylvania garden seemed ideal for growing Arctic kiwi, but year after year they would die during winter. After several attempts, I finally discovered that my biggest mistake was failing to provide sufficient drainage and failing to water plants during dry spells. It's worth preparing a raised bed above your indigenous soil so the plant can resist the chances of root rot.

KEY CHARACTERISTICS

Origins: Native to Siberia

Zones: 5–9

Propagation: By air layering, soil layering, and softwood or hardwood cuttings

Pests and Diseases: Japanese beetles and root rot caused by Phytophthora, avoidable by good drainage

Height: Up to 30 feet

Supports: Use a strong trellis or 4-foot-wide × 6-foot-tall section of builder's wire between two posts. Also consider training over arches, arbors, and pergolas. In areas of borderline hardiness (Zone 7 and north), plant in a sheltered courtyard and train the top of the vine along a sunny roofline.

KIWIFRUIT, NEW ZEALAND

The New Zealand kiwi is actually native to the Yangtze River Valley of China, but was pioneered by New Zealand farmers as a commercial crop in 1940. The flowers are creamy white and resemble clematis. Kiwis have male and female flowers on separate plants, and a male is usually required as a pollinator for every six females. The fruits are variable in shape depending on variety, but are generally the size of a hen's egg, with brown fuzzy skin that must be peeled. The inside is bright green with black seeds and a tart-sweet flavor, but its sweetness improves when perfectly ripe.

Fruit growers offer several varieties, including the golden kiwi, with a flavor similar to pineapple. Its egg-shaped fruit has a fuzzless and tender edible skin. The variety 'Hayward' is the most popular of regular fuzzy kiwi fruits, because of its large size (as big as a goose egg).

Gardeners in most locations in California and the Pacific Northwest can grow the New Zealand kiwi. In the northeast corridor, gardeners as far north as Wilmington, Delaware, have had success growing kiwifruit outdoors, but trunk cracking during freezing winters will kill the vines. Planting the vine in a sheltered location where it can benefit from house heat and piling mulch against its trunk can improve the chances of a New Zealand kiwi surviving the winter in Zone 7. Generally, New Zealand kiwis will not tolerate temperatures below 10°F. Provide them with full sun and a fertile, well-drained soil.

Dormant rooted cuttings are best planted in spring after frost danger has passed. If the cutting shows multiple shoots or long broken shoots, prune it back to one healthy stem 6 to 12 inches long. In home gardens, grow vines up the wall of a building, up an arbor or arch, or along a split-rail fence, and be sure the support is strong, since the plant produces vigorous, tangled, heavy vines. Orchardists grow kiwifruit on a system of double wires strung between two posts, with the top wire 6 feet above the ground and the bottom wire 3 feet aboveground. Space plants 10 feet apart. As the vine grows, select one or two main shoots to train along the wires and prune away all remaining

New Zealand kiwis are suitable for mild winter areas of California and the Pacific Northwest as well as parts of the Southeastern US.

side shoots. A bamboo cane is ideal for training the plant's lead shoots up to the wires. Both summer and winter pruning is needed to keep the vines from strangling themselves and reducing fruit production. Thin crowded branches by pruning them flush with the main trunk. During winter, remove all wood that fruited the previous year, leaving only two new canes to continue growing for next season's crop.

A single New Zealand kiwi vine can produce a hundred or more fruit by fall frost, so it's worth erecting a special structure to accommodate it. This can be in the form of a square, flat, 4 × 4-foot, slatted wooden roof raised above head height on posts. The main trunk of the kiwi vine can be trained up one of the posts and pruned of lower branches. Then allow a topknot of vines to spread out over the slatted roof, with the kiwifruits hanging below the foliage for easy picking.

KEY CHARACTERISTICS

Origins: Native to China

Zones: 7–9

Propagation: By air layering, soil layering, and softwood or hardwood cuttings

Pests and Diseases: Winter kill and root rot, avoidable by good drainage

Height: Up to 30 feet

Supports: Use a strong trellis or 4-foot-wide × 6-foot-tall section of builder's wire between two posts. Also consider training over arches, arbors, and pergolas. In areas of borderline hardiness (Zone 7 and north), plant in a sheltered courtyard and train the top of the vine along a sunny roofline.

RASPBERRIES

Cultivated raspberry varieties have resulted from crossing two species of wild raspberry—the red (*Rubus ideaus*) and the black (*R. occidentalis*). Purple-hued raspberries are the result of crossing the red and the black, while yellow raspberries are a mutation of the red. The key to growing a good crop of raspberries is to understand that most varieties bear fruit only on 2-year-old canes. (An exception is the so-called everbearer raspberry—with varieties such as 'Heritage' and 'Summit'—which bears fruit on old canes in early summer and on new canes in late summer and early fall.) It is fairly easy to tell the two canes apart—new canes are smooth and green or gray-green, while 2-year-old canes are brown. Once the 2-year-old canes have borne fruit, they can be removed to allow more new canes to replace them. Since regular raspberry varieties (such as 'Latham') bear fruit only on old canes, the cropping period is confined to just 4 weeks, whereas an everbearer can crop for 8 weeks or more.

If fruit size matters, then choose varieties such as 'Titan' (a large-fruited red raspberry) or 'Royalty' (a large-fruited dusky purple variety). Neither of these are everbearers, but the large berry size and fruity flavor make them worth growing for fresh eating and pie fillings. Two good yellow raspberries are 'Kiwi Gold' and 'Fallgold'; both are exceedingly sweet.

Raspberries multiply by aggressive underground runners, so one cane planted this year can produce 12 new plants next season. To prevent raspberries from spreading into unwanted areas, plant inside a sunken container or in a raised bed, and use a trellis or heavy-gauge reach-through garden netting to hold the canes erect.

Raspberry canes can become top-heavy with fruit and arch out into pathways, so secure them to a support with twist ties to keep the canes vertical. A simple way to do this is to create parallel trellises; just crisscross bamboo canes opposite each other in two rows 3 feet apart; plant the raspberries between the bamboo rows. You can also mount double strands of wire in two rows spaced 3 feet apart, and plant raspberries between them.

Not many raspberry canes are needed for a worthwhile harvest. I have four everbearer plants inside a 3-foot-diameter × 6-foot-high cylinder of builder's wire, and each plant will supply a quart of fruit in spring and another quart in fall. As the mother plants produce new offspring outside the cylinder, I dig them up and transplant them to the edges of my property, where they can proceed to establish new colonies among wild plantings of blackberry and black raspberries.

Origins: Native to North America and Europe

Zones: 4–9

Propagation: By root division

Pests and Diseases: Fruit rot (called mummy berry) from wet weather at time of ripening

Height: Up to 7 feet

Supports: Use a trellis or a section of builder's wire, either freestanding or mounted against a wall, and splay out the canes like a fan. Can also plant within a 3-foot-wide × 6-foot-tall wire cylinder to help keep the canes erect rather than arching out into pathways.

STRAWBERRIES

Standard strawberries can be planted in tower pots, one plant to a pot, and the runners allowed to cascade down the sides of the pot and bear fruit in decorative clusters. Strawberries are also suitable for growing in hanging baskets, to create a decorative curtain of foliage, runners, flowers, and fruit. There are also special tall, barrel-shaped strawberry planters for growing strawberry plants in side pockets. A new race of climbing strawberries can be trained up traditional vertical gardening supports to bear clusters of fruit even when the runners are not rooted in soil.

Strawberries can be classified as *June bearers* (fruiting over a 3- to 4-week period in spring), *everbearers* (fruiting twice a year—in spring and then again in fall), and *day-neutral* (fruiting in several flushes in spring, summer, and fall). In general, it is the June bearer, such as 'Earliglow', that produces the largest fruit—some as big as a small peach.

Dr. Gene Galetta, a strawberry breeder at the USDA Fruit Breeding Center in Beltsville, Maryland, is the person responsible for breeding a series of day-neutral strawberries, one of which is 'Tristar'. The day-neutral strawberry does not quit bearing after June, unlike regular strawberries that seem to have a built-in time clock that turns off their flowering and fruiting ability. The day-neutrals do not appear to measure day length, and will continue flowering and fruiting even after days turn hot and humid.

They will bear in flushes from late spring through summer and into fall, a truly remarkable breeding achievement made possible by the discovery of a day-neutral wild strawberry in Brighton Canyon, Utah.

'Earliglow' is the June bearer capable of producing very large fruit. It is the variety most often grown by farmers for pick-your-own strawberry operations. The scarlet red fruits are not only big, but are also produced in clusters of a dozen or more.

'Jewel' is a June bearer, later bearing than 'Earliglow', but capable of even larger fruit. This is the variety you often see sold in supermarket egg containers, with one large berry and a stalk cradled in each compartment. It is also the favored variety for that most delectable of all treats, the chocolate-covered strawberry.

'Tristar' and 'Tribute' are day-neutral strawberries developed by Dr. Galetta at the USDA Fruit Breeding Center in Maryland. Both varieties produce medium-size, mostly conical fruits, in spring, summer, and fall. Check with your extension service to see which of the two varieties it recommends for your area. I have found 'Tristar' especially fruitful.

The new Dutch day-neutral strawberry 'Everest' is capable of bearing fruit throughout the growing season on extremely long (up to 4 foot) runners. Because of this ability, it is popular for growing in a hanging basket, planted in a fertile potting soil so the runners drape over the sides to produce a curtain of fruit, and also for training up a short trellis as a climbing strawberry. In order for these new climbing strawberries to climb, they need to be trained up like a vining tomato, using twist ties to keep the runners up in the air. These so-called climbing strawberries were developed specifically to create decorative hanging baskets, but as breeders managed to elongate the runners to as much as 4 feet, the idea of using them as climbing strawberries was born.

Strawberries are grown from year-old roots and also from seed. From roots, you can expect to produce berries within 60 days of planting. Growing from seed generally takes at least 12 weeks to create a transplant that's ready to bloom, and 4 more weeks for its berries to start to ripen, so you must plan far ahead when starting strawberries from seed.

The seed is small and should be covered lightly with potting soil, just enough to anchor it. Do not try direct seeding. Rather, start a group of seeds in a seed tray at 70°F and when large enough to handle, transfer to individual 4-inch transplant pots. Never allow the soil to completely dry out, and be sure to provide bright light—but not direct sunlight—until the plants are ready to be placed outdoors. For a curtain effect with the strawberry runners, place three to five plants around the perimeter of a hanging basket. Water daily and feed weekly with a diluted general purpose liquid fertilizer in a 1-2-1 ratio of NPK plant nutrients (nitrogen, phosphorus, potassium), such as 5-10-5.

For a climbing effect in your vertical garden, plant three to five plants in a circle around a scaffold or pyramid of 4-foot-tall bamboo stakes with cross members for added stability. As the runners develop, gently train them to grow upward, allowing the fruit clusters to form around the sides of the scaffold or pyramid. In fall, after frost ends the harvest, the vertical gardening stakes can be dismantled and the runners laid out flat on the ground and lightly covered with straw to help them survive winter.

You can advance earliness among strawberries by up to 2 weeks by growing them through black plastic mulch and covering them with horticultural fleece. For extra-large fruit, professional strawberry growers provide strawberry plants with a 1-2-1 balance of nutrients as a liquid spray (such as 5-10-5 or 10-20-10) at time of flowering.

KEY CHARACTERISTICS

Origins: Native to North America and Europe

Zones: 4–11 (grow strawberries during the winter months in Zones 9–11)

Propagation: By seed or runners after first season

Pests and Diseases: Rust and various leaf spots, fruit rot during excessively wet weather, birds, turtles, and deer

Height: Up to 5 feet in tower pots, with one plant to each pot

Supports: For vertical plantings, grow in special terra-cotta strawberry pots or tower pots with one plant to each planting station. For climbing strawberries, train up the middle of a wire cylinder or a cluster of twiggy branches to hold the runners erect.

HOW TO ESPALIER BERRIES AND
FRUIT TREES IN A VERTICAL GARDEN

Most fruit trees and berry bushes, because they have pliable branches, can be trained flat against a wall or against a trellis to save space. This training is known by the French term *espalier* (pronounced *is-PAL-yay*), because it was French orchardists who developed the training of fruit trees into a fine art. The French word *cordon* (pronounced *coor-DON*) means rope, and so a form of espalier that imitates a rope strung between posts to create a low border or fence is called a cordon. Other forms of training can create decorative patterns, allowing for a large harvest from a compact space. For example, the pliable branches of apples and peaches can be trained on a diagonal to create a diagonal pattern or

The branches of this pear tree are espaliered as a cordon, with pairs of branches splayed out like ropes along posts for support.

splayed out to form a fan pattern. The following is a list of the best fruit trees for espalier and examples of the espalier patterns best suited for each type.

Apples. The best use of apple trees in an espalier that I've ever seen is at the historic garden of Eleutherian Mills, near Wilmington, Delaware, where an entire wooden arch is covered with the branches of apples. The trees were planted on opposite sides of the arch to meet overhead in the middle. In Claude Monet's garden in Giverny, France, apple trees are trained as cordons (ropes) to edge a lawn. Apple branches also can be easily trained as parallel laterals or oblique laterals to create a fan shape on a trellis or flat against a sunny wall.

Apricots. Since apricot trees bloom early, and often the fruit embryo (immature fruit) is killed by a freeze, apricot trees are best trained flat against a wall for protection against late spring frost. Walls often retain sufficient heat to protect the blossoms or developing fruit. Also, when flat against a wall, apricot trees can be given the extra protection of a sheet draped over the branches when cool temperatures occur.

Cherries. Cherry trees are best trained in a fan pattern flat against a freestanding trellis or a wall. It's stunning to alternate red and yellow varieties.

Nectarines and peaches. Just as I do with apricot trees, I train nectarine and peach trees flat against a sunny wall for protection, because the buds are often endangered by late spring frosts.

Pears. Most varieties of pear trees will take some shade, much more than those of apples or other fruits. I have grown them flat against lightly shaded walls, training their branches in parallel laterals and in a fan shape. However, the best espaliered pear trees I have ever seen are at the Chateau de Villandry, in France's Loire Valley, where they are pruned into conical forms, the outstretched branches creating a wedding-cake effect.

Plums. The best example of espaliered plum trees I've seen is at Longwood Gardens in Pennsylvania, in their fruit-growing demonstration area, where the plum trees are trained as cordons (ropes) to edge a vegetable

Fruit trees have pliable branches and can be trained (known as espalier) against a wall; choose dwarf and semidwarf varieties of trees for best results. Freestanding cordon-type espalier is also suitable for a small space or a vertical garden and works best with dwarf and semi-dwarf fruit tree varieties.

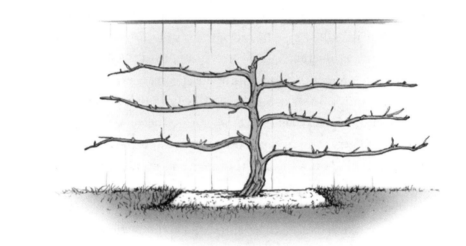

plot. Plum trees can also be trained flat against a sunny wall in a fan pattern or parallel laterals.

When choosing varieties for espalier in a limited space or for the edge of a vertical garden, consider the three-in-one grafted kinds, with three varieties of the same fruit on one tree. For example, it's possible to purchase a three-in-one pear, a three-in-one apple, or a three-in-one cherry. The big advantage (in addition to three varieties of fruit in the space of one tree) is the ability of the varieties to pollinate one another. Beware of advertisements for the fruit cocktail tree, however. Theoretically, it should be possible to graft five stone fruits (for example, a peach, apricot, nectarine, cherry, and plum) onto the same trunk, but I have never seen one of these trees actually bear more than one kind of fruit—and I have tried growing them many times at Cedaridge Farm. I'm told that the problem with these mail-order trees is that the grafts are on too young a root stock (usually a peach), and that the peach tends to dominate after the first season.

While not espalier, another good space-saving idea for a vertical garden is the upright and narrow Colonnade fruit trees—mostly bearing apples and pears. These trees grow to about 8 feet in height with a very slender outline—a straight trunk and short branch spurs that face upward. With a fruit tree this narrow, you can easily grow three or four of them as vertical accents in the space normally occupied by one full-size fruit tree. Full sun along the house foundation often suits them best. Look for varieties on the Internet and in mail-order catalogs.

Ornamental
Annual Vines

12

Who among gardeners wouldn't prefer a column of flowers, like a dramatic "pillar of fire" when you plant orange and red climbing nasturtiums, rather than a small mounded bedding plant, like French marigolds? The planting effort is the same. The only difference is that you add a support to allow the climbing plant to grow upward.

Vertical vining plants can carry colorful flowers well above eye level, so that your entire field of vision is filled with color. The Impressionist artist Claude Monet felt that color high in the sky was so important to the aesthetic appeal of his flower garden that he filled his 5-acre property in Giverny, France, with special metal trellises and arches, allowing climbing roses, clematis, silver fleece vines, and Mexican flame vines to mingle their colors and frame his house. In his water garden, he even built a special canopy over an arched Japanese-style footbridge so that two colors of wisteria could cover it and drape their blue and white flower panicles through the slats to hang like bunches of grapes.

Monet also sought textural interest from foliage plants, covering the gables of his house with Virginia creeper to soften large expanses of masonry with ivylike leaves that are lush, glossy green in summer and molten red in autumn.

The easiest flowers for vertical growing are annual vines. These grow quickly from seed, and many are capable of flowering from early summer to fall frost. These climbing vines are a mix of cool season annuals, such as sweet peas that will tolerate mild frosts, and warm season annuals, such as morning glories and nasturtiums that are sensitive to frost.

The next best flowering vines are hardy perennials (such as perennial sweet peas) and tender perennials that can be grown like annuals. Tender perennials, such as vining ivy-leaf geraniums, mandevilla, and allamanda, can be discarded at the end of the season; they can also be trimmed back almost to the soil line, potted to be brought indoors, and watered sparingly until the following spring, when they can be taken outdoors when all danger of frost has passed. Descriptions of them and my other favorite flowering annual vines follow in this chapter. Hardy perennial and woody vines also offer a large selection of plants to choose from (including clematis, rambling roses, and trumpet creeper) and are described in the next chapter.

BALLOON VINE

This tender, woody evergreen perennial is normally grown as an annual and bears small greenish-white flowers, but its main attraction are the quantities of conspicuous bright green balloonlike seed capsules that follow the flowers. This is an oddity that is often included in children's gardens, as the balloons never fail to please children, who like to clap their hands around them and make them pop. The vine's oval toothed leaves are borne in pairs, and the stems are light and airy looking. Grow balloon vine up a tall trellis or garden netting. The plants tolerate poor soil if it's well drained and prefer full sun.

KEY CHARACTERISTICS

Botanical Name: *Cardiospermum halicacabum*

Origins: Native to Africa and India

Zones: 4–11 as an annual

Propagation: By seed

Pests and Diseases: Relatively carefree, but sometimes colonized by aphids

Height: Up to 12 feet

Supports: Trellis, garden netting, and chain-link fencing. Thread the vines through picket fences.

BLACK-EYED SUSAN VINE

This tender perennial is mostly grown as an everblooming annual from seed started indoors. The vigorous, lightweight vines grow quickly to create a curtain of bright flowers the first season. Transplanted to the garden after frost danger and spaced at least 12 inches apart, the vines knit together to form a dense screen of small spear-shaped leaves, and literally hundreds—even thousands—of mostly yellow, orange, or pink 1-inch flowers with black centers. These are highly attractive to hummingbirds.

Plant black-eyed Susan vine against a trellis, on netting, or on chain-link fencing, where the vines will climb unaided by twining. In frost-free locations, the black-eyed Susan vine will overwinter to rebloom the following season, especially if the vines are cut back to the soil line. These plants make attractive hanging baskets, with the vines draping down the sides of the basket like a curtain. Seed is sold in separate colors and as mixtures. Black-eyed Susan vines require full sun and good drainage, but will tolerate light shade like you'd have under a slatted patio roof.

KEY CHARACTERISTICS

Botanical Name: *Thunbergia alata*

Origins: Native to tropical Africa

Zones: 5–11 as an annual

Propagation: By seed started 6 to 8 weeks before outdoor planting when frost danger has passed

Pests and Diseases: Relatively carefree, but sometimes colonized by spider mites

Height: Up to 15 feet

Supports: Trellis, garden netting, chain-link fences, arbors, and arches. Encircle a tree with chicken wire to support a column of flowers all the way up the trunk into the tree canopy.

CANARY CREEPER

A type of nasturtium, this fast-growing, twining vine produces hundreds of bright yellow flowers that resemble a bird in flight. The flowers occur continuously from early summer to fall frost. Seed may be direct-sown after frost danger has passed in spring. The leaves are decorative and resemble clover, and the stems twine to climb unaided up garden netting or tall trellis. For a really unusual display, consider pairing the cheerful yellow flowers of canary creeper with the bold red flowers of cardinal creeper.

KEY CHARACTERISTICS

Botanical Name: *Tropaeolum peregrinum*

Origins: Native to Ecuador and Peru

Zones: 4–11 as a tender annual

Propagation: By direct-sown seed, or started indoors 4 to 6 weeks before outdoor planting

Pests and Diseases: Slugs and aphids

Height: Up to 12 feet

Supports: Trellis, garden netting, arbors, and arches

CARDINAL CREEPER

Also known as cypress vine, because its delicate feathery green leaves resemble those of the evergreen cypress tree, this easy-care tender annual is related to morning glories. From early summer to fall frost, the rapidly growing vines produce hundreds of small red flowers highly attractive to hummingbirds. Seed may be direct-sown after frost danger has passed in spring. Plants grow erect by twining up garden netting or tall trellis.

Cardinal creeper is actually related to morning glories, but it's better known as cypress vine because its foliage resembles the threadlike leaves of the cypress tree.

Botanical Name: *Ipomoea × multifida*

Origins: Native to South America (a hybrid between two South American species)

Zones: 4–11 as an annual

Propagation: By direct-sown seed after frost danger has passed, or started indoors 4 weeks before outdoor planting

Pests and Diseases: Slugs and aphids

Height: Up to 15 feet

Supports: Trellis, garden netting, chain-link fences, arches, and arbors

CUP-AND-SAUCER VINE

This rampant tender annual vine is pollinated by bats as well as insects and easily grown from seed. The cup-shaped flowers in mostly white, green, pink, and blue are attached to green calyxes resembling saucers and bloom on extremely long stems that climb by tendrils. Seed packets mostly offer mixtures of colors. In areas with a Mediterranean climate, such as coastal California, the plant can be invasive. Cup-and-saucer vine requires full sun, tolerates poor soil as long as drainage is good, and blooms continuously from early summer to fall frost. The long stems allow you to cut the flowers for vases and arrangements. Cup-and-saucer vine is a decorative way to cover high chain-link fencing (like the kind that surrounds a tennis court) or a tall trellis attached to a wall.

KEY CHARACTERISTICS

Botanical Name: *Cobaea scandens*

Origins: Native to Mexico

Zones: 4–11 as a tender annual

Propagation: By direct-sown seed, or started 6 weeks before outdoor planting when frost danger has passed

Pests and Diseases: None serious, and rarely bothered by spider mites

Height: 15 feet

Supports: Tall trellis, garden netting, tall chain-link fencing, arches, arbors, and pergolas

ORNAMENTAL ANNUAL VINES

FLAME VINE, MEXICAN

Related to morning glories but with tubular blooms, these red and yellow flowers are highly attractive to hummingbirds. Flame flower is an annual tropical vine that twines like a morning glory to create a curtain of dazzling flowers up garden netting or a tall trellis. A dozen or more florets can occur on each flower spike, with hundreds of flower spikes open at one time. The French artist Claude Monet grew this in urns supported by ladderlike trellises. Plants flower continuously from early summer to fall frost, tolerate drought, and are especially beautiful for covering chain-link fencing. Create a spectacular plant partnership by planting flame flower and 'Heavenly Blue' morning glories close together so their flowers entwine.

KEY CHARACTERISTICS

Botanical Name: *Ipomoea lobata*

Origins: Native to Mexico

Zones: 4–11 as a tender annual

Propagation: By direct-sown seed after frost danger has passed, or started 6 weeks before outdoor planting

Pests and Diseases: Root and stem rot in poorly drained soil

Height: 15 feet

Supports: Trellis, garden netting, chain-link fencing, arches, and arbors

GERANIUM, IVY-LEAF

In northern states, ivy-leaf geraniums are most commonly grown as annuals to climb up walls and fences or to cascade from balcony and window box planters. But ivy-leaf geraniums are really tender perennials that will overwinter in moderately frost-free areas. In northern states, plants can be cut back to their roots and transferred to a pot to overwinter indoors in a sunroom or even a sunny window, then placed back in the garden the following spring.

Although there are varieties of vining ivy-leaf geraniums that can be grown from seed to flower the first year, the preferred method of propagation is from tip cuttings taken at least 10 weeks before outdoor planting after frost danger has passed in spring. It is a lot easier to just buy rooted cuttings or transplants. Space plants at least 12 inches apart. As the lead shoot grows, tie it to netting or a trellis with twist ties. The best trellises for vining ivy-leaf geraniums are tall wooden or fan trellises. Available mostly in red, pink, and white, the flowers are everblooming until fall frost.

The flexible stems of ivy-leaf geraniums will cascade elegantly, and so a curtain of flowers is possible by growing in window box planters. In Switzerland, these geraniums are seen everywhere decorating the balconies of chalets.

Derived from crosses mostly between *Pelargonium crispum* and regal geraniums (*P. domesticum*), the color range includes red, pink, white, purple, salmon, orange, and bicolors. The leaves resemble English ivy, often velvety to touch and lemon scented. Plants need a sunny location in fertile, well-drained soil. The Balcon Family of ivy-leaf geraniums is so free-flowering it can create a pillar of blooms.

KEY CHARACTERISTICS

Botanical Name: *Pelargonium peltatum*

Origins: Native to South Africa

Zones: 4–11 as a tender annual

Propagation: By seed started in winter and early spring at least 10 weeks before outdoor planting, and by softwood cuttings rooted over winter, summer, or fall

Pests and Diseases: Root rot in poorly drained soil; also thrips, spider mites, mealybugs, caterpillars, mildew, and botrytis

Height: Up to 15 feet, depending on variety

Supports: Tall trellis, fan trellis, chain-link fencing, walls, arches, and arbors

GLORIOSA CLIMBING LILY

Although this beautiful flowering vine is classified as a tender perennial bulb, it is often grown as an annual to flower the first year; after frost kills the top growth, its bulbous roots are lifted in fall and stored indoors over winter in a cool, frost-free location. In spring, cut the long, fleshy roots into 2-inch, sausage-shaped bulbs for planting 1 inch deep. These will sprout topgrowth soon after watering and flower within 9 weeks. The mostly crimson red flowers have swept-back petals like a Turk's cap garden lily, with yellow edging and prominent arching stamens that project far out. These blooms certainly live up to their name "Gloriosa." Plants flower continuously all summer. The variety *'Rothschildiana'* has flowers up to 4 inches across, and 'Citrina' is all yellow.

Plants prefer a fertile, well-drained or slightly moist soil in full sun. The leaves are lancelike, curled, with terminal tendrils that allow the vine to climb up garden netting or a short trellis. This stunning beauty also makes an excellent container plant, grown up the center of a wire cylinder or bamboo scaffold. The tubers are poisonous and can irritate skin, so handle them with gloves when planting or moving them.

KEY CHARACTERISTICS

Botanical Name: *Gloriosa superba*

Origins: Native to Africa and northern India

Zones: 5–11 as a tender annual; 8–10 as a perennial

Propagation: By bulbs planted in spring after frost danger

Pests and Diseases: Aphids, anthracnose, and bulb rot in cold or wet soil

Height: Up to 6 feet

Supports: Short trellis, garden netting, wire cylinders, and chain-link fencing

GOURD, BOTTLE

The fast-growing bottle gourd vine has tendrils that allow it to climb aggressively up a trellis or netting and over arches and arbors. The large, velvety, heart-shaped leaves are tropical looking, as are the white trumpet-shaped flowers that can be male or female. The females bear gourds after pollination from a male. In their immature stage, the fruits are edible like summer squash; simply slice thinly and use raw in salads or stir-fry. The bottle-shaped dark green gourds can be removed from the vine when mature or when the vine is killed by frost. After harvesting the fruit, hang them up off the ground in an airy, sheltered area. They can be air dried to make bird nesting boxes; just cut a hole in the dried shell with a sharp knife and shuck out the seeds.

Provide plants with full sun and a fertile soil that drains well. A high nitrogen organic fertilizer helps the vines to grow vigorously and to set a large number of fruit. Plants tolerate heat, high humidity, and drought. Space them at least 12 inches apart, so the vines knit together. When harvesting, leave a section of the stem intact, as this prolongs storage.

There are many different selections and varieties; some popular ones are the crookneck type called a goose gourd and the long, straight-neck 'Hercules Club' gourd with a bulbous base.

KEY CHARACTERISTICS

Botanical Name: *Lagenaria siceraria*

Origins: Native to India and Africa

Zones: 5–11 as a tender annual

Propagation: By direct-sown seed after frost danger has passed, or started from seed 6 weeks before outdoor planting

Pests and Diseases: Susceptible to mildew and borers

Height: Up to 20 feet

Supports: Tall, strong wooden or metal trellis; heavy-gauge garden netting; chain-link fencing; arches, arbors, and pergolas

GOURDS, ORNAMENTAL LARGE

Seed companies usually sell mixtures of seeds for large or small ornamental gourds. The large gourd mixture invariably includes varieties of 'Turk's Turban', crookneck cushaws (both the brown and green striped), blue Hubbard, orange Boston, and even some fancy pumpkins like 'Rouge Vif d'Etampes'. Most of them are edible as winter-storage squashes. Also, many of the popular kinds—like the Turk's Turban—can be purchased individually in seed packets. Generally, when grown vertically, the large ornamental gourds require a stronger support than the small ornamentals and sometimes supportive slings to suspend the weight of fruits that form off the ground. Create a striking display by growing these large vining gourds over sturdy arches and pergolas, so they form a shady tunnel and let their fruit hang down beneath the leaf canopy.

Ornamentally, large gourds are used for Thanksgiving decorations, piled up against cornstalks or on straw bales, and displayed in wooden carts. Because of their larger size, the vines need extra-fertile soil, high in nitrogen.

KEY CHARACTERISTICS

Botanical Name: *Cucurbita maxima*

Origins: Native mostly to Central and South America

Zones: 5–11 as a tender annual

Propagation: By direct-sown seed after frost danger has passed, or started indoors 4 weeks before outdoor planting

Pests and Diseases: Mostly borers, mice, mildew, and various wilt diseases

Height: Up to 15 feet

Supports: Strong, tall trellis; also heavy-gauge garden netting, chain-link fencing, arches, arbors, and pergolas

GOURDS, ORNAMENTAL SMALL

These fast-growing, tender annuals are related to cucumbers and have tendrils that allow them to climb naturally. The mostly yellow flowers can be male or female, with the females bearing fruit after pollination from a male. Pollinated mostly by bees, the flowers are followed by multicolored fruits of various shapes, some round like a tennis ball and others egg-shaped, pear-shaped, star-shaped, or even crooknecked. In addition to being mostly yellow, orange, green, or white, the gourds can be striped and mottled.

Generally sold as seed mixtures, some varieties can be purchased individually, such as one called the nest egg gourd or Easter egg gourd with fruits shaped like chickens' eggs. Gourds require full sun and are best grown up netting or chain-link fencing and over arches. In fertile soil, the vines can reach as high as a ranch house the first season; with regular feeding of a general-purpose organic fertilizer, the vines can be induced to cover a pergola with their beautiful assortment of fruit hanging down like tree decorations.

The seeds are large, easy to handle, and usually direct-sown after frost danger has passed. Provide full sun and a fertile, well-drained soil. Harvest the gourds in late summer and early fall when their colors turn bright and before frost kills the vines. Be sure to keep a length of stem section attached to each fruit, as this aids storage and staves off rotting. It's also possible to shellac the fruits to give them a glossy shine and to help preserve them as Thanksgiving and Christmas decorations.

KEY CHARACTERISTICS

Botanical Name: *Cucurbita pepo*

Origins: Native mostly to Central and South America

Zones: 5–11 as a tender annual

Propagation: By direct-sown seed after frost danger has passed, or started indoors 4 weeks before outdoor planting. The vines will root on contact with soil, so layering is an effective way to propagate more plants.

Pests and Diseases: Borers, mildew, and various wilt diseases

Height: Up to 12 feet

Supports: Tall, strong trellis; chain-link fencing; arches, arbors, and pergolas; also A-frame supports

HYACINTH BEAN

Although the pods are considered edible when young and are used in Asian stir-fries, mature hyacinth beans are considered poisonous if eaten raw, so I recommend the plants be used only as an ornamental. At Cedaridge Farm, hyacinth beans grow mostly up trellises to decorate a sunny wall. The vines are extremely eye-catching, possessing not only purple flowers but also purple stems, purple leaves, and later shiny purple seed pods. The plants are suited for many types of growing supports, including fan trellises and lampposts encircled with chicken wire. The pea-shaped flowers are formed in pyramid-shaped clusters and attract hummingbirds. Hyacinth beans are also a good choice for a container planting, especially grown up the center of a wire cylinder for support.

KEY CHARACTERISTICS

Botanical Name: *Dolichos lablab*

Origins: Native to Asia

Zones: 5–11 as a tender annual

Propagation: By direct-sown seed after frost danger has passed, or started indoors 4 weeks before outdoor planting

Pests and Diseases: Mostly slugs and Japanese beetles

Height: Up to 15 feet

Supports: Tall trellis, garden netting, chain-link fencing, lampposts, arches, and arbors

IVY, SWEDISH

A tender perennial vine, Swedish ivy is so fast-growing that in all parts of North America it is used as an annual, often clambering over the edge of balcony planters to create a curtain of velvety leaves and beautiful white or pale blue flowers. The most popular form has gray-and-white variegated ivylike leaves on trailing stems that become crowded with clusters of small trumpet-shaped flowers. Although the long stems can be trained to climb, plants are best used in window boxes and hayrack planters, where they can cascade freely to create a curtain of decorative flowers and foliage. At the end of the growing season, the plant can be cut back to the soil line, potted, and taken indoors to overwinter during freezing weather. In spring, replant outdoors in a sunny position after frost danger has passed. In order to climb, the vines need to be attached to a support, such as a fan trellis, using twist ties to hold the stems erect.

KEY CHARACTERISTICS

Botanical Name: *Plectranthus australis*

Origins: Native to Australia and Indonesia

Zones: All as an annual, 9–11 outdoors as a tender perennial

Propagation: By taking cuttings that have aerial roots (at any time); plants will root in plain water

Pests and Diseases: Mostly whiteflies and mealybugs when taken indoors

Height: Up to 10 feet (longer when allowed to cascade)

Supports: Short trellis, or allow vines to cascade from balcony or window box planters

MOONFLOWER

This fast-growing annual vine climbs unaided by twining through netting or up a trellis. It produces large, decorative, heart-shaped leaves and large trumpet-shaped white flowers up to 5 inches across. Moonflowers bloom at night and last until early morning, have a strong pleasant fragrance, and are especially well suited to porch and patio plantings, where you can enjoy their scent in the evening hours. Plants are everblooming until fall frost and perform as perennials in frost-free locations such as southern Florida (where they can be invasive) and southern California.

Fragrant moonflower vine opens in the late afternoon and closes by noon the next day.

MORNING GLORY

Of all flowering vines, morning glories are the most popular, even more popular than sweet peas and climbing nasturtiums. They are an old-fashioned flower widely used in European cottage gardens for covering walls of outbuildings, such as barns, gazebos, and outhouses, long before colonists arrived in America. The most popular morning glory is 'Heavenly Blue', which produces sky-blue trumpet-shaped blooms on twining stems covered in attractive heart-shaped leaves. Other favorite morning glories include 'Scarlett O'Hara' (red) and 'Pearly Gates' (white). There are also bicolors such as 'Grandpa Otts', which is a beautiful deep blue with purple petal markings. 'Tie-Dye' has striped flowers in a mixture of red, pink, and blue; 'Mt. Fuji' has a white rim around and a white strip down the middle of each petal.

In addition to their covering conventional supports such as tall trellises and garden netting, I have seen morning glories planted to cover rusting old farm machinery and unsightly piles of brushwood, to climb up stairways, to encircle windows, to climb through the branches of boring forsythia bushes after they have finished flowering, and to creep along picket fencing.

For a really spectacular curtain of bloom, plant several varieties in different colors, so that the vines intermingle. Morning glories generally flower in the morning, stay open on cloudy days, and close up in the after-noon sun. At Cedaridge Farm, I like to plant morning glories at the feet of sunflowers, so they can climb up the tall sunflower stems; the sunflowers provide strong support, and the yellow sunflower heads contrast with the blue of 'Heavenly Blue' morning glory for a striking color combination. Another striking plant partnership is 'Heavenly Blue' morning glory part-nered with climbing orange, red, and yellow nasturtiums. Try this in a whiskey half-barrel with a wire cylinder for the morning glories and nas-turtiums to climb up and mingle their blooms.

KEY CHARACTERISTICS

Botanical Name: *Ipomoea purpurea*

Origins: Native to Mexico

Zones: 4–11 as an annual

Propagation: By direct-sown seed after frost danger has passed, or started indoors 4 weeks before outdoor planting. Soak the seed overnight before planting to speed germination, or nick the seed coat with a razor to aid moisture penetration.

Pests and Diseases: Slugs will eat the leaves.

Height: Up to 15 feet

Supports: Tall trellis, fan trellis, garden netting, chain-link fencing, arches, and arbors; and any wall of a garden building, such as a summerhouse, barn, or toolshed

NASTURTIUM, CLIMBING

Although there are many dwarf varieties of nasturtiums, old-fashioned climbing types are still available from seed companies. These have decora-tive parasol-shaped leaves and are mostly sold as mixtures that include red, yellow, orange, lemon, white, and mahogany. Plant a mixture to grow up a trellis or netting for a tapestry of hot colors and a stunning display. To help make your garden plantings distinctive, it's worth searching out spe-cial colors of climbing nasturtiums. 'Ladybird', a single-color variety with yellow flowers and red markings at the petal base, flowers generously on lightweight vines; grow it with 'Heavenly Blue' morning glory to create a beautiful harmony in yellow, red, and blue. 'Milkmaid' has white flowers with yellow throats. There are also climbing varieties, such as 'Empress of India', with bronze-colored leaves and dark red flowers. Climbing nasturtiums will climb by twining without support and will flower nonstop from late spring to fall frost. Seed can be direct-sown after frost danger has passed in spring. The flowers are edible, with a peppery flavor, and good to use in salads and egg dishes.

Perhaps the most famous planting of nasturtiums is in the French painter Claude Monet's garden at Giverny. Here, instead of climbing, the nasturtiums are allowed to spread horizontally across the broad path under the Grande Allée, helping to carpet a flowering tunnel, with roses overhead on metal arches and tall perennials such as sunflowers forming the sides.

A very beautiful perennial nasturtium from Chile—*T. speciosum,* commonly called the flame nasturtium for its crimson flowers—can be grown in mild winter areas, particularly where summers are cool, like in the Pacific Northwest and coastal Maine. Some of the finest specimens can be seen in the famous topiary garden of Levens Hall, in the north of England, where they have been planted to grow up over topiaries of clipped boxwood. I have even seen tall specimens flowering riotously in the Shetland Islands, between Scotland and Norway.

KEY CHARACTERISTICS

Botanical Name: *Tropaeolum majus*

Origins: Native to South America

Zones: 4–11 as an annual

Propagation: By direct-sown seed after frost danger has passed, or started indoors 4 weeks before outdoor planting. The double-flowered variety 'Hermine Grasshof' can be propagated only from stem cuttings.

Pests and Diseases: Mostly aphids

Height: Up to 12 feet

Supports: Tall trellis, garden netting, and chain-link fencing; also in a whiskey half-barrel, with a wire cylinder for support

PETUNIA, CLIMBING

Most petunias have a spreading habit that allows them to cascade over planters to create a curtain of color, or to climb up a vertical column to form an impressive tower. The small-flowered purple species petunia, *Petunia integrifolia,* will climb 3 feet or more, or cascade to form an airy waterfall of blooms and foliage. A similar hybrid multiflora petunia, 'Purple Wave', also produces unusually long vines that can be trained to climb or allowed to cascade, creating a curtain of blooms in either case. Give 'Purple Wave' a short trellis to hold its stems erect, and consider growing it as the main accent plant in a mixed-container planting.

Petunia integrifolia *has small flowers but a vining habit that makes it suitable for growing in hanging baskets and balcony planters.*

Most petunias are classified as grandiflora (large flowered) or multiflora (smaller flowered). The famous Double Cascade series of petunias—ideal for hanging baskets and balcony planters—belongs to the grandiflora group. Petunias like full sun and fertile, well-drained soil. They will also tolerate light shade. Their biggest enemy is heavy rain, as this saturates the petals and makes them limp; it can take a week or more for plants to recover. The multifloras are less susceptible than the grandifloras to rain damage.

Although petunias come in a vast range of solid colors, notably in shades of red and blue plus white, there are a number of unusual bicolors, including 'veined' varieties (with a light-colored petal, such as white or pale blue, that is streaked with intricate darker-colored veins). Another group has starry-looking blossoms; you'll notice a white stripe that runs the length of each petal, creating a starburst effect in each flower. Yet another color group has a rim of white around each petal; this is particularly striking with blue, red, and purple varieties.

A number of petunia look-alikes are known as mini petunias. These include the extremely free-flowering series known as 'Million Bells' (botanically called *Calibrachoa*). They are not presently grown from seed, although several plant breeders are working on a seed-grown series. They are grown from cuttings, and the color range is one of the most beautiful among flowering annuals, including white, pale blue, sky blue, dark blue, yellow, orange, terra-cotta, red, pink, and salmon. Many of them have a contrasting dark or bright eye. Nothing is quite so spectacular as a grouping of 'Million Bells' colors cascading from balcony planters to create a kaleidoscope effect; when so many flowers are open at one time, they almost completely hide the foliage.

Petunias are particularly effective in cylindrical soft plastic pouch planters, in which six or more transplants are grown in pockets surrounding a contained column of soil. Also consider planting petunias in metal hayrack planters, with the planters fixed to a sunny wall in a staggered pattern. When each hayrack planter features a different color, the cascading flowering stems can merge into each other to create a curtain of mixed colors. Provide full sun, fertile soil, and good drainage.

KEY CHARACTERISTICS

Botanical Name: *Petunia integrifolia*

Origins: Native to South America

Zones: 4–11 as a tender annual

Propagation: By seed started indoors 8 weeks before planting outdoors when frost danger has passed; also by tip cuttings

Pests and Diseases: Mostly aphids and various fungus diseases following wet weather

Height: Up to 3 feet; also cascades

Supports: Short trellis, or draped to form a curtain from window box and balcony planters

SNAIL VINE

This is a plant oddity that never fails to delight children, since nature has engineered an intricate cluster of flowers that are spiraled, resembling the swirling pattern of a snail's shell. Although it's a moderately hardy perennial, the plants are mostly grown as annuals to flower the first year. A legume related to pole beans, snail vine has mostly white flowers tinged with pink. In areas where the ground freezes, the roots can be dug up and potted to overwinter indoors before frost kills the vine. The second-season growth will result in many more flower clusters than the previous season. Plants climb by twining and will grow to 12 feet high in one season. Provide full sun and fertile soil with good drainage. Consider growing snail vine in a whiskey half-barrel, planted so the vine can climb up the center of a wire cylinder or against a fan trellis. A simple wooden trellis and garden netting are also suitable supports. Although there is much disagreement over its hardiness, some fans of snail vine in Maryland (Zone 7) report vines dying back after frost, but after being cleaned up in spring, sprouting new shoots—allowing it to perform as a true perennial.

KEY CHARACTERISTICS

Botanical Name: *Vigna caracalla*

Origins: Native to India

Zones: 5–11 as a tender annual, 7–11 as a perennial

Propagation: By direct-sown seed after frost danger has passed, or started indoors 4 weeks before planting outdoors

Pests and Diseases: Leaves can be discolored by powdery mildew.

Height: Up to 12 feet

Supports: Tall trellis, garden netting, chain-link fencing, arches, and arbors

SWEET PEAS

For decades before World War II, the sweet pea was the most popular flowering annual in North America, valued both for its flamboyant flowering display on climbing vines and for its sweet fragrance. European immigrants remembered sweet peas from cottage gardens back home and planted them faithfully early each spring. Sweet peas are still as much a part of British culture as Yorkshire pudding, but in North America their popularity began to decline as the plants fell victim to soil fungus diseases.

Such was the demand for sweet peas worldwide that thousands of acres had been devoted to seed production in the Lompoc Valley of California, where cool mists and a sandy soil with excellent drainage produced ideal growing conditions. Truckloads of sweet peas were sent east for planting in early spring for early summer flowering. But there, nasty root diseases, such as Pythium, Phytophthora, and Thielaviopsis, often killed the vines before they had a chance to flower. The demise of sweet peas after these fungus diseases took hold was so rapid that plant breeders turned their attention to improving other promising annuals, and marigolds, zinnias, and petunias quickly replaced the sweet pea in popularity for sunny spaces.

Unfortunately, these diseases are still widespread across North America, and there are no sprays to control them and no resistant plant varieties. But you still can enjoy sweet peas by planting them in a different location each season (to avoid infected soil) or by planting them in containers with sterile soil. At Cedaridge Farm, I can pick armloads of sweet pea flowers for indoor floral arrangements because I grow clumps of them in sunken 10-gallon plant pots. I fill the pots with potting soil that I sterilize myself, by baking batches of regular topsoil mixed with peat and sand in a disposable aluminum pan in an oven at 450°F for 40 minutes. I also ensure that the potted soil dries between watering to diminish the risk of root rot.

Sweet peas were first discovered in Sicily in 1695 near Palermo by a Franciscan monk, Francisco Cupani, who passed seed along to botanist friends in England and Holland. The seed grew highly fragrant, small, bicolored flowers with purple upper petals and blue lower petals. His original find is still available to home gardeners under the name 'Cupani'. I discovered that one of the delights of traveling the highways and byways of

New Zealand was to find it growing wild, especially along the scenic coast road between Blenheim and Christchurch.

The British took a special interest in sweet peas, and a Scotsman, Henry Eckford, began a breeding program at his farm on the English/Welsh border. He introduced a whole new race with large flowers known as grandifloras. More than 20 of Eckford's introductions are still commercially available in the United States. In 1901, Silas Cole, head gardener to the Earl of Spencer, discovered a larger mutation with ruffled petals on the earl's English estate. Using this as a parent, Eckford created the famous Spencer race of extra-large sweet peas. He shared his expertise with W. Atlee Burpee, founder of Burpee Seeds, and over the years the Burpee Company produced the popular Galaxy group of climbing sweet peas with up to six large flowers per stem.

Sweet peas offer an extensive color range, including all shades of red, maroon, navy blue, lavender blue, all shades of pink, and pure white. There are also striped varieties and bicolors. To enjoy a fruity, old-fashioned fragrance, choose one of the heirloom varieties, such as 'Eckford's Finest Series', also known as 'Old Spice Series'. Some new varieties grown by Dr. Keith Hammett, a New Zealand breeder, are also highly fragrant, including a striped mixture called 'Streamers' and the solid-color 'High Scent'. In the United States, Renee Shepherd of Renee's Garden in California sells a complete range of the best individual colors, in addition to several highly fragrant mixtures. Her Web site features 'Cupani's Original' and many of Dr. Hammett's introductions, including 'North Shore', a rich claret and violet-blue bicolor; 'Saltwater Taffy Swirls', a candy-striped variety; 'April in Paris', a pale yellow sweet pea with violet-blue ruffled edges; and 'Watermelon', with blooms the color of a freshly sliced red watermelon. All have long, strong, wiry stems excellent for cutting.

Instructions for growing sweet peas can be confusing. Many seed packets recommend the European method of sowing seeds in fall, which is unsuitable for the northeastern United States. Northern gardeners should start seed indoors 4 weeks before outdoor planting in early spring. Since the sweet pea seed has a hard coat, soak the seed overnight in a cup of lukewarm water, and plant only those seeds that have swelled by morning, indicating viability. Wait until after severe frosts have passed to transplant. Choose a spot where neither edible peas nor sweet peas have grown previously. Ensure the soil has good drainage, because water puddling around roots will induce rot. In heavy clay soils, mix in plenty of organic matter beforehand.

Space plants 4 to 6 inches apart and provide garden netting for the vines to climb up with their tendrils. From germination to flowering, you'll need at least 50 days of cool temperatures to grow sweet peas. For generous flowering, choose a fertilizer with a high phosphorus content, such as 10-20-10, since phosphorus is the nutrient responsible for flower initiation. The deeper the roots can go, the cooler they will remain when days turn hot. A mulch of organic material, such as shredded leaves or straw, will help maintain a cool soil temperature. In addition to those offered by Renee's Garden, a good selection of sweet pea varieties is offered by Baker Creek Heirloom Seeds (www.rareseeds.com).

KEY CHARACTERISTICS

Botanical Name: *Lathyrus odoratus*

Origins: Native to Sicily

Zones: 4–11 as a cool season annual

Propagation: By direct-sown seed, or started 4 weeks before planting outdoors when danger of severe frosts has passed

Pests and Diseases: Various root rots that are difficult to control

Height: 3–6 feet, depending on variety

Supports: Tall trellis or garden netting. Also consider growing around a wire cylinder and up twiggy branches arranged to create a tall pyramid.

VERBENA, TRAILING

Wild species of verbenas usually grow in deserts and tolerate drought; modern garden varieties are mostly hybrids bred to create beautiful hanging baskets. Many varieties have stems that can exceed 4 feet, with flowers that look like clusters of tiny primroses. I especially like to see them placed in window box planters or hanging baskets to cascade down for spectacular vertical accents. You also can train these vines to grow up a trellis for display in containers. The color range

Hanging baskets of trailing verbena can be hung at various heights to create a curtain of color.

is vibrant—not only vivid blues and reds and dazzling white, but also purple, orange, salmon, and chocolate brown. Many flower with a contrasting white eye, and some are bicolored for a sparkling candy-cane appearance. For a particularly attractive plant combination, combine trailing verbena with 'Million Bells' mini petunias *(Calibrachoa)*.

Trailing verbenas demand full sun, good drainage, and a fertile soil. In order to climb vertically, guide the stems up a pyramid of short bamboo canes, held in place with twist ties.

KEY CHARACTERISTICS

Botanical Name: *Verbena × hybrida*

Origins: Native to South America

Zones: 4–11 as a tender annual

Propagation: By seed started 8 weeks before planting outdoors, or from tip cuttings

Pests and Diseases: Aphids and rot following wet weather

Height: Up to 4 feet

Supports: Short trellis, or allow to cascade like a curtain from balcony or window box planters

Ornamental Perennial and Woody Vines

CHAPTER

13

In the following section, you'll find hardy perennial vines, woody vines, and tender perennial vines grown for their beautiful flowering or foliage effect. Many will add immense aesthetic appeal to a garden at the same time they save space. They will take floral color, leaf color, texture, and decorative leaf shapes well above the height of flowering annual vines and also beyond most bushy perennials and shrubs. This sky-high decoration can be achieved by growing the vines against a wall or fence and also over arches, arbors, and pergolas. Hardy evergreen kinds like English ivy can be used to cloak a boring or ugly expanse of wall or fence, while deciduous kinds like Virginia creeper and Boston ivy will provide lush spring and summer foliage and brilliant fall color.

You'll need to take much greater care when choosing supports for perennial and woody vines, because some—like wisteria and trumpet creeper—can be so aggressive and heavy that they will quickly rot a flimsy wooden structure. A metal support might be a better choice. Other woody

ORNAMENTAL PERENNIAL AND WOODY VINES

285

vines—like clematis and silver fleece vine—will eventually rot a flimsy wooden structure, but not as quickly, especially if pruned at the end of each season to lighten the load. Another consideration when planting these types of vines is the aggressive root systems they have. Their roots can spread rapidly and into unwanted areas, extending out from the mother plant up to 6 feet in a single season.

You can be much more creative with perennial and woody vines than with annual vines. For example, two colors of wisteria—a blue and a white—can be planted so their branches entwine over a bridge canopy to create a mass of flowers at a greater height than annual vines. With clematis and roses, even wider ranges of colors can be planted to entwine; you can even mix the two species for an especially beautiful plant partnership.

I have included a number of tender perennials that will survive in frost-free locations, but they must be taken inside where freezing occurs during winter. The practice of growing a tropical or subtropical vine in a pot—or digging up its rootball to place in a pot—for overwintering indoors is a simple procedure and well worth the trouble. I've selected vines that will tolerate having their stems pruned back to the soil line and then being left to rest in a dormant or semi-dormant state, watered just enough to keep them alive. In late winter and early spring, as day length increases and the vines start to sprout new top growth, you can increase watering and fertilizing and, after your last frost date, take your plants outdoors to flower.

AKEBIA, FIVELEAF

The leaves of this semi-evergreen, tall climber are composed of five oval leaflets, giving the vine a decorative appearance even when not in bloom. Also known as chocolate vine, its small, spicy-scented, chocolate- or purple-colored cup-shaped nodding flowers appear in spring, almost hidden by the dense foliage cover. Plants prefer full sun or partial shade and a well-drained but humus-rich, fertile, moist soil. Suitable for training up trellises and posts as tall as telephone poles, it can also be trained on walls, arbors, and pergolas. Male and female flowers occur among the clusters. When the females are pollinated, they may produce sausage-shaped purple fruits, but this generally requires two vines. Plants self-climb by twining.

KEY CHARACTERISTICS

Botanical Name: *Akebia quinata*

Origins: Native to Eastern Asian countries of China, Japan, and Korea

Zones: 4–8

Propagation: By seed, softwood cuttings, root division, and layering

Pests and Diseases: Mostly winter dieback: Prune away dead stems.

Height: Up to 30 feet; can become invasive

Supports: Tall trellises, heavy-gauge garden netting, chain-link fences; also tree trunks that allow it to climb up into the leaf canopy

BITTERSWEET, AMERICAN

The berry-laden fall branches of American bittersweet are valued for Thanksgiving and Christmas decorations; they look rustic and charming circled into wreaths, displayed on windowsills, and arranged on cabinet tops at holiday gatherings. The flowers of this hardy, deciduous rampant climber are small, green, and inconspicuous, so it's all about the show of the orange-red berries in fall, which take the stage after the leaves drop. Plants tolerate impoverished soil, thrive in sun or light shade, and are best grown up trellis or fencing. In New England states, this plant is considered a noxious weed because of its ability to self-seed and choke competing vegetation, especially in lightly wooded areas along roadsides. The berries are produced only on female plants, so a male is required to ensure pollination. The Oriental bittersweet *(Celastrus orbiculatus)* is equally hardy and aggressive, and its flowers are self-fertile, with a subsequent berry display very similar to the American bittersweet.

Botanical Name: *Celastrus scandens*

Origins: Native to North America

Zones: 5–8

Propagation: By seed, root division, and softwood cuttings

Pests and Diseases: Powdery mildew

Height: Up to 30 feet

Supports: Strong, tall trellises; split-rail and chain-link fences; robust trees like maple and river birch that have rough bark and low-spreading branches to provide support way up into the leaf canopy

BLUE SKY VINE

Related to the black-eyed Susan vine, this is one of the most beautiful vines in all of nature, producing curtains of sky-blue trumpet-shaped blooms up to 3 inches wide. The tender perennial plants are mostly grown outdoors in frost-free locations, like southern Florida and southern California, to create a curtain of arrow-shaped leaves and long spring-flowering flower clusters. The vines are extremely vigorous, with leaves overlapping to cloak walls like fish scales, and are most suitable for growing up a trellis on the sunny side of a building and over arbors. Provide full sun and good drainage. In areas with winter freezes, it is worth growing the plant in a pot to transfer indoors before fall frost.

KEY CHARACTERISTICS

Botanical Name: *Thunbergia grandiflora*

Origins: Native to India

Zones: 10–11

Propagation: By softwood and semi-hardwood cuttings and soil layering

Pests and Diseases: Scale insects

Height: Up to 30 feet

Supports: Tall metal trellises, arches, arbors, and pergolas; also tall chain-link fences, such as security fences and those surrounding tennis courts

BOUGAINVILLEA

A common sight in frost-free locations like southern California and southern Florida, bougainvillea is a tender perennial, producing woody vines capable of flowering continuously. The most commonly grown bougainvillea is a gaudy flowering vine in magenta. Three tiny cream-colored flowers are nestled within each grouping of three papery bracts. It is the bracts that give the plant its dazzling color. The plants have long, thorny stems that are best trained up a strong trellis, pillar, or over an arbor. There are also bushy forms that stay compact as well as spreading groundcover varieties. Plant breeders have extended bougainvillea's color range from its true magenta to yellow, orange, dusky red, salmon, pink, purple, white, and bicolors. Provide full sun and a fertile, well-drained soil. Constant pruning of the lead shoots and irrigation will keep plants blooming.

If you live in a frost-free area, purchase containerized rooted cuttings to grow up strong supports, or obtain mature tree-form plants that have been shaped into topknots. Left to grow naturally, bougainvillea will extend its stems into the tops of tall trees, as they have on my Sanibel Island property in Florida. In colder regions, plants are also suitable for hanging baskets, capable of creating a colorful sphere or curtain of color. Even gardeners in cold winter areas will find bougainvillea readily available in local nurseries. When taking plants indoors, prune back the vines to the soil line and water just enough to keep them alive. Increase watering in March and fertilize, setting outside again after your last spring frost date.

KEY CHARACTERISTICS

Botanical Name: *Bougainvillea spectabilis*

Origins: Native to Brazil

Zones: 9–11, tolerates some frost

Propagation: By tip cuttings in spring and summer

Pests and Diseases: Stress from drought can cause bacterial and fungus problems.

Height: Up to 60 feet

Supports: A tall metal trellis, or a strong stone wall, arch, arbor, or pergola

BOWER PLANT

If you like the orange-red trumpet-shaped flower clusters of trumpet creepers, you'll love the bower plant, as its flowers are similar but have a throat color of adorable soft pink with red veins that attracts hummingbirds. This plant resembles the hardy trumpet creeper (*Campsis radicans*) in habit, but it is a tender tropical vine suitable for growing as an annual in northern gardens or as a perennial in frost-free areas. Trumpet-shaped flowers are borne in clusters on woody vines that twine. The most common colors are white with a pink throat or light pink with a red throat, although there is also a pure white. Provide plants with a sunny, well-drained location and a fertile soil for generous flowering. While the vine is suitable for all kinds of supports with rough surfaces, I especially like to see it trained up into small trees, so the vines can scramble up a rough trunk into the canopy.

KEY CHARACTERISTICS
Botanical Name: *Pandorea jasminoides*
Origins: Native to Australia's eastern seaboard
Zones: 9–11
Propagation: By seed, softwood cuttings, and soil layering
Pests and Diseases: Harbors spider mites, especially if taken indoors
Height: Up to 15 feet
Supports: Tall trellises, stone walls, tall chain-link fences, arches, arbors, and pergolas

CALICO VINE

I don't know of any other flowering vine that is capable of creating such awe among children, since its size, shape, and coloring are so captivating. In bud form, its flower resembles a goose; an old common name for it is the "great goose flower." This is one of the largest-flowered and most unusual of a larger family of tender tropical vines. The flower of the calico vine is composed of a single petal that's shaped like a blaring trumpet and is

The heart-shaped leaves of Dutchman's pipe, a close relative of calico vine, turn beautiful shades of rose and taupe when the weather turns brisk in the fall.

speckled maroon and white with a dark, almost-black throat. It is a fast-growing climber with long, twining stems, suitable for growing up a trellis against a wall or to cover a pergola. The flowers are malodorous to attract flies as pollinators, but you need to be close to the flower to notice its smell. Several other species look like the calico vine, including *Aristolochia gigantea* and *A. grandiflora.* Mix several kinds along a chain-link fence for a really spectacular display.

Provide full sun or partial shade and a fertile, well-drained soil. These plants can become invasive; in southern Florida, they have escaped into the wild. If you live in a frost-free area where calico vine has invasive tendencies, avoid growing this plant. Calico vine has a hardy relative, the Dutchman's pipe vine (*A. durior,* also known as *A. macrophylla*), whose small white pipe-shaped flowers are generally hidden by the large heart-shaped leaves.

Botanical Name: *Aristolochia littoralis*

Origins: Native to South and Central America (*A. durior* is native to the United States)

Zones: 9–11 (*A. durior* is hardy from Zones 4–8)

Propagation: By seed, root division, and semi-hardwood cuttings

Pests and Diseases: Aphids, and root rot when drainage is poor

Height: Up to 30 feet

Supports: Tall metal trellises, stone walls, chain-link fences, arches, arbors, and pergolas

CAT'S CLAW VINE

For sheer quantity of bloom, this attractive tender vine is one of the best, its bright yellow trumpet-shaped flowers crowded so closely together that they almost hide the foliage. Its common name refers to its pairs of hooked tendrils that grasp rough surfaces. This aggressive ornamental vine, closely related to *Thunbergia*, creates a dense curtain of slender, willow-like leaves and bright yellow 4-inch-wide blooms that appear in spring. I have seen it covering garage roofs in the historic districts of Charleston and New Orleans. I have always admired its glorious springtime display, but the Internet is full of warnings by home gardeners in frost-free areas to be wary of its aggressive habit.

KEY CHARACTERISTICS

Botanical Name: *Macfadyena unguis-cati*

Origins: Native to Mexico

Zones: 8–11

Propagation: By beanlike seeds, softwood cuttings, or soil layering

Pests and Diseases: Can harbor spider mites

Height: Up to 30 feet

Supports: Tall metal trellises, chain-link fences, walls, arches, arbors, and pergolas

CHALICE VINE

You are unlikely to find a more spectacular flowering vine than this, although you will need to live in a relatively frost-free location to enjoy its huge, 6-inch-wide, cup-shaped yellow blooms that are striped brown along the inside of each petal. A single specimen of this plant, also called cup of gold, will produce hundreds of blossoms among large, leathery, spear-shaped leaves that resemble those of a rhododendron. A variegated selection has its leaves outlined with a creamy yellow border. The flowers mostly occur in spring, but the vine will bloom intermittently throughout the year. A strong support such as a pergola or wall is needed for the heavy tangle of sinuous stems. Provide full sun and a fertile soil with good drainage. The vines can be heavily pruned almost to their roots to restrict their size. In areas with frost, the plant can be pruned back, its roots dug up and placed in a container, and moved indoors for winter.

KEY CHARACTERISTICS

Botanical Name: *Solandra maxima*

Origins: Native to Mexico and Central and South America

Zones: 9–11

Propagation: By seed and air layering in spring, also semi-hardwood cuttings in summer

Pests and Diseases: Scale insects and spider mites when moved indoors

Height: Up to 20 feet

Supports: Tall metal trellises, high walls, chain-link fences, arbors, arches, and pergolas

CLEMATIS SPECIES AND HYBRIDS

Is it *clem-AH-tis, CLEM-ah-tis,* or *clem-AY-tis*? According to the world authority on this popular flowering perennial vine, UK breeder Raymond J. Evison, it is *clem-AH-tis*. With the possible exception of climbing roses, few plants are more cherished for growing vertically than clematis. They climb by twining their long, thin stems, making them suitable for growing up freestanding trellis or netting, around tree trunks, up walls and fences, and over arbors. Clematis also perform well when allowed to climb up bamboo stakes inserted into roomy containers, such as whiskey half-barrels. In a large container, there is sufficient room to grow several colors so that they entwine. This way, an eye-catching patriotic red, white, and blue effect can be created.

Known as the queen of vines, species of clematis can be bushy and classified as herbaceous perennials, but the most glorious are long-lived woody vines that can produce generous quantities of flowers in a wide assortment of colors. These include white, blue, purple, red, yellow, and bicolors. The number of petals in a standard flower can range from four to eight. There are also doubles with more than 50 overlapping petals. Indeed, there are so many variations in flower form that they can resemble single-flowered dahlias, double-flowered water lilies, tulips, and bellflowers. A great deal of hybridization has occurred among the species, so that today there are about 3,000 varieties, with different degrees of hardiness, from which to choose.

It is especially appealing to see clematis partnered with climbing roses—for example, a purple 'Jackmanii' clematis threading its stems through a climbing 'Blaze' rose, or a pink-and-white bicolored 'Nelly Moser' clematis embracing an orange 'Westerland' rose. There are varieties that bloom early (such as 'Nelly Moser'), midseason (such as red 'Ernest Markham'), and late (such as the fragrant white sweet autumn clematis that drapes itself in thousands and thousands of tiny fragrant white flowers). Some clematis bloom on new wood, but most bloom on previous season's growth and so dictate the method of pruning to use. With a vine like 'Jackmanii' that blooms on new wood, I simply thin out tangled stems if the vine becomes too top-heavy and threatens to suffocate itself, or I cut the entire plant back to within 3 feet of the soil line. With a vine like 'Nelly Moser' that blooms on old wood, I generally selectively prune the mass of stems to five main uprights. For more sophisticated instructions for pruning the many different kinds of clematis, I recommend Raymond Evison's book, *Clematis for Everyone*.

A maxim for growing clematis well is to keep their roots in the shade and their heads in the sun, although the blooms will tolerate light shade. Where summers are hot, a good practice is to lay a covering of flat fieldstone, gravel, or terra-cotta tile over the roots.

Clematis flowers best in a humus-rich, well-drained soil with trellis or netting for support. Most produce decorative fluffy seed heads that persist into fall. A common problem with clematis—especially among spring-blooming varieties—is clematis wilt, a disease that can affect an entire plant, causing it to turn brown and shrivel to its roots, or may affect only part of the plant. There is a tendency for all clematis to show signs of wilt from stress—especially drought—by shedding their lower leaves, but you'll recognize true wilt if the vine's growing tips collapse and die.

Clematis flowers come in a wide range of shapes and sizes, some of them quite bizarre when the crown of stamens at the center of the flowers

Clematis 'Nelly Moser' is the perfect choice for growing up a chain-link fence.

is especially pronounced. Some clematis are delightfully doubled, similar to double-flowered dahlias in appearance, although the doubles never seem to be quite so free-flowering as the singles, in my experience. Here are some of my favorite species and hybrids.

Clematis montana is from northern India and China and is perhaps the tallest climber of all clematis. There are several colors, including a pure white, light pink, deep pink, and a delightful pink-and-white bicolor, 'Freda'. A single vine can grow to 60 feet and almost smother itself in four-petaled flowers. In addition to growing up, the vines like to drape down like a curtain. Claude Monet so admired the curtain effect of this vigorous clematis that he erected special high metal trellises for them to climb up and along. This way the white and pink flowers could hang down like a lace curtain. One of the finest decorative effects can be achieved by allowing *C. montana* to climb up into wide-spreading trees such as beech and birch. Zones 6–9.

Clematis terniflora (sweet autumn clematis) has had many names. I wish taxonomists (learned professors who decide upon the botanical names for plants) would make up their minds about what to call the sweet autumn clematis. When I began gardening, it was *C. paniculata*, then *C. maximowicziana*, then *C. dioscoreifolia;* and now more recently it is *C. terniflora* (a name which very few nursery catalogs use, preferring instead the original *C. paniculata*, even though that name has been given to a larger-flowered white New Zealand clematis that is not as hardy). Native to Russia and China (and naturalized in many regions of North America, including my Cedaridge Farm in Pennsylvania), the sweet autumn clematis flowers the first season from seed. It is extremely fast growing and likes to latch onto bushy shrubs, cloaking them completely with starry white flowers in late summer. Zones 5–9.

'Dr. Ruppel' is similar in appearance to 'Nelly Moser' (an old garden clematis named for a French nurseryman's wife), but with a deeper and wider pink coloring on the petals. Both are large flowered (up to 6 inches across). Both are extremely free-flowering and among the first to bloom in

Fragrant white flowers of sweet autumn clematis decorate the balcony of a white gingerbread gazebo at Cedaridge Farm.

spring. They are so early, in fact, that I have plants growing among azaleas, so that they flower simultaneously. Zones 5–9.

'Etoile Violette' is similar in color to the old garden clematis called 'Jackmanii', named for a British nurseryman. While the deep purple-blue 'Jackmanii' has mostly four or five petals and is larger-flowered (up to 5 inches across) than 'Etoile Violette' (4 inches across), 'Jackmanii' is considered a bit too common by clematis connoisseurs, due to overuse by homeowners. 'Etoile Violette' has up to eight petals, with a more conspicuous crown of yellow stamens, and offers better mildew resistance. The vine is fast-growing and can reach the roof of a ranch house in a single season. It's a perfect candidate for growing through climbing roses, especially pink rose varieties like 'America' and 'Eden'. Zones 5–9.

'Henryi' is my favorite white clematis, with some individual flowers up to 6 inches across. The eight petals are perfectly symmetrical, flowering in early summer. 'Henryi' clematis grows to 10 feet high in a single season. Zones 4–9.

Venosa Violacea, though small-flowered (up to 3 inches across), oozes with charm. The six-petaled star-shaped flowers are blue-mauve with a flash of white along the petal center, making it sparkle. Add to this a black ring of stamens, and the color combination is one of the most beautiful among clematis. Zones 5–9.

'Ville de Lyon' is my favorite clematis among the reds. The carmine-red six-petaled flowers bloom in early to midsummer and measure up to 5 inches across. It's similar in appearance to 'Ernest Markham' (also midsummer flowering), which has slightly smaller flowers but more of them and up to 4 inches across. Zones 4–9.

'Vyvyan Pennell' is a large midsummer-flowering double lavender-blue clematis and one of two double-flowered clematis that I admire. The second is 'Duchess of Edinburgh', an early summer-flowering large white that resembles a double water lily. Zones 5-9.

KEY CHARACTERISTICS

Botanical Name: *Clematis* species and hybrids

Origins: Clematis are mostly native to Asia and North America, but also to Europe, Australia, and New Zealand.

Zones: Depends on species or hybrid; largely 5–9

Propagation: By seed, root division, layering, and soft or semi-hardwood cuttings

Pests and Diseases: Mostly clematis wilt, dieback from various causes of stress, and root knot nematodes

Height: Varies according to species and hybrid, mostly to 15 feet, but some (like *C. montana*) up to 60 feet

Supports: Tall trellises, garden netting, chain-link fences, walls, arches, arbors, and pergolas

CORAL PEA

Small purple flowers hang in generous clusters like grapes on the coral pea vine. This vigorous woody climber is a tender perennial that can be grown in a pot and overwintered indoors in northern states. In early summer, the twining vines produce masses of pea-shaped purple flowers in dense pendant clusters among lancelike leaves. Pink and white varieties are also available. It's popular for growing up arches and arbors and as sentinels at the entrance to a house. Plants are suitable for growing in containers, planted inside a wire cylinder or against a tall trellis. Provide full sun and a fertile, moist, but well-drained soil. When taken indoors in winter, cut the stems back to within 6 inches of the soil line and water just enough to keep the plant alive.

KEY CHARACTERISTICS

Botanical Name: *Hardenbergia violacea*

Origins: Native to Australia

Zones: 10–11

Propagation: By seed, pregerminated by soaking; also from softwood cuttings taken in spring

Pests and Diseases: Mostly spider mites and aphids

Height: Up to 10 feet in a single season, taller in frost-free areas

Supports: Tall trellises, garden netting, chain-link fences, arches, arbors, and pergolas

CORAL VINE

Coral vine's small coral-pink flowers are clustered on arching stems and make a beautiful, airy display that can last all summer. This tender perennial climber has tendrils to climb to great heights. Its heart-shaped leaves and climbing habit resemble those of the silver fleece vine and Japanese knotweed, to which it is closely related. Even in poor soil and deprived of water for long periods, its flowering display can be quite spectacular, especially in full sun, and its stems can easily cover a pergola or climb to the top of a chain-link fence surrounding a tennis court. In northern gardens with frost danger in fall, it's possible to dig up the rootball, transfer it to a pot, prune the stems back to the soil line, and keep it alive in a dormant state by sparse watering until early spring. Then increase the watering to force a new flush of leaves, and transfer the rootball to the garden after frost danger. Plants are aggressive even in poor soil and potentially invasive in frost-free areas.

KEY CHARACTERISTICS

Botanical Name: *Antigonon leptopus*

Origins: Native to Mexico

Zones: 9–11

Propagation: By seed, root division, and tip cuttings

Pests and Diseases: Aphids, spider mites, and whiteflies

Height: Up to 40 feet

Supports: Tall trellises, garden netting, chain-link fences, high walls, arches, arbors, and pergolas

CRIMSON GLORY VINE

Given its alluring common name, and the sight of it turning brilliant molten red in British gardens during fall, I wondered why this member of the grape family is hardly ever seen in North American gardens, except in the Pacific Northwest. The answer lies in its extreme susceptibility to mildew disease in most other areas of the United States, causing it to defoliate before it can turn on its fall brilliancy. The leaves resemble grape leaves, and the vine produces small black clusters of inedible grapes. Where it will survive mildew and Japanese beetle depredations, it is suitable for covering arbors and pergolas. A striking plant partnership is possible by growing crimson glory vine through the berried branches of a firethorn.

KEY CHARACTERISTICS

Botanical Name: *Vitis coignetiae*

Origins: Native to Japan

Zones: 5–8

Propagation: By hardwood cuttings in winter, softwood cuttings in spring, or soil layering

Pests and Diseases: Mildew, Japanese beetles, and a host of other diseases that affect grapes

Height: Up to 20 feet

Supports: Strong, tall trellises, heavy-gauge garden netting, chain-link fences, arches, arbors, and pergolas

VERTICAL GARDENING

CROSS VINE

For the life of me I can't understand why such a beautiful and distinctive spring-flowering vine doesn't have a more appealing common name. This extremely aggressive native vine is one of a family of trumpet vines that can be tender or hardy, depending on the species. Cross vine closely resembles the hardy orange-red trumpet creeper (*Campsis radicans*), but the cross vine can be variable in its flower coloration. The tubular flowers are mostly a combination of chocolate in the throat and a rim of yellow around the petal tips and petal reverse, but there are forms with ruby-red or salmon-pink flowers. Plants climb by tendrils (unlike the trumpet creeper that has aerial roots for climbing) and need strong support, such as a wall or a pergola. Provide full sun and fertile soil with good drainage. At one time, all of the following were named a species of *Bignonia,* but they have now been reclassified:

Bignonia grandiflora (now Campsis grandiflora)

B. jasminoides (now Pandorea jasminoides)

B. pandorana (now Pandorea pandorana)

B. radicans (now Campsis radicans)

B. stans (now Tecoma stans)

B. unguis-cati (now Macfadyena unguis-cati)

KEY CHARACTERISTICS

Botanical Name: *Bignonia capreolata*

Origins: Native to North America, especially Virginia and the Carolinas

Zones: 6–9

Propagation: By seed started 10 weeks before outdoor planting after frost danger has passed. Also by stem layering and semi-hardwood cuttings

Pests and Diseases: Mostly black mildew, powdery mildew, and leaf spots that rarely damage the vine

Height: Up to 30 feet

Supports: Strong, tall trellises, stone walls, chain-link fences, arches, arbors, and pergolas. Will also use trunks of trees to climb up into the leaf canopy

FIG, CREEPING

This plant is a familiar sight on brick walls in the historic sections of southern cities, particularly Charleston, Savannah, and New Orleans. It's an evergreen climber, mostly seen affixing its aerial roots to walls. Here in Pennsylvania, a neighbor of mine with a conservatory has creeping fig covering an entire wall, creating an easy-care sheet of greenery. The wiry stems are massed and knit together with small, oval green leaves that overlap to create a dense curtain. Tiny, insignificant figs are produced in late summer. It's fast growing in full sun in fertile, well-drained soil.

KEY CHARACTERISTICS

Botanical Name: *Ficus pumila*

Origins: Native to China and Japan

Zones: 7–11

Propagation: By cuttings peeled off walls and rooted in water or moist, sandy soil

Pests and Diseases: Mealybugs, spider mites, and scale insects

Height: Up to 30 feet

Supports: Walls and trees with rough surfaces and stone columns

FIRETHORN

The selection of berried vines is quite small, and firethorn is undoubtedly the best for sheer quantity of brightly colored berries and long-lasting display. This hardy, tall-growing shrub is one of my favorite woody plants for creating an ornamental espalier display against a wall. Although not really a vine, its long, pliable thorny branches can be trained to climb to the roof of a ranch house. Plants produce a blizzard of small, fragrant, hawthornlike flowers in spring, followed in fall by bright red, orange, or yellow berry clusters, depending on the variety. The semi-evergreen leaves are small and oval. Provide full sun and good drainage. A particularly fine series of fire-blight-resistant varieties has Native American names, released by the National Arboretum: It includes 'Apache' with red berries that persist into December.

Botanical Name: *Pyracantha coccinea*

Origins: Native to Northern Italy and Serbia

Zones: 6–9

Propagation: By seed and softwood cuttings taken in spring or summer

Pests and Diseases: Fire blight and scab

Height: Up to 18 feet

Supports: Walls, tall trellises, chain-link fences, split-rail fences

GLORY BOWER

Although the genus *Clerodendron* has a number of species known as glory bowers, *C. thomsoniae* is my favorite, because its dense clusters of white flowers have red pokerlike protrusions that make it distinctive among flowering vines. This tender, tropical vine climbs by twining and features flower clusters that hang down like grapes and consist of white, papery calyxes surrounding small red flowers. The dull green oval leaves are evergreen in frost-free areas; even if the plant is nipped briefly by frost, it will generally send up new shoots from the roots. Grow in fertile, humus-rich soil in full sun. Use glory bower to climb up trellises and posts. Plants can be grown in containers, and at the approach of fall frosts, the stems can be pruned back to the soil line to overwinter indoors.

KEY CHARACTERISTICS

Botanical Name: *Clerodendron thomsoniae*

Origins: Native to West Africa

Zones: 9–11

Propagation: By seed, root division, and softwood cuttings taken in summer

Pests and Diseases: Whiteflies and mealybugs

Height: Up to 12 feet

Supports: Tall trellises (especially fan trellises), heavy-gauge garden netting, chain-link fences, arches, and arbors

ORNAMENTAL PERENNIAL AND WOODY VINES

GOLDEN CHAIN TREE

Although the golden chain tree is not a vine, its pliable branches can be trained like vines so that its long, yellow wisteria-like flower clusters can hang down to create a curtain of dazzling blooms. In Monet's garden in Giverny, France, a golden chain tree is partnered with a blue wisteria vine to create a stunning yellow and blue color harmony. The most famous vertical accent using *Laburnum* is in Bodnant Garden, North Wales, where these small trees are planted on either side of a metal framework, forming an enclosed allée high enough for visitors to walk under. The rubbery branches arch over the metal canopy, and in early June the tunnel is covered with a mass of golden yellow blooms that seem to be dripping from the ceiling. It's thrilling to pass through. *L.* x *watereri* is a hybrid that produces extra-long flower panicles. A Dutch clonal selection from this hybrid, known as 'Vossii', has the longest blossom clusters of all—up to 2 feet long. Provide full sun and good drainage. To stimulate the best flowering display, plant in fertile soil.

KEY CHARACTERISTICS

Botanical Name: *Laburnum* × *watereri*

Origins: Native to European alpine regions

Zones: 3–9

Propagation: Although the species are easily grown from seed, the hybrid forms require softwood cuttings or air layering.

Pests and Diseases: To avoid root rot, plant in soil with excellent drainage. Avoid wind damage by planting in a sheltered location.

Height: Up to 25 feet

Supports: Trellises (especially fan trellises), arches, arbors, and pergolas; can be espaliered flat against a wall

GOLDEN TRUMPET

A well-grown golden trumpet is capable of more bang for the buck than any other flowering vine that I know. I have seen plants so densely covered with golden yellow saucer-size blooms that they look like large yellow morning glories. Although this prolifically flowering, tropical evergreen or semi-evergreen woody plant is not really a vine but a shrub, it produces exceedingly long, arching, woody canes that can be trained high up a trellis to create a nonstop floral display. The spear-shaped bright green leaves form a dense background for the masses of large flowers. The flowers of *Allamanda cathartica* can be 4 inches across. The closely related species *A. violacea* has smaller purple flowers. 'Cherries Jubilee', a hybrid involving *A. blanchetii*, has dusky red flowers with dark centers. 'Hendersonii' has red-tinted buds, while 'Nobilis' has the largest flowers, up to 5 inches wide. Provide full sun and a fertile, well-drained soil. Plants are commonly sold as annuals in bud, although they are perennial in frost-free areas. Overwinter in other areas by pruning the canes to the soil line and digging up the rootball for potting and moving indoors. Water sparingly—just enough to keep the plant alive until frost-free days return in spring. Golden trumpet is suitable for growing in containers, like a whiskey half-barrel with a fan trellis for support. I can grow golden trumpet year-round in Florida on my Sanibel Island property, usually having to cut it back every year in winter to keep it under control.

KEY CHARACTERISTICS

Botanical Name: *Allamanda cathartica*

Origins: Native to South America

Zones: 10–11

Propagation: By seed and tip cuttings

Pests and Diseases: Spider mites, aphids, and whiteflies

Height: Up to 25 feet

Supports: Tall trellises (especially fan trellises); also heavy-gauge garden netting, chain-link fences, arches, and arbors

HAWAIIAN WEDDING FLOWER

Its strong, gardenia-like fragrance is reason enough to grow this vigorous tropical climber. The woody plant produces clusters of tubular white flowers among glossy, spear-shaped leaves. The flowers resemble white jasmine, but are larger. Plant in full sun and provide a fertile soil with good drainage. An excellent choice for containers, these plants climb by twining and are especially suitable for growing in a container up a fan trellis. Plants will flower all summer, but must be taken indoors before frost kills the vine. During the short-day months in winter, the plant may go dormant and drop its leaves. Before moving my vine indoors, I like to cut it back to the soil line. I water it sparingly until the warmer days of early spring, when I increase watering and fertilizing to produce a new flush of growth prior to flowering outdoors.

KEY CHARACTERISTICS

Botanical Name: *Stephanotis floribunda*

Origins: Native to Madagascar

Zones: 10–11

Propagation: By semi-hardwood cuttings in summer and air layering

Pests and Diseases: Scale insects and mealybugs

Height: Up to 20 feet

Supports: Strong trellis, especially fan trellis. In frost-free areas, it is suitable for growing up chain-link fencing and over arches and arbors.

HERALD'S TRUMPET

Imagine a vigorous vine with leaves shaped like rhododendron's and huge, fragrant, white lilylike flowers that seem to glow in the moonlight in spring. That's what this incredibly beautiful plant can provide, especially splayed out against a wall. The 5-inch-wide flowers of this tender perennial occur in clusters with four or five open at one time. Evergreen, glossy, spear-shaped leaves are decorative year-round in frost-free locations. The heavy, rampant, woody vine climbs by twining and needs an exceedingly strong support, such as a sunny wall or a pergola. Herald's trumpet is a good choice to cover the roof of a gazebo or arbor. Grow it in a pot and move it indoors over winter in locations with frost.

Botanical Name: *Beaumontia grandiflora*

Origins: Native to India

Zones: 10 and 11

Propagation: By seed and tip cuttings

Pests and Diseases: Spider mites

Height: Up to 30 feet

Supports: Strong trellis, stone wall, chain-link fencing, arches, arbors, and pergolas

HONEYSUCKLE, GOLD FLAME

The Honeysuckle family has numerous hardy and tender species and hybrids suitable for growing vertically. My personal favorite among the hardies is *Lonicera* x *heckrottii* (commonly called the gold flame honeysuckle). A hybrid involving the trumpet honeysuckle, *L. sempervirens*, it is valued for its masses of fragrant pink and yellow flower clusters that are arranged in a crown and produced in spring. These tubular flowers contain a sweet nectar highly attractive to hummingbirds. The paired, oblong leaves are blue-green and deciduous. Plants climb by twining and are most suitable for covering chain-link fences, a trellis, or garden netting. Plant in full sun and fertile soil with good drainage. Top-heavy vines can be cut back to the soil line to sprout new growth. At Cedaridge Farm, I have partnered gold flame honeysuckle with 'Jackmanii' clematis and 'Blaze' climbing rose.

KEY CHARACTERISTICS

Botanical Name: *Lonicera × heckrottii*

Origins: A naturally occurring hybrid involving a Japanese and an American species

Zones: 5–9

Propagation: By layering and tip cuttings

Pests and Diseases: Mostly powdery mildew and scale insects

Height: Up to 15 feet

Supports: Strong trellises, heavy-gauge garden netting, chain-link fences, arches, arbors, and pergolas

HONEYSUCKLE, HALL'S

This vigorous semi-evergreen, fast-growing vine can suffocate every plant in its path, including small trees, unless controlled by rigorous pruning. In many states, it is considered a noxious weed because of its tendency to displace native vegetation. However, in gardens it is widely used as a summer-flowering, care-free vine trained up chain-link fencing and other strong supports. The fragrant yellow tubular flowers have a splash of white in the throat. Plants prefer full sun and tolerate poor soil and drought. Black, round berries in fall can self-seed readily to become invasive. At Cedaridge Farm, Hall's honeysuckle is in all the hedgerows, where I occasionally eradicate it by grubbing out the roots. Most reference books caution against using this invasive plant, yet time and again I see it used in sophisticated gardens, mostly on a patio in a container or climbing a pillar where its habit can be controlled. At Hershey Gardens in Hershey, Pennsylvania, miles of the vine are used as a slope cover along entrance roads.

KEY CHARACTERISTICS

Botanical Name: *Lonicera japonica*

Origins: Native to Japan

Zones: 4–10

Propagation: By seed, root division, and soil layering

Pests and Diseases: None. Virtually indestructible, except by digging up the entire root system

Height: Up to 25 feet

Supports: Strong, tall trellises, heavy-gauge garden or wire netting, chain-link fences, arches, and arbors

HONEYSUCKLE, TRUMPET

I have seen columns of this honeysuckle in southern gardens appear to be pillars of fire, with hundreds of red flower clusters in bloom at one time. Trumpet honeysuckle is popular for home gardens not only for its rich red flowers, but also for its attraction to hummingbirds. It's a deciduous, twining vine with blue-green smooth, spear-shaped leaves. There is also a yellow clone. Plants thrive in full sun and tolerate high heat and humidity. Plant them in fertile soil with good drainage. A high phosphorus fertilizer will produce the best flowering display. 'Superba' is an extra-vigorous, generously flowering selection. When the vine becomes top-heavy, it can be pruned back to the roots to be rejuvenated. At Cedaridge Farm, I partner the red trumpet honeysuckle with the pink and white clematis 'Nelly Moser'.

KEY CHARACTERISTICS

Botanical Name: *Lonicera sempervirens*

Origins: Native to the eastern United States, particularly southern states, where it can be seen climbing up into lofty pine trees

Zones: 4–10

Propagation: By seed and softwood cuttings taken in spring

Pests and Diseases: Mostly scale insects and powdery mildew

Height: Up to 15 feet

Supports: Strong, tall trellises, especially fan trellises; also heavy-gauge garden or wire netting, chain-link fences, arches, and arbors

HYDRANGEA, CLIMBING

The hydrangea family of flowering shrubs has produced a lot of confusion with regard to hardiness and flowering performance. The bushy mophead hydrangea from Japan often fails to flower in severe wintery areas, because most varieties produce their flowers on second-season growth that can be killed to the ground by severe freezing. The more robust climbing hydrangea hails from Russia. It is hardier and climbs by means of aerial roots that affix to rough surfaces, flowering profusely in early summer. The flat or dome-shaped white flowers resemble Queen Anne's lace and can measure up to 5 inches across, borne among lush, leathery, ivylike leaves. Plants prefer full sun but will tolerate light shade. Give them a slightly moist, well-drained fertile soil and strong support such as a wall or pergola.

Climbing hydrangea climbing the wall of a ruin

KEY CHARACTERISTICS

Botanical Name: *Hydrangea anomala* subsp. *petiolaris*

Origins: Native to Russia, China, and Japan

Zones: 4–9

Propagation: By softwood cuttings in summer and hardwood cuttings during fall and winter

Pests and Diseases: Mostly slugs and powdery mildew

Height: Up to 30 feet

Supports: Strong, tall trellises, stone walls, tall chain-link fences, arches, arbors, and pergolas

HYDRANGEA VINE, JAPANESE

This aggressive, heavy vine looks so much like a climbing hydrangea (*Hydrangea anomala* subsp. *petiolaris*) that it is difficult to tell the two apart. They have similar large, heart-shaped, veined, serrated leaves, and the same white flower form—a cluster up to 10 inches across of small, fragrant white flowers surrounded by larger white spoon-shaped sepals—that blooms at the same time in early summer. There is also a pink form. Japanese hydrangea vine is an excellent choice for covering a large expanse of wall or creating a flowering canopy over a pergola—although I personally prefer the climbing hydrangea, since its flowers seem to have slightly more substance.

KEY CHARACTERISTICS

Botanical Name: *Schizophragma hydrangeoides*

Origins: Native to Japan

Zones: 5–9

Propagation: By tip cuttings in late summer, or soil layering

Pests and Diseases: Slugs are a minor problem. Beware of wasp nests among the dense foliage when pruning.

Height: Up to 40 feet

Supports: Strong, tall trellises; walls with rough surfaces; trees with rough bark; arches, arbors, and pergolas

---

IVY, BOSTON

The mention of ivy often brings a scowl to the faces of many people, as ivy is considered so common and is associated with cemeteries and haunted houses. But Boston ivy has become such a popular substitute for the rather course, common English ivy, especially in New England, that it has become most associated with its namesake city—even though the wild species is native to Japan. Of the two *Parthenocissus* species described in this chapter, Boston ivy is a little more refined than Virginia creeper (*P. quinque-folia*). But like Virginia creeper, its small green flowers and blue-black fruits are inconspicuous. The handsome maplelike deciduous leaves overlap like the scales of a fish and present a magnificent cloaking effect for high, wide walls. Plants climb strongly by means of sticky tendrils. This is the plant to choose when you wish to cover an entire gazebo or pergola with foliage. The shiny green leaves open bright green in spring, darken during summer, and turn brilliant shades of red and pink in fall. Provide full sun and good drainage.

Botanical Name: *Parthenocissus tricuspidata*

Origins: Native to Japan, in spite of its common name

Zones: 4–10

Propagation: By seed, semi-hardwood cuttings taken in summer, or soil layering; any stem section with a node will root.

Pests and Diseases: Sometimes minor slug damage, canker, powdery mildew, and scale insects, but mostly carefree

Height: Up to 40 feet

Supports: Strong metal trellises or strong stone walls; also arbors, arches, and pergolas. Plants will easily cover a gazebo.

IVY, ENGLISH

Though shunned by many gardeners as boring and destructive of masonry (its aerial roots penetrate rough surfaces such as wood and stone and can cause it to crack), numerous varieties of hardy English ivy can add beautiful textural interest to a garden, especially the variegated kinds of ivy that combine green and gold and green and white. The shape of their leaves can vary considerably, from that of a maple leaf to heart shaped, slender, and curled. I particularly like the miniatures, such as 'Little Diamond' with blue-green and white leaves and 'Needlepoint' with delicate slender, pointed leaves. The variety 'Buttercup' is almost completely yellow with just a hint of green at the leaf edges. A good place to display a collection of ivies is around a ruin.

Many of the miniature ivies are suitable for making topiary figures. You can make a topiary by creating a form of chicken wire, filling it with sphagnum moss, and planting ivy in it to cover the frame.

Ivy leaves are evergreen, and though trees might not like their trunks cloaked in ivy, healthy trees can tolerate the imposition. The flowers are mostly green and inconspicuous, occurring in spring, followed by clusters of small black berries. An old saying about English ivy is "First it sleeps, then it creeps, and then it leaps," referring to the fact that it can take up to

3 years for new plantings to become sufficiently established to start covering a wall or fence.

At Cedaridge Farm in my woodland areas, I have a collection of English ivies growing up the trunks of trees. In spite of English ivy's reputation as being deer proof, it is, in fact, a favorite food of deer in winter, so I must protect it with deer repellent.

Ivies tolerate a wide range of conditions, including sun or shade and fertile or poor soil, but they do prefer a fertile, well-drained soil. Established plants grown on buildings often need pruning to keep them from encroaching on windows, doors, gutters, and overhangs, where they will induce rot. Plants can be cut to the ground to rejuvenate.

KEY CHARACTERISTICS

Botanical Name: *Hedera helix*

Origins: Native to Europe

Zones: 5–11

Propagation: By cuttings, as any stem section with an aerial root will create a rooted cutting; also by layering

Pests and Diseases: Numerous, including spider mites, mealybugs, and scale. Although deer favor ivy as a winter food, they do not eat its main stem, allowing the vine above their reach to remain evergreen.

Height: Up to 30 feet

Supports: Tall, strong trellises, rough wall surfaces, chain-link fences, arches, arbors, and pergolas; also uses tree trunks to climb up into the leaf canopy

IVY, PERSIAN

Of all ivies available for vertical growth, Persian ivy is surely the most tropical in appearance. This aggressive climber also makes a weed-suffocating groundcover. It has much larger leaves than English ivy, and though not as hardy, it survives winters south of Philadelphia. In California and the Pacific Northwest, it is used extensively along highways to cover embankments and retaining walls. The somewhat floppy leaves can be dark glossy green, green-and-white variegated, or green-and-gold variegated. Plants prefer full sun but tolerate light shade, and require a fertile soil high in humus content with good drainage.

KEY CHARACTERISTICS

Botanical Name: *Hedera colchica*

Origins: Native to Turkey

Zones: 7–9

Propagation: By cuttings. Cut 5-inch semi-hardwood stem sections with several nodes in spring or early summer, lay them flat on moist potting soil, and allow to root.

Pests and Diseases: Mostly scale insects, mealybugs, and spider mites; also a favorite winter food of deer

Height: Up to 30 feet

Supports: Strong, tall trellises, stone walls, heavy-gauge wire netting, chain-link fences, arches, arbors, and pergolas

JASMINE, CAROLINA

One of my fondest memories of a visit to Magnolia Plantation and Gardens in Charleston, South Carolina, was walking in the early morning along paths beneath live oaks cloaked in Spanish moss. I breathed in the scent of jasmine pervading the air and found the vine draped up and over flowering azaleas and camellias. I also encountered jasmine climbing walls in historical areas of Charleston and Savannah. A beautiful, tender perennial evergreen, Carolina jasmine climbs by twining, and almost smothers itself in spring with bright yellow, sweetly scented tubular flowers. Small, lancelike leaves give it a graceful appearance. It's ideal for training over pergolas, arbors, and arches to form a canopy. Plants prefer full sun (but will tolerate light shade) and a fertile, moderately moist but well-drained soil. Carolina jasmine can be pruned almost to the soil line to rejuvenate it. 'Pride of Augusta' is a double-flowered mutation.

KEY CHARACTERISTICS

Botanical Name: *Gelsemium sempervirens*

Origins: Native to the southeastern United States, where it is seen mostly growing up trees at the edge of woodland

Zones: 7–9

Propagation: By seed in spring or semi-hardwood cuttings in summer

Pests and Diseases: Scale and whiteflies

Height: Up to 25 feet

Supports: Tall trellises, ornate metal fences, chain-link fences, arches, arbors, and pergolas

JASMINE, COMMON

The heavenly fragrance of its white star-shaped flowers is the reason for this plant's popularity, especially in southern gardens (it is tender to freezing temperatures). The variety 'Affine' has flowers tinted pink, while

Common jasmine is an ideal choice for covering a fence. The fragrant white flowers bloom over several months and create a vertical garden around a swimming pool.

'Aureum' has mottled green and yellow foliage. Plants are deciduous or semi-evergreen, displaying smooth, lance-shaped leaves clustered in five or more leaflets. Common jasmine is most often grown up and along chain-link fences and pillars, especially to decorate a gazebo, and its fragrance can add a romantic touch to a tranquil retreat. I once saw a pergola in California whose entire structure from end to end was covered in white jasmine.

KEY CHARACTERISTICS

Botanical Name: *Jasminum officinale*

Origins: Native to Northern India and China

Zones: 8–11

Propagation: By softwood cuttings in spring or summer

Pests and Diseases: Carefree outdoors; mealybugs and spider mites indoors

Height: Up to 15 feet

Supports: Tall trellises, heavy-gauge garden netting, chain-link fences, arches, arbors, and pergolas

JASMINE, CONFEDERATE

Famous for its clouds of fragrant white flowers in spring, this tender ever-green perennial, also known as Star jasmine, climbs by twining. Clusters of 1-inch-wide star-shaped white flowers have a pink tint. In southern states, it is grown up pillars and ornate metal fencing, pervading the air with a pleasant vanilla fragrance. The vines are lightweight and suitable for growing up a trellis. Plants grow elegant, green, spear-shaped leaves and prefer fertile soil, good drainage, and full sun. Suitable for growing in containers, the vines can be pruned back to the roots and protected indoors in areas with harsh winters. The name "jasmine" can be applied to a wide range of flowering vines, some of which are not true jasmines but look like jasmines—the Confederate jasmine is one of these.

Botanical Name: *Trachelospermum jasminoides*

Origins: Native to China and Japan

Zones: 8–10

Propagation: By semi-hardwood cuttings in summer

Pests and Diseases: Avoid root rot with excellent drainage.

Height: Up to 30 feet

Supports: Tall wood or metal trellises, garden netting, chain-link fences, arches, arbors, and pergolas

JASMINE, WINTER

The common name "winter jasmine" describes this plant's ability to bloom before the last snowfalls of spring, usually during the first sunny warming trend, even ahead of forsythia and early daffodils. The star-shaped yellow flowers are borne on long arching canes that can be trained to climb. The leaves are attractive and composed of three oval leaflets. Although the name "jasmine" usually conjures up a gardenia-like fragrance, winter jasmine has none. The hardy plants prefer full sun and tolerate poor soil, and they are also drought resistant. If left unsupported, the plant's arching canes will not grow more than 5 feet, but given the support of a sunny wall or trellis, a plant can grow to 15 feet.

KEY CHARACTERISTICS

Botanical Name: *Jasminum nudiflorum*

Origins: Native to China

Zones: 6–9

Propagation: By softwood cuttings in spring and summer

Pests and Diseases: Root rot in poorly drained soil; also scale insects and mealybugs

Height: Up to 15 feet

Supports: Tall trellises, heavy-gauge garden netting, chain-link and ornate metal fences, arches, arbors, and pergolas

KIWI VINE, VARIEGATED

This ornamental Arctic kiwi is a tough winter-hardy species grown mostly for its white- and pink-variegated juvenile leaves. The small white, fragrant flowers appear in spring and are usually hidden by the leaves. Small edible fruits occur on female plants if pollinated by a male. The most intense coloring occurs in spring when nights are cool and in summer in locations where nights remain cool, such as in the Pacific Northwest and coastal Maine. A primary reason for failure to survive the first year is the plant's susceptibility to root rot and trunk injury from alternate thawing and freezing. The trunk becomes more winter hardy with age. Here in Pennsylvania—and in the case of a few plantings I have seen in Ohio—fruiting Arctic kiwis are best grown along a sheltered, sunny wall with excellent drainage. The survival rate can be increased by growing the Arctic kiwi in a 5-gallon container for its first year. Move the container to a sheltered area close to the house during winter to protect its roots from freezing, and transplant to its permanent position only in its second season. For more on kiwifruit and kiwi vines, see Fruits for Vertical Gardens chapter, beginning on page 237.

KEY CHARACTERISTICS

Botanical Name: *Actinidia kolomikta*

Origins: Native to Siberia

Zones: 4–9

Propagation: By air layering, soil layering, and softwood or hardwood cuttings

Pests and Diseases: Japanese beetles and root rot caused by Phytophthora, avoidable by good drainage

Height: Up to 30 feet

Supports: Use a strong trellis or 4-foot-wide by 6-foot-high section of builder's wire between two posts. Also consider training along chain-link fences or over arches, arbors, and pergolas. In areas of borderline hardiness (Zones 3 and 4), plant in a sheltered courtyard and train the top of the vine along a sunny roofline.

MANDEVILLA

Also known by the genus name *Dipladenia*, this tender woody hybrid is a twining evergreen vine that produces beautiful trumpet-shaped flowers resembling those of a hibiscus, up to 4 inches across. The variety 'Alice du Pont', the most commonly cultivated, is an everblooming pale pink that flowers from early summer to fall frost. Other mandevillas are available in white and red. Plants are suitable for containers with a trellis for support. Although the best flowering occurs in full sun, mandevilla will tolerate light shade. Plants can be potted to be overwintered indoors, or they can be pruned to within 6 inches of the ground to be rejuvenated for successive seasons of bloom.

KEY CHARACTERISTICS

Botanical Name: *Mandevilla × amabilis*

Origins: Native to Jamaica

Zones: All zones as a tender perennial; Zones 9–11 outdoors all year

Propagation: By softwood cuttings in spring, and by layering

Pests and Diseases: Harbors spider mites and mealybugs, especially when taken indoors

Height: Up to 8 feet

Supports: Tall wooden or metal trellises, heavy-gauge garden netting, chain-link and ornate metal fences, arches, and arbors

NASTURTIUM, FLAME

If I were asked to name my most coveted perennial vine, it would be the flame nasturtium. Its stunning flowers are like a cloud of scarlet butterflies rising into the sky, but it is challenging to grow. Ideally, it likes full sun to flower all summer, and prefers cool nights like you find in the Pacific Northwest. Famous for its bright crimson flowers, it is something of an enigma regarding hardiness. I have seen the best flowering specimens in the Shetland Islands located between northern Scotland and Norway in

Zone 6, yet it is classified as a Zone 8 plant in most plant encyclopedias. Some other fine specimens can be seen in the famous topiary garden of Levens Hall, in the north of England (a Zone 7 garden), where they are planted to grow up over shapes of clipped boxwood. Though they prefer full sun, they will tolerate light shade. Give them good drainage and garden netting or twiggy branches to climb up.

KEY CHARACTERISTICS

Botanical Name: *Tropaeolum speciosum*

Origins: South America

Zone: 8 (with cool summers)

Propagation: By seed

Pests and Diseases: Slugs and aphids

Height: Up to 10 feet

Supports: Tall trellises, especially fan trellises; also chain-link and ornate metal fences; bushy shrubs

ORCHID CACTUS

Also known as "queen of the night," orchid cactus is one of numerous night-blooming forest cacti with spectacular, fragrant white flowers pollinated by bats. The flowers grow from long, flexible, straplike vines capable of climbing up into the leaf canopy of trees by means of aerial roots. (*Hylocereus undatus* is very similar and is also called "queen of the night" for its large, fragrant white flowers.) Orchid cactus can be grown outdoors in Zones 10 and 11, and is suitable for growing up walls and trellises. The flowers of this vining cactus are so beautiful and their scent so powerful that many gardeners will invite neighbors over to watch the flowers open (often within a matter of minutes). It is obvious when a bud is likely to flower, because it swells up during the day and at about 5:00 p.m. starts opening its petals. In northern areas, orchid cactus is popular as a houseplant, grown in a pot and overwintered easily if watered sparingly. Place it outdoors during frost-free months.

PASSION VINE, BLUE

The common name "blue passion vine" derived from early missionaries to South America who likened the flower parts to elements of Christ's passion at the crucifixion: 10 petals representing the apostles present, an arrangement of spiky filaments representing the crown of thorns, five stamens representing Christ's wounds, and three styles representing the nails on the cross. The vine's tendrils represent the cords used to bind Christ, and the lobed leaves the hands of his tormentors. I doubt there is a more intricately formed or more fascinating flower to admire in all the plant kingdom than the passion vine. With continuous blooming during warm, sunny weather, the flowers can be all shades of blue—plus scarlet, pink, coral, and white—followed by round or oval yellow fruit that dries to the texture of a brown, wrinkled prune.

Most passion vines are tropical and frost tender, but two are reasonably hardy. They are *Passiflora caerulea,* which generally survives outdoors south of New York City, and *P. incarnata*—commonly called maypop—which is a zone hardier and survives in Zone 5. The blue passion vine has larger flowers—up to 4 inches wide—than the maypop's. The flowers of blue passion vines have a complex arrangement of outer petals, an inner ring of stamens resembling a sea anemone, and a central arrangement of pistils that resembles a pinwheel. Yellow fruit up to the size of a golf ball ripen in fall. The skin of the fruit is leathery, but when peeled away, it reveals a colony of tightly packed black seeds surrounded by a yellowish jellylike substance that is sweet and delicious, especially spooned over vanilla ice cream.

Plant passion vines in full sun and fertile soil with good drainage. Feed with a high-phosphorus fertilizer to encourage generous bloom production and fruiting. Depending on the variety (the hardy kinds are less aggressive), passion vines can create a heavy burden of vines that will quickly rot lightweight wooden structures. Stone walls or metal supports are preferred. I have seen some tropical passion vines cover a large barn. To overwinter tropical kinds, grow them in pots and cut the vines back to the soil line before moving them indoors.

KEY CHARACTERISTICS

Botanical Name: *Passiflora caerulea*

Origins: Blue passion vine is native to Brazil; maypop is native to North America.

Zones: 6–10 for blue passion vine; 5–9 for maypop

Propagation: By seed, softwood cuttings, and soil layering

Pests and Diseases: Relatively carefree grown outdoors. Can suffer winterkill after long periods of freezing. Mulch heavily in fall to protect roots.

Height: Up to 15 feet

Supports: Use strong, tall metal trellises or metal arbors, arches, and pergolas with rot-resistant wooden crossbeams; also split-rail fences and tall chain-link fences, such as those used around tennis courts.

PASSION VINE, RED

For a fine collection of passion vines, visit the Fairchild Tropical Botanic Garden in Coral Gables, Florida, where a large number are grown in a display area. Most impressive of all is the red (or scarlet) passion vine, a vigorous summer-flowering climber that displays dark red star-shaped flowers with dark green filaments around a green center. Sausage-shaped yellow fruit ripen in late summer. Provide full sun and fertile, well-drained soil. Grow on supports such as arches and arbors that keep the flowers at eye level for maximum visual impact. Although plants are sensitive to frost, northern gardeners can grow the red passion vine in pots, cutting it back to soil level and moving it indoors during winter.

KEY CHARACTERISTICS

Botanical Name: *Passiflora coccinea*

Origins: Native to South America

Zones: 10–11

Propagation: By seeds, softwood cuttings, and soil layering

Pests and Diseases: Minor slug damage; spider mites when moved indoors

Height: Up to 15 feet

Supports: Strong trellises or heavy-gauge garden netting; also chain-link fences, arches, arbors, and pergolas

PLUMBAGO, BLUE

There are not many blue-flowering vines, which is understandable since flowers must stand out against the blue sky in order to attract insect pollinators. But when vines have good green foliage cover, blue flowers can be conspicuous. This species is not only a rare sky-blue color, but is also continuously flowering. Although it is a tropical fast-growing vine tender to frost, it is often sold as an annual to create a stunning everblooming blue accent in midsummer until fall frost. Mostly sold as a trailing plant to cascade from hanging baskets or as a bushy shrub, the variety 'Monet' can be trained to climb and cover an arbor. Plants like full sun and well-drained soil and tolerate drought. The flowers are borne in generous clusters among slender, lance-shaped light green leaves.

KEY CHARACTERISTICS

Botanical Name: *Plumbago capensis*

Origins: Native to South Africa

Zones: 9–11, and all zones as an annual

Propagation: By cuttings

Pests and Diseases: Slugs

Height: Up to 25 feet

Supports: Tall trellises, arches, and arbors; also chain-link fences

POTATO VINE

On trips to the United Kingdom, I see almost as many potato vines used to cover walls as I see wisteria. The same is true in California and the Pacific Northwest. This tender perennial woody vine is closely related to eggplant, tomatoes, peppers, and other solanaceous plants. Its common name is derived from its star-shaped white flowers that resemble those of the potato. Plants climb by twining and are suitable for growing up walls and over arbors. From a distance, the generous flower clusters look like clouds of white jasmine. Plants tolerate impoverished soil and prefer full sun and good drainage. Potato vine is very popular for growing up trellises and arches.

KEY CHARACTERISTICS

Botanical Name: *Solanum jasminoides*

Origins: Native to Brazil

Zones: 8–10

Propagation: By seed, and softwood and semi-hardwood cuttings in summer

Pests and Diseases: Mostly powdery mildew, botrytis, and aphids

Height: Up to 20 feet

Supports: Tall trellises, especially fan trellises; also walls and chain-link fences, arches, arbors, and pergolas

POTATO VINE, CHILEAN

Chilean potato vine is a tender perennial woody vine that is a common sight in the gardens of Britain, decorating old stone walls around house foundations. It's also popular throughout California for growing over arbors. The fragrant flowers are blue with prominent yellow stamens and are produced in summer. They are borne in generous clusters, resemble those of the potato, and are followed by inedible yellow fruit. Even young plants can be covered in the bright blue star-shaped flowers, making them a popular impulse purchase in British and California garden centers. Provide full sun, a humus-rich soil, and good drainage for the Chilean potato vine. In areas with frost, plants can be grown in a container, pruned back almost to the soil line, and moved indoors during winter.

KEY CHARACTERISTICS

Botanical Name: *Solanum crispum*

Origins: Native to Chile

Zones: 8–10

Propagation: By seed and softwood or semi-hardwood cuttings in summer

Pests and Diseases: Powdery mildew

Height: Up to 20 feet

Supports: Tall trellises, especially fan trellises, and heavy-gauge garden netting; also high walls, chain-link fences, arches, arbors, and pergolas

QUEEN'S WREATH

The first time I saw this plant in flower, covering an arch in a Florida garden, I thought it was a miniature wisteria (the flowers being miniature, not the vine). It makes a beautiful evergreen flowering vine capable of producing clouds of small blue, star-shaped flowers clustered in long panicles. It's a perfect candidate for decorating arbors and arches. Though queen's wreath can be mistaken for wisteria from a distance, the leaves of queen's wreath are smooth and slender and the vine not nearly as aggressive. It climbs by twining. Plant in full sun in fertile soil with good drainage. While the plant overwinters outdoors only in frost-free locations, it can be grown in a pot and the vines cut back to the soil before bringing indoors for protection from cold. There is also a white-flowered form, and when the two are grown to intertwine their flowers, the effect is magnificent.

KEY CHARACTERISTICS

Botanical Name: *Petrea volubilis*

Origins: Native to Mexico and Central America

Zones: 9–11 (also Zone 8 in a sheltered location)

Propagation: By semi-hardwood cuttings, air layering, and soil layering

Pests and Diseases: Aphids, scale insects, mealybugs, and spider mites, especially when grown indoors

Height: Up to 40 feet

Supports: Tall trellises or heavy-gauge garden netting; also chain-link fences, arches, and arbors

ROSES, CLIMBING

I know of no place in North America where roses do not grow well. Indeed, there are few places in the world—even the tropics—where roses do not enjoy a strong following. More countries (including the United States) have adopted the rose as their national floral emblem than any other flower. Though the rose has been cultivated for thousands of years (in its earliest years as a source of fragrant oils), it was not until Empress Josephine, wife of Napoleon, began collecting roses for her garden at Malmaison, north of Paris, that the rose began its rise to popularity as a flowering ornamental in Europe and then the United States.

Also important in the rose's journey to international acceptability was the endorsement of the great French Impressionist painters, particularly Renoir, Monet, and Henri Fantin-Latour. They grew roses in their gardens

To frame a window with climbing roses, attach three sections of trellis to the wall.
Prune the rose canes to five strong upright stems each year during winter dormancy.

not only for display, but also to make still-life arrangements to paint indoors when the weather was too bad to work *en plein air*. Monet liked to see roses reach their flowering canes high into the sky, and he created special metal structures for climbers to extend horizontally long distances, as well. Renoir liked to begin each day by dashing off a small vignette of a rose before starting a more complicated study of a nude. The colors of roses became the flesh tones of his models, whom he often posed with a bouquet of roses or with a rose in their hair, echoed in their rosy cheeks.

Fantin-Latour made a profession of painting roses, sending most of each season's output to an English dealer for sale to wealthy British merchants and aristocrats. In particular, the artist liked old roses—the wild-looking musk roses, the multi-petaled 'Apothecary' rose, and cabbage roses with their swirling petals—painted with a romantic atmosphere so a viewer could almost smell their scent.

Monet's favorite roses were all climbers, like the large yellow-flowered single 'Mermaid', the small pink button-flowered 'Belle Vichyssoise', and 'American Pillar', a single-flowered magenta rose with a white eye. He called the latter his Pennsylvania rose, because it was introduced into France by rose growers Conard-Pyle, of West Chester, Pennsylvania. Today, it is the most prolific rose in Monet's garden, trained high over arches that shade the boat dock in his water garden and covering long stretches of trellises at the bottom of his flower garden.

When Monet would step into his garden, which he did several times a day to evaluate the plantings and the light, he liked to see his entire field of vision filled with color. Climbing roses achieved this goal better than any other flowering vine. To train them to a great height, Monet built metal arches to span a wide gravel path leading from the front door of his house to the bottom of his garden. He also had a metalworker create special supports that meet in a peak and then splay out like an umbrella, to support a fountain of canes and a topknot of blooms.

Be aware that roses do not have tendrils or a twining habit to climb like a clematis or wisteria; rather, they have thorns that can hook onto other plants, allowing the canes to form an erect bush that can reach a great height. In the wild, there are often plenty of small trees and shrubs for roses to cling to for support, but in the garden, climbing roses generally need training to be able to climb. You must guide the canes into a particular position, then secure them to a support by means of a twist tie or string. It is important that the canes are secured tightly, as wind can otherwise cause them to flap about like whips and become damaged.

Climbing roses are generally purchased by mail order from a specialist catalog or locally from nurseries and garden centers. Mail-order plants are generally shipped bareroot, with the canes pruned back to within 8 inches of the rootball. Nursery stock is generally sold in a container, usually with the canes cut back to within 8 inches of the soil line. Bareroot stock should be steeped in a bucket of water overnight before planting. Choose a location with full sun and good drainage. Dig a hole to accommodate the roots when they are spread out sideways, and ensure good soil contact when you fill in the hole. Leave a depression as a catchment for water. Allow the canes to put on as much growth as possible the first season. Following winter dormancy, when the canes start to break bud with new foliage growth, examine the condition of the plant and remove any canes that are dead. If more than five canes survive, trim away the weakest so the plant's energy goes into the five strongest canes.

In addition to the aforementioned climbers, the following are varieties that can be trained to a great height, some vigorous enough to cover a small building like a garden shed.

'Cecile Brunner' is classified as a climbing polyantha rose. This pale pink variety is proof that size is no way to determine a rose's value. What this prolific rose lacks in flower size (the double flowers measure just 2 inches across), it more than makes up for in charm and density of bloom. It is ideal for training up walls, over arches, and along frames to create a lace curtain effect.

'Climbing Iceberg' is a selection from the famous everblooming shrub rose 'Iceberg'. This climbing form attains 10 feet in height and is popular for decorating white gazebos to create an all-white theme for weddings. The generous flush of blooms in late spring is followed by intermittent repeat bloom until fall frosts.

'Crepuscule' in French means dusk, and the double flowers do indeed resemble a beautiful apricot sunset. An old garden rose that blooms in early summer, it is especially beautiful partnered with a blue clematis like 'Ramona' so the two mingle their blooms.

'Gloire de Dijon' is classified as a climbing tea rose. Monet grew this large-flowered orange-pink French rose on metal frames. Today, a similar variety, 'Westerland' (a floribunda), has largely replaced the 'Gloire de Dijon', since 'Westerland' is a repeat bloomer. Both plants grow to 15 feet high.

'Lady Banks' rose is popular for covering arches and arbors and training up into pine trees, such as loblolly pines, where it will reach up to 20 feet. There are basically two color forms—a bright yellow and a pure white. Both are a common sight in southern states, and especially in cities like Charleston, New Orleans, and San Antonio. The almost thornless, slender canes are studded with thousands of buttonlike blooms up to 1½ inches across, creating a curtain of color. This variety is not reliably hardy above Zone 7.

'Nevada' is classified as a shrub rose. It is planted in Monet's garden around his water lily pond, where its long, arching canes, studded with saucer-size single white flowers, are allowed to extend up and out to dip their tips into the water. 'Nevada' is similar in appearance to the wild species rose from China, *R. laevigata,* popular in southern gardens and commonly called the Cherokee rose. The Cherokee rose is not quite so hardy as 'Nevada', nor so large flowered, but it has longer canes, up to 20 feet.

'Paul's Scarlet Climber' is a prolific flowering rose that won a gold medal from the National Rose Society in 1915 and another at the test gardens in the Parc de Bagatelle, near Paris. Monet seized on it and planted it throughout his garden, training it along metal crossbars to frame a garden view. This variety was followed by 'Paul's Scarlet Improved', sold in the

United States as 'Blaze'. Described as repeat blooming, the first flush of flowers occurs in early summer, followed by sporadic flowering when watered at regular intervals.

'Veilchenblau', also called 'Blue Rambler', is the closest to blue that I have seen of any rose. Its cupped flowers are small, fragrant, and borne in clusters like grapes. It is extremely free flowering and capable of reaching the roof of a two-story house.

'Wedding Day' is an incredibly free-flowering climber that bears mostly single white flowers and has reached the roof of a two-story home near my Zone 6 garden.

'Zéphirine Drouhin' is classified as a Bourbon rose. Introduced by a French rose breeder in 1868, this vigorous plant is probably the most heavily scented climbing rose you can grow. The large double, deep pink flowers can measure 4 inches across. At Monet's garden in Giverny, it is trained over arbors and allowed to scramble along the eves of a roof.

KEY CHARACTERISTICS

Botanical Name: *Rosea* species and hybrids

Origins: Most climbing roses are hybrids of species native to China.

Zones: 4–11

Propagation: By tip cuttings and soil layering

Pests and Diseases: Mostly black spot, powdery mildew, and Japanese beetles

Height: Varies according to variety. Many will grow to 30 feet high. I have seen 'Lady Banks' reach 50 feet at Magnolia Plantation and Gardens in Charleston, South Carolina.

Supports: Strong, tall trellises, chain-link fences, high walls, arches, arbors, and pergolas

SILVER FLEECE VINE

If you need to cover something quickly with spear-shaped foliage and clouds of summer-flowering white flowers, this hardy lightweight, aggressive vine is a good prospect. Also known as mile-a-minute vine for the

Silver fleece vine (top right) starts to bloom in late summer when other plants are losing their luster. Provide a strong support and this twining vine will provide a lush covering in a matter of weeks.

rapidity with which it can grow, a single plant can produce thousands of white flower clusters that have a frothy appearance among deciduous leaves. The plant prefers a framework of netting or a trellis for support, lifting itself skywards by twining. A single vine can quickly cover an arbor and even a gazebo, flowering in late summer. In Monet's garden in Giverny, France, silver fleece vine is trained high on wires to create a lace-curtain effect. The closely related, tender pink-flowering species *Polygonum reynoutria* is not reliably hardy north of Zone 9, but resembles silver fleece vine in all other respects. Plants are worth growing in a pot, trimming to the soil line after fall frost, and moving indoors to survive winter in a semi-dormant condition, watered just enough to keep the plant alive.

Botanical Name: *Polygonum aubertii,* also listed botanically as *Persicaria aubertii* and *Fallopia aubertii*

Origins: Native to China

Zones: 5–9

Propagation: By seed, root division, and hardwood cuttings

Pests and Diseases: Almost none; vine is almost indestructible, although sometimes leaves are disfigured by leaf miners

Height: Up to 60 feet

Supports: Strong, tall trellises, heavy-gauge garden or wire netting, and chain-link fences; also arches, arbors, and pergolas

SNAIL VINE

This is a contender for the "weird but wonderful" category among flowering vines, a plant oddity that delights adults and children alike, since the pendant flower clusters are spiraled, resembling the swirling pattern of a snail's shell. Although it's a moderately hardy perennial, this plant, sometimes called the corkscrew plant, can be grown as an annual to flower the first year from seed. The mostly white flowers are fragrant and tinged with pink. In areas where the ground freezes, the roots can be dug up and potted to overwinter indoors before frost kills the vine. The second-season growth will result in a taller plant and many more flower clusters than the previous season. Plants climb by twining and will

This snail vine close-up shows its unique coiled flower structure.

grow to 12 feet high in one season. Provide full sun and fertile soil with good drainage. Consider growing snail vine in a whiskey half-barrel, planted so it can climb up the center of a wire cylinder or against a fan trellis. A simple wooden trellis or garden netting is also a suitable support. Although there is much disagreement over its hardiness, some fans of snail vine in Maryland (Zone 7) report vines dying back after frost, but after being cleaned up in spring, sprouting new shoots—allowing it to perform as a true perennial.

KEY CHARACTERISTICS

Botanical Name: *Vigna caracalla*

Origins: Native to India

Zones: 5–11 as a tender annual, 7–11 as a perennial

Propagation: By direct-sown seed after frost danger has passed, or started indoors 4 weeks before planting outdoors

Pests and Diseases: Leaves can be discolored by powdery mildew.

Height: Up to 12 feet

Supports: Tall trellises, garden netting, chain-link fences, arches, and arbors

SWEET PEA, PERENNIAL

If you have trouble growing annual sweet peas, take heart—it's almost impossible to kill their perennial relative. Although annual sweet peas flower within 70 days of sowing seed, the perennial sweet pea usually produces foliage the first year after its seed is planted and then flowers the following spring. The perennial sweet pea is much easier to grow, since it tolerates heat, drought, and diverse soil conditions. Plus, the biggest advantage of the perennial sweet pea over annual kinds is its resistance to root diseases, which usually afflict the annuals. While the perennial is not as large-flowered as its annual counterpart and not fragrant, it is everblooming from early summer to fall frost. Colors include red, pink, white, and purple—not as extensive as the colors of annual sweet peas, but adequate. Like its annual counterpart, the perennial uses tendrils to climb. In addition to climbing up a trellis, the plants can be grown on a sunny bank in poor soil to control soil erosion. They are easily grown in containers when planted inside a wire cylinder for support.

KEY CHARACTERISTICS

Botanical Name: *Lathyrus latifolius*

Origins: Native to southern Europe and the Mediterranean

Zones: 5–9

Propagation: By seed and root division

Pests and Diseases: Slugs and snails attracted to young plants

Height: Up to 8 feet

Supports: Tall trellises, especially fan trellises, and heavy-gauge garden netting; also chain-link fences, arches, and arbors

TRUMPET CREEPER

I once visited a garden in Cornwall, England, after the local newspaper announced that a rare plant was in bloom. It caused hundreds of visitors to line up under the eaves of a chapel and stretch their necks to glimpse a trumpet creeper with a few sparse blooms—a plant that is so common in the United States, it is often regarded as a rampant weed! A fast-growing woody vine with aerial roots that can attach to any rough surface, trumpet creeper is the hardier of two garden-worthy species, the other being *Campsis grandiflora* from China. Although the Chinese species is not as hardy (suitable for Zones 7–9), it has been crossed with the North American species to create a hardy hybrid, *C.* x *tagliabuana* 'Mme. Galen' (Zones 5–9), bearing flowers twice the size of the North American species. Also known as hummingbird vines, these trumpet creepers have trumpet-shaped blooms that are mostly orange and are highly attractive to hummingbirds that feast on their sweet nectar. A yellow variety, 'Flava', is also available.

The leaves resemble those of wisteria, and drape down the vine like a curtain. Plants prefer full sun and a fertile, well-drained soil. Specimens often produce too much vine for their own good, causing poor flowering. To rejuvenate, cut all but one main stem, or prune to the ground to force multiple juvenile growth. Train up a wall, a pergola, or along a split-rail fence.

KEY CHARACTERISTICS

Botanical Name: *Campsis radicans*

Origins: Native to North America

Zones: 5–9

Propagation: By seed, soil layering, and tip cuttings

Pests and Diseases: Although susceptible to powdery mildew and scale insects, this is a tough survivor with plenty of vigor to overcome all kinds of stress.

Height: Up to 40 feet

Supports: Strong, tall trellises, fences, and walls with rough surfaces; also chain-link fences, arbors, arches, and pergolas. Climbs trees with rough bark to flower in the leaf canopy

VIRGINIA CREEPER

Virginia creeper is an American native, but it is so widely adapted to a range of climate conditions that I have seen it used universally in every great gardening country I have visited, including those in Europe, Japan, Canada, and New Zealand. At Cedaridge Farm, Virginia creeper covers the stone walls of my farmhouse and is naturalized at the edge of the woodland and in the hedgerows. Even on Sanibel Island, Florida, a Zones 10–11 location, this creeper is naturalized along the roadsides, growing up into the tops of palm trees. Although its small green flowers and subsequent black berries are inconspicuous, Virginia creeper is admired for its lustrous bright green, ivylike leaves in spring and summer and its dazzling fall color, when the five-fingered deciduous leaves turn molten red. The plant climbs by means of suction cups at the ends of its tendrils and creates a cloaking effect; it adheres to any rough surface, growing fast. Plants prefer full sun and good drainage, tolerating high heat, drought, and impoverished soil. Virginia creeper is mostly used to cover high, wide walls.

KEY CHARACTERISTICS

Botanical Name: *Parthenocissus quinquefolia*

Origins: Native to North America, especially the eastern seaboard, where it climbs up into the loftiest trees

Zones: 3–10

Propagation: By seed or by semi-hardwood cuttings taken in summer, or by soil layering. Any stem section with its suction cup can be rooted in soil.

Pests and Diseases: Minor slug damage in its juvenile stage. This vine is almost indestructible, except by pulling it up by its roots.

Height: Up to 30 feet

Supports: Strong, tall trellises, walls and fences with rough surfaces, tree trunks with rough bark, chain-link fences, arches, arbors, and pergolas

Hardy Virginia creeper covers a wall of the farmhouse at Cedaridge Farm. The vine is deciduous and turns beautiful russet colors in fall.

WAX FLOWER

What an enchanting vine this can be! A vine just 6 feet tall can have a hundred flower clusters open at any one time. Although variable in color—from white to pink, red, or cinnamon—the waxy star-shaped flowers are arranged in tight clusters to create a pendant dome or even a sphere. In my Zone 10 garden on Sanibel Island, Florida, I have a wax flower growing up a coconut palm, with its cinnamon-red flower clusters draped over its

The sphere-shaped flower clusters of wax flower appear from spring to summer and gently bob on their vines when breezes are aloft.

glossy, lancelike leaves like a curtain. This tender evergreen vine produces generous clusters of nodding flowers in spring and summer. In areas with frost, the plants are easily grown in a container for overwintering indoors. Wax flower climbs by producing long, erect stems and aerial roots that attach to rough surfaces. Long, cylindrical seedpods may occur after flowering. Plants prefer full sun and fertile, well-drained soil, but they will tolerate light shade.

KEY CHARACTERISTICS

Botanical Name: *Hoya carnosa*

Origins: Native to tropical China and India

Zones: 10–11 (grown as a houseplant elsewhere)

Propagation: By semi-hardwood cuttings in spring or summer, or by soil or air layering

Pests and Diseases: Mealybugs, scale insects, and whiteflies indoors

Height: Up to 30 feet

Supports: Strong, tall trellises, especially fan trellises; also heavy-gauge garden netting, chain-link fences, tree trunks with rough bark, arches, arbors, and pergolas

WINTERCREEPER

This clinging vine is grown mostly for evergreen foliar effect. My favorite use for it is to cloak tree trunks: The variegated gold and silver forms, such as 'Emerald 'n' Gold' and 'Silver Queen', are perfect for this. Even though the greenish-yellow flowers are small and inconspicuous, the smooth, oval, shiny leaves provide more visual interest than those of most ivies. Plants prefer full sun and a fertile soil, but tolerate light shade, too. Aerial roots allow the woody stems to climb. In addition to growing it up tree trunks, use wintercreeper to cloak walls by growing it up trellises, and allow it to spill over rock ledges for a vertical accent in rock gardens. Partner a gold-variegated variety with a silver-variegated variety, and allow the vines to intermingle for a beautiful mosaic effect.

KEY CHARACTERISTICS

Botanical Name: *Euonymus fortunei*

Origins: Native to Asia

Zones: 5–9

Propagation: By semi-hardwood cuttings in summer, and by soil or air layering for the evergreen forms

Pests and Diseases: Mostly scale insects and mildew; a favorite food of deer

Height: Up to 15 feet

Supports: Tall, strong trellises, especially fan trellises; also walls with rough surfaces, trees with rough bark, arches, arbors, and pergolas

WISTERIA, AMERICAN

The introduction of the free-flowering variety of American wisteria, 'Amethyst Falls', has propelled this beautiful native wisteria into the spotlight in the nursery trade. The fragrant lilac-blue flowers smell like fresh basil and are borne in clusters that are shorter and more tightly packed than those of Japanese wisteria and that begin blooming up to 4 weeks later. In all other respects, the plant resembles a Japanese wisteria, coiling its erect stems up trees, poles, and other strong supports. The variety 'Amethyst Falls' is noted for its copious number of purple-blue flowers and its ability to flower the second season after being planted as year-old rooted cuttings. 'Nivea' is a white-flowered variety. Give this wisteria full sun, a fertile soil, and good drainage.

Wisteria frutescens is a native American wisteria suitable for growing over arbors or pergolas.

KEY CHARACTERISTICS

Botanical Name: *Wisteria frutescens*

Origins: Native to North America, mostly Virginia to Florida

Zones: 5–9

Propagation: By seed, cuttings from side shoots, and soil layering

Pests and Diseases: Mostly carefree, but can attract scale insects; also stem cankers and powdery mildew

Height: Up to 40 feet

Supports: Strong, tall trellises, strong canopies, heavy-gauge wire netting, chain-link fences, arches, arbors, and pergolas; also tall tree trunks

WISTERIA, CHINESE

In appearance, the Chinese wisteria is barely distinguishable from the Japanese variety, but it is the latter that is mostly sold in garden centers. The Chinese variety is not quite as vigorous as the Japanese, not as fragrant, and its flower panicles are not as long. Another small detail that observant gardeners will notice is that the twining habit of the Chinese wisteria is counterclockwise, whereas the Japanese is clockwise. The leaves of both are composed of many serrated, spear-shaped leaflets that turn yellow in fall. Flowering time—spring—is the same for both. Plants prefer full sun and a fertile soil with good drainage, and are suitable for covering arbors, arches, and pergolas.

WISTERIA, JAPANESE

Japanese wisteria is possibly the most rampant vine you can grow, capable of reaching to the tops of tall trees by coiling around the trunks and twining up into the leaf canopy. It's also possibly one of the longest-lived vines, able to survive for 100 years and more. The long, pendant flower clusters are mostly blue or white, often up to 24 inches long and highly fragrant. These bloom in early spring for 2 weeks. The leaves are composed of a dozen or more leaflets that turn yellow in fall and then drop. Plants are popular for covering pergolas, arches, arbors, and long sections of fences and walls. Plants prefer a fertile, well-drained soil in full sun. Late spring frosts can nip the buds and prevent flowering. In Monet's garden in France, two colors of Japanese wisteria are partnered on a canopy above a Japanese-style arched footbridge.

KEY CHARACTERISTICS

Botanical Name: *Wisteria floribunda*

Origins: Native to Japan

Zones: 6–9

Propagation: By seed, cuttings from young side shoots, and layering

Pests and Diseases: Mostly carefree, but can attract scale insects; also stem cankers and powdery mildew

Height: Up to 60 feet

Supports: Strong trellis or a strong canopy, preferably metal; also chain-link fences, tree trunks, arches, arbors, and pergolas

Designing with Ornamental Vines

14

To show some originality of design, whether you have a small backyard space or a long vista, think beyond a tomato vine on a traditional fan trellis in a whiskey half-barrel, or standard English ivy to cover a long expanse of wall. Even in the smallest garden, you can create a mosaic of color using a combination of wall planters, so that trailing vines can hang down like a curtain to meet erect vines growing up supports along the wall's foundation. This type of green or flowering wall will look even more beautiful if you can introduce a water cascade. A simple, slender thread of water arching out from an overhead bamboo or metal pipe can descend to a small pool or other catchment to create spray and a musical splashing sound, the water recirculated by means of a small hidden pump. In a small space, also consider adding a small sculptural accent placed on a shelf or tall pedestal—perhaps the head of Pan (the Greek god of shepherds and flocks) playing his pipes for a whimsical accent, a nymph, or Eve for a romantic touch.

When you need to design a garden from scratch, you have two basic choices: Create an informal plan in which plants and views can develop over time, or lay out a formal garden plan in which every detail is carefully considered in the early stages. Informal designs blur the edges of a garden; mix woody plants with annuals and perennials; may be located in shaded areas like woodlands; and may involve water in the form of a wildlife pond or a stream. Formal gardens consist mainly of geometric shapes, often built around a rectangular reflecting pool. They are generally sunny, open spaces that reflect the architecture or lines of the house on the property. Formal gardens are often associated with large spaces (consider the ostentatious formal gardens of Versailles Palace outside Paris). But a cozy formal garden also can be made within a small enclosed courtyard or a confined backyard space by using a small rectangular or circular reflecting pool as its focal point accented by boxwood as low hedges and tall topiary sentinels as vertical accents.

When people start to garden (in both small and large spaces), they often become too close-up conscious, buying and planting everything that grows knee high or waist high. It's only after some experience that beginner gardeners realize the importance of taking color to eye level and above, using ornamental vines. Visiting well-established public gardens can be great inspiration. When I visit a garden, I like my entire field of vision to be filled with color, something I refer to as the tapestry effect of varying leaf color, form, and texture. Especially in composing my photographs of gardens, I look for several levels of interest. Don't think that the tapestry effect applies only to large gardens; even tiny gardens, such as a city courtyard garden or the area around a patio, benefit from multiple levels of planting. When I'm taking photos, I like a stroll through any garden to be an experience of "hide and reveal" or "compression and release." Vines can produce these sensations by giving height to a certain area, by screening something you want to disguise or keep hidden, by softening a hard surface or view, or by being trained to create a verdant tunnel connecting different parts of the garden. Whether a vine-laden tunnel is short, in the case of an arbor or pergola, or long, like the avenues or allées so popular in botanical and

European gardens, stepping out of these tunnels—even on a cloudy day—is like stepping from shade into sunlight. Vines can also be one of the essential plants to create the relaxing sensation of a sanctuary—a private, secluded place you can go to shut out all the cares of modern life.

Another edict I value in gardens is to avoid bare soil. Unless the space between tall plants is covered with a decorative organic mulch such as shredded leaves, I like to see bare soil covered with a living, spreading groundcover. Even common groundcovers like 'Purple Wave' petunias in sun and evergreen blue periwinkle in shade are better than bare soil. At garden centers and nurseries, you will mostly find ankle-high, knee-high, waist-high, and even chest-high plants, often identified on plant labels as dwarf (such as alyssum), semi-dwarf (such as columbine), standard-size (such as New England asters), and tall (such as foxgloves and delphinium). Vines are more of a rarity, because most gardeners haven't experimented enough with them to know all of their wonderful attributes.

Even if you've planted or are planning to plant your garden with bedding or tall plants, consider adding ornamental vines to any bare space above chest height, and definitely think about including vines in addition to tall shrubs or trees to create the vertical component so necessary in a field of vision. In wide-open, sunny spaces, vertical accents are often needed to create a background, even on the skyline—either to develop a sense of sanctuary and privacy, or to create interesting skyline silhouettes and vistas. In a shaded area, such as woodland, a tree canopy may already provide that sense of enclosure, in which case the space between the canopy and the ground is your canvas for filling in with several levels of interest.

When I first moved to Cedaridge Farm in Pennsylvania, a woodland area of mostly sugar maples already existed along a stream, but the understory was choked with brambles and poison ivy, and the space between the woodland floor and the canopy was a tangle of fox grapevines and a mess of broken or dying maple branches. It would be a big project to tackle, but I realized that I had the opportunity to remove the undesirable plants and create the tunnel-like vistas I love so much in woodlands. Immediately, I cleared the weeds by grubbing out their roots with a spade and garden fork, exposing bare soil. I trucked in loads of topsoil to improve the soil depth above the exposed tree roots, and brought in a crew to prune away all the lower branches of the trees, opening up views through the woodland and admitting precious light. I left the fox grapes in place, as these etched beautiful sinuous lines up into the canopy, but I pruned the vines' side growth so the snaking coils became the focal point, like liana vines in a tropical rain forest.

I then looked at the site as a potential layer cake and started building its layers. I brought in shade-loving groundcovers and wildflowers to color the woodland floor, then shade-loving shrubs and small trees like azalea, rhododendron, mountain laurel, and dogwood to fill the void above the wildflowers. Finally, I planted vines at the base of the tallest sugar maples and allowed them to climb up into the tree canopy, soon filling in the blank spaces above head height. I planted various varieties of English ivy—not the course common ivy, but others including the more delicate miniature ivy called *Hedera helix* 'Needlepoint'. Although ivy doesn't have any noticeable floral display, it is the leaf color, leaf texture, and leaf shape that add visual interest. A good ivy substitute is euonymus, especially the variegated silver and gold varieties. The tall-growing kinds can reach up to the tree canopy and help stitch together the two main levels of interest—the floor and the canopy. For woodlands, there are few shade-loving vine choices that will fill visual voids, but clematis, honeysuckle, and wisteria are three that I have found to be tolerant of light shade. I have trained some of them to use the fox grapevines for support.

If you have a woodland setting or a few very tall trees clustered on your property, consider adding fast-growing medium-height trees with decorative bark to help fill that floor-to-ceiling visual void. Surely, white birch is one of the most desirable, since its pale silvery or white bark stands out magnificently against darker tree bark and leaf shadows. Also consider the 'Heritage' variety of river birch. It is fast growing (up to 5 feet a year) and has honey-colored, flaking bark from the top of the tree to ground level. Moreover, it will not only tolerate boggy soil, but because of its long taproot, it will also survive in dry locations like on a slope. Other choices include canoe birch with its white bark, stewartias with their green and white marbled bark, the coral bark Japanese maple, and the bronze paperbark maple; they all grow to medium height and produce a colorful trunk.

When you garden out in the sun, the choice of ornamental vines is extensive. Hardy woody vines with "flower power" are my first choice, especially climbing roses and clematis, but also wisteria, silver fleece vine, trumpet creeper, flame honeysuckle, and hardy passion vine. Annual vines pack a punch, too—notably morning glories, climbing nasturtiums, sweet peas, and Mexican flame flower.

When I first arrived at Cedaridge Farm, there were no flowering plants, but there were several outbuildings that begged to be covered with decorative vines and other vertically grown plants. These buildings included a garden shed, a guest cottage, and a Colonial springhouse—all with slate roofs—plus a barn with a cedar-shingled roof. I mounted simple, inexpensive sections of tall trellis against the walls of these buildings to support a collection of climbing roses, including not only red, but also pink, yellow, orange, white, and bicolors. Beside them I planted varieties of clematis in mostly red, white, and blue, so the two climbers would mingle their blooms. Along sections of bare fence, I planted honeysuckle and clematis to mingle their flowers. And I installed several arches to connect garden spaces and to support blue and white wisteria and orange trumpet creeper.

To create a vibrant sunny garden with layer-cake levels, turn to the vining annuals. Even though many annual flowering vines are tender to frost, they are capable of nonstop flowering from late spring to fall frost and are easily grown from seed (direct-sown into their flowering positions) or added as transplants. I grow a variety of annual vines on my wisteria arches, because the annuals flower after the wisteria vines have finished blooming. On the top of my list for flowering annual vines are morning glories, as they grow rapidly and create a curtain of trumpet-shaped flowers in blue, red, pink, white, and bicolors. Good companions for morning glories are climbing nasturtiums that predominate in colors at the other end of the color spectrum—orange and yellow. When the two knit together to mingle their flowers, the effect is enchanting, especially when 'Heavenly Blue' morning glory is partnered with 'Orange Jewel' climbing nasturtiums.

IN SMALLER GARDENS

The smaller the garden space, the more you need to think "vertical gardening." Even a narrow passageway between your property and your neighbor's can usually accommodate an arbor or even a pergola that can connect the side passage to your backyard. Pergolas are perfect structures to support a tunnel of wisteria, climbing roses, or clematis. Consider placing a garden mirror at the end of a narrow space and framing it with a variegated euonymus vine or 'Needlepoint' ivy; the mirror form and outline will be immediately evident, but the reflection will make the space seem much longer than it really is.

In small spaces, think in terms of "color echoes" or repetitions of color—perhaps a white garden bench at the end of a narrow garden space framed by the pendant blossoms of a white wisteria. My friend Robyn Kilty's tiny city garden in Christchurch, New Zealand, uses this simple color scheme, and it makes her garden design distinctive.

Where French doors open out onto a small backyard space, consider a canopy to support a grapevine, so that your view into the garden is framed by foliage and grape clusters at the end of summer.

Screening

What would you rather have for a screen to create privacy: a wall of brick or stone, a wooden fence, a hedge, or a curtain of vines? My choice would be a curtain of vines every time. Expanses of bare brick and wood can be monotonous, and hedges can look too stiff and regimented and are often in need of timely pruning and feeding. But vines can be relatively carefree, and their leaf shapes and textures and the frothy appearance of those with white, airy flowers are soothing to the senses. Moreover, you can choose from a wide variety of vines: evergreen vines like ivy for four seasons of green, flowering and fragrant vines like honeysuckle, and even fruiting vines like the hardy kiwi and grapes.

Green Wall Covers

Frank Lloyd Wright once quipped that a doctor could bury his mistakes and an architect could hide them with vines. Wright rarely used vines along the walls of his houses, though, because he designed his buildings to be works of art in their own right, without the need for leafy adornment. However, he liked to frame his buildings with the branches of trees, and he did use vines to sometimes break up vast, monotonous expanses of stone, especially along retaining walls set back from his houses. With these retaining walls, he created terraces up or down hillsides, and he liked to plant vines like clematis to cascade down them like a curtain.

Home gardeners can be inspired by the ways Wright and other architects have used Boston ivy and Virginia creeper to embellish walls. Their serrated leaves are attractive in summer and turn brilliant red in autumn. Think of using wall planters or pouches to create "living walls." The highly engineered "green walls" pioneered by Frenchman Patrick Blanc for mostly large commercial buildings can be realized on a much smaller scale for home gardens by attaching long, tubular plastic pouches to walls in a checkerboard pattern, so vining plants like strawberries, Swedish ivy, 'Wave' petunias, and vining verbena can drape down and mingle their leaves and flowers. Or attach brackets to a wall at high, medium, and low heights for a collection of hanging baskets to drape their flowering vines and mingle their flowers. Use not only cascading petunias but also coleus, weeping fuchsias, and pendant tuberous begonias.

Windbreaks

In addition to creating a vertical garden to provide screening and privacy, a vertical screen of greenery may be needed as a windbreak, especially in coastal locations. Be aware that a solid windbreak like a wall is never as good as a foliage screen to break the force of a high wind. Gale-force winds can hit a solid wall and propel right over it with equal force, whereas a structure covered with a foliage cushion—such as Virginia creeper or Persian ivy—can more effectively break and absorb the force of the wind. (Keep in mind that even when a plant is considered a good candidate for a windbreak, in its juvenile state it may need the protection of a temporary wind barrier. A wall of hay bales or a section of snow fence on the windy side can blunt the force of the wind.)

A windbreak can be provided by either trees or vines. Make sure to choose a plant suited to your environmental conditions. For example, for a coastal property, you may need plants with a tolerance to salt, since winds off the ocean can carry salt long distances and kill plants that are sensitive to it.

Of course the best windbreaks are evergreen, and many evergreen conifers have been bred to create a column of dense foliage, such as blue 'Skyrocket' juniper, 'Green Giant' arborvitae, weeping Norway spruce, and weeping white pine; broadleaf evergreens like tall American holly and English holly are good choices, too.

Where you have large expanses to fill, consider some of the more aggressive vines planted against an existing wall or against a construction of trellis. For example, trumpet creeper and many climbing roses can reach more than 6 feet high in a year. The same is true of wisteria and some ivies—especially Boston ivy and Virginia creeper. A long section of wall or trellis can be a perfect place to plant a collection of climbing roses, or even alternate climbing roses with clematis.

Naturalizing

In nature, vines scramble up trees, they push their sinuous stems through bushy shrubs, they cling to steep rock faces, they creep up ruined walls, and they threaten to suffocate neglected buildings. In the garden, vines can add visual texture to other plants and to structures. Look around your garden and property and see where you might plant a *Clematis montana* to twine up into a tree canopy, draping curtains of starry white or pink flowers from the loftiest branches all the way to the ground. Choose a vigorous heritage climbing rose like 'Belle Vichyssoise' or 'American Pillar' to cover a dilapidated old barn, or a Concord grapevine to run riotously up and over the trees and shrubs in a hedgerow. Where you have a high field-stone wall, consider planting the perennial sweet pea in a mixture of colors. Ambitious and artful gardeners may even consider building a garden "folly" like a ruin in order to display a collection of ivies, allowing them to creep into window spaces and doorways.

Tree Cloaks

Most trees offer only a tall stretch of brown bark and aren't nearly as ornamental as the birches mentioned above, making them the ideal backdrop for a vertical covering of vines. Black walnuts, many types of poplar, and even oaks are generally a dull gray color and perfect candidates for a cloak of ivy, euonymus, creeping fig, or another decorative, fast-growing vine. In order to help a climbing plant get started up the trunk of a tree, provide a collar of wire netting around the trunk. This is particularly important for clematis, which do not have aerial roots or holdfasts like ivies and can find it difficult to climb unaided.

Although ivy, euonymus, and creeping fig may be a burden that a tree might not relish, a healthy tree will not be killed by having its trunk wrapped in vines and leaves. If you notice that a tree is suffering with poor leaf coverage, is dropping an abnormal number of dead branches, or seems to be in danger of complete suffocation, you may need to remove the vine and give the tree a chance to recover. Avoid using more aggressive vines like wisteria, Japanese honeysuckle, and kudzu as tree cloaks, because they can suffocate or strangle a healthy tree.

IN GRANDER SPACES

Where you have large spaces to fill with vines, consider some of the more aggressive kinds and build special supports for them. A vine-decorated gazebo can be a beautiful accent at the end of a vista, for example, especially partially covered with a vine that produces lightweight stems that don't tend to rot wood, like sweet autumn clematis or silver fleece vine. With a metal structure like a wire gazebo, you can consider the use of vines with heavier stems, such as trumpet vine and wisteria.

If you happen to have a stream dissecting an expanse of lawn, consider building a bridge with a canopy for vines like Impressionist painter Claude Monet's famous wisteria-covered Japanese-style footbridge. Vine-covered pergolas are wonderful devices to add interest to long vistas, too, especially when situated at the edge of a spacious lawn or meadow; then garden visitors are presented with a choice of walking across the sunlit grass or under the cooling shade of the vine-covered pergola. For long stretches of boring chain-link fence, especially the tall kinds surrounding tennis courts and swimming pools, consider Boston ivy and Virginia creeper. The molten red fall foliage display can even outshine the impact of thousands of red roses in bloom.

Cliff and Steep Slope Gardens

Many kinds of climbers are suitable for climbing up a cliff or steep slope, or else cascading down like a curtain. In frost-free areas, vining ivy-leaf geraniums and bougainvillea, both of which have an extensive color range, can be used to create a polychromatic color harmony (or rainbow effect). In order for stems to twine and become self-supporting on steep spaces, it's good to lay a net over the face of the slope or cliff. The hardy woody vine *Clematis montana* is especially good to consider for covering a cliff or steep slope. It is available in three colors—white, pale pink, and deep pink—and at the Cross Hills Gardens in Kimbolton, New Zealand, the three cover an entire side of a cliff, knitting their stems and colors together.

Tapestry Gardens

A tapestry garden is a garden of foliage tints, tones, and shades, using the colors of leaves (rather than flowers) to create a beautiful pattern across a steep slope or against a cliff. The most beautiful tapestry garden I have seen is at Kerdalo Gardens, near the French port of Tré-guier on the Brittany coast. There, a collection of trees and shrubs with gold, silver, blue, bronze, and every imaginable shade of green leaves (from dark black to bright emerald) creates a multihued landscape. Another fine example of a tapestry garden can be seen along the Normandy coast at the garden of Bois des Moutiers, Varengeville. The founder of the garden, Guillaume Mallet, owned a textile tapestry manufacturing business and used swatches of cloth to decide on the colors of tree foliage for the landscape beyond

This beautiful green wall at the Naples Botanical Garden in Florida features moisture-retaining Woolly Pockets to hold plants in this vertical garden display. The "woolly" felt and the moisture barrier are made from recycled plastic bottles and are then filled with potting soil. Here, the pockets hang from metal hooks on a screen of builder's wire.

his house. Noteworthy in his garden are the glossy dark green paddle-shaped leaves of rhododendron contrasting with the blue foliage of Atlas cedar and the reddish leaves of copper beech.

Vertical Water Gardens

In all of nature I doubt there is anything so alluring as a waterfall cascading from a great height. Even if your landscape doesn't feature water or a waterfall (and obviously most do not), you should consider creating a vertical water feature with falling water. Contrary to popular belief, it need not be a costly project involving multiple levels of water, construction with boulders, and electrical and mechanical expertise. It can be as simple as a silvery thread of water arching down to a small pool or basin catchment, the water recirculated by a small hidden pump. During visits to Japan, I have seen tiny open-air courtyard meditation gardens that use the full height of the wall enclosing them to feature a cascade of water that falls down among evergreens and stones. A vertical water garden—no matter how small—is a show-stopping centerpiece in a garden or landscape.

In the lexicon of garden terms used by Japanese landscape designers— supreme masters of creating water features—different styles of waterfalls have different names. For example, a thin stream of water is called a *silver thread,* while a wide sheet of water is known as *falling cloth.* You can also have *broken cloth* falls, whereby a single broad curtain of water is split into two narrower widths by a *divider stone.* A silver thread falls can be made into *multiple threads,* also by using divider stones. *Stepped falls* usually descend a slope over a series of slabs, narrow at the top and wider at the bottom. *Broken falls* have divider stones that will divert a flow of water to the left and right for a more natural appearance.

The stones used in the construction of a Japanese waterfall also have special names. For example, a *mirror stone* is a smooth flat stone behind the falls, often used as a viewing platform or as a stepping-stone. *Flanking stones* are large heavy stones that anchor the falls and frame the cascade of water. *Base stones* are used along the foundation for extra support. *Water-dividing stones* can be used as stepping-stones, as well as a device to divert water. *Wave-dividing stones* can be used as stepping-stones to cross a narrow section of the stream above or below the falls. *Edging stones* are used to prevent erosion of the bank, while *fill stones* are mostly used behind the falls for rigid support. *Observation stones* are usually flat stones upon which a person can stand and admire a view; they can even jut out over the water. A *bridge stone* can be a flat slab laid across a narrow section of stream to connect the opposite banks. *Stepping-stones* not only provide a means of crossing a stream; they also can provide access to an island in the stream. Be aware that it is not a good idea to have a long section of stepping-stones (people can lose their balance negotiating a long stretch), but they are suitable for crossing a short stretch of water or boggy area.

It's important to have plants not only edging a waterfall, but also arching out over it and as a tall vertical backdrop behind the falls in order to make it look natural. A bare pile of boulders with a waterfall emanating from a stream of recirculated water can look contrived, but if the boulders are made to appear like an outcrop or rocky cliff at the edge of woodland, the effect can be so beautiful that visitors will think it is entirely natural.

Some of the most beautiful waterfall designs were created by the late Roberto Burle Marx, a Brazilian landscape architect. Examples of his work can be seen at Longwood Gardens in Kennett Square, Pennsylvania. All of his designs involve tropical plants, and although the examples at Longwood are in a conservatory, his ideas can still be used outdoors in areas with freezing winters by moving the tender plants indoors before frost strikes the garden.

Some excellent plants to consider for planting atop waterfalls to cascade down over rocks and create a curtain or cloaking effect include weeping Norway spruce, weeping white pine, weeping forsythia, weeping dogwood, and weeping redbud. For summer-long color, plant trailing-type annuals, such as 'Wave' petunias, vining nasturtiums, and some trailing perennials like creeping Jenny (which will even extend its stems and yellow cup-shaped flowers into the water, where they will float).

SOURCES

There are dozens of reputable garden suppliers to be found on the Internet by entering your plant category as a search. Here are some I have found most helpful.

NATIONAL PLANT SOCIETIES

AMERICAN BAMBOO SOCIETY
315 South Coast Highway 101, Suite U
PMB 212
Encinitas, CA 92024-3555
www.americanbamboo.org

AMERICAN CLEMATIS SOCIETY
PO Box 17085
Irvine, CA 92623
www.clematis.org

AMERICAN GOURD SOCIETY
PO Box 2186
Kokomo, IN 46904-2186
www.americangourdsociety.org

AMERICAN HYDRANGEA SOCIETY
PO Box 53234
Atlanta, GA 30355
www.americanhydrangeasociety.org

AMERICAN IVY SOCIETY, INC.
PO Box 163
Deerfield Street, NJ 08313
www.ivy.org

AMERICAN POMOLOGICAL SOCIETY
(FRUIT AND NUTS)
103 Tyson Building
University Park, PA 16802-4200
www.americanpomological.org

AMERICAN ROSE SOCIETY
PO Box 30,000
Shreveport, LA 71130
www.ars.org

CACTUS AND SUCCULENT SOCIETY
OF AMERICA
Gunnar Eisel
PO Box 1000
Claremont, CA 91711
www.cssain.org

HERB SOCIETY OF AMERICA
9019 Kirtland Chardon Road
Kirtland, OH 44094
www.herbsociety.org

PERENNIAL PLANT ASSOCIATION
3383 Schirtzinger Road
Hilliard, OH 43026
www.perennialplant.org

ANNUAL FLOWER and VEGETABLE SEEDS

BAKER CREEK HEIRLOOM SEEDS
2278 Baker Creek Road
Mansfield, MO 65704
www.rareseeds.com

BURPEE & CO., W. ATLEE
300 Park Avenue
Warminster, PA 18974
www.burpee.com

HARRIS SEEDS
355 Paul Road
PO Box 24966
Rochester, NY 14624-0966
www.harrisseeds.com

JOHNNY'S SELECTED SEEDS
955 Benton Avenue
Winslow, ME 04901
www.johnnyseeds.com

PARK SEED
1 Parkton Avenue
Greenwood, SC 29647
www.parkseed.com

PINETREE GARDEN SEEDS
PO Box 300
New Gloucester, ME 04260
www.superseeds.com

SEED SAVERS EXCHANGE
3094 North Winn Road
Decorah, IA 52101
www.seedsaversexchange.org

SEEDS OF CHANGE
PO Box 15700
Santa Fe, NM 87592-1500
www.seedsofchange.com

THOMPSON & MORGAN SEEDSMEN, INC.
PO Box 397
Aurora, IN 47001-0397
www.tmseeds.com

TOMATO GROWERS SUPPLY COMPANY
PO Box 60015
Fort Myers, FL 33906
www.tomatogrowers.com

BULBS

BRENT AND BECKY'S BULBS
7900 Daffodil Lane
Gloucester, VA 23061
www.brentandbeckysbulbs.com

VAN BOURGONDIEN
PO Box 2000
Virginia Beach, VA 23450-2000
www.dutchbulbs.com

FRUIT TREES

MILLER NURSERIES
5060 County Road 16
Canandaigua, NY 14424-8904
www.millernurseries.com

RAINTREE NURSERY
391 Butts Road
Morton, WA 98356
www.raintreenursery.com

STARK BRO'S NURSERIES
    & ORCHARDS CO.
PO Box 1800
Louisiana, MO 63353
www.starkbros.com

HERBS

NICHOLS GARDEN NURSERY
1190 Old Salem Road NE
Albany, OR 97321
www.nicholsgardennursery.com

WELL-SWEEP HERB FARM
205 Mount Bethel Road
Port Murray, NJ 07865
www.wellsweep.com

PERENNIALS

BLUESTONE PERENNIALS
7211 Middle Ridge Road
Madison, OH 44057
www.bluestoneperennials.com

WHITE FLOWER FARM
P.O. Box 50
Litchfield, CT 06759-0050
www.whiteflowerfarm.com

SHRUBS

FOREST FARM
990 Thetherow Road
Williams, OR 97544
www.forestfarm.com

MUSSER FORESTS, INC.
1880 Route 119 Highway N
Indiana, PA 15701
www.musserforests.com

WAYSIDE GARDENS
1 Garden Lane
Hodges, SC 29695
www.waysidegardens.com

SUPPLIES

GARDENS ALIVE!
5100 Schenley Place
Lawrenceburg, IN 47025-2100
www.gardensalive.com
Biological controls of garden pests

HYDRO HARVEST FARMS
1101 Shell Point Road East
Ruskin, FL 33570-5003
www.hydroharvestfarms.com
Hydroponic growing system using tower
    pots

KINSMAN COMPANY
PO Box 428
Pipersville, PA 18947-0428
www.kinsmangarden.com
Vertical gardening units and containers

THE CEDAR STORE
5410 Route 8
Gibsonia, PA 15044
www.CedarStore.com
Vertical gardening structures including
    arches, arbors, and trellises

About the Author

Derek Fell is a prolific garden writer and garden photographer. The author of more than 80 garden books and hundreds of articles, as well as the photographer for dozens of garden calendars, he has won more awards from the Garden Writers Association than any other person. The owner of historic Cedaridge Farm in Bucks County, Pennsylvania, for more than 20 years, he has used 15 themed areas to test a wide variety of plants and gardening techniques featured in several shade gardens, sunny perennial borders, a cottage garden, a large vegetable garden, and a water garden open to the public. He worked with the White House during the Ford Administration as chairman of a task force to plant an inflation-fighting vegetable garden. He is married with three grown children, Tina, Derek Jr., and Victoria. His wife, Carolyn, is a landscape designer who helps maintain the gardens at Cedaridge Farm.

Derek Fell's book *Vegetables: How to Select, Grow, and Enjoy* won a best book award from the Garden Writers Association. Its companion volume, *Annuals: How to Select, Grow, and Enjoy,* also received national acclaim.

Acknowledgments

Thanks to the late E. O'Dowd Gallagher, who taught me to write; the late Harry Smith, who taught me how to photograph plants; and the late David Burpee, who taught me how America gardens.

INDEX

Boldface page numbers indicate photographs or illustrations. Underscored references indicate boxed text, charts, and graphs.

Netting, garden, 44–46, **210**
Newspapers, as mulch, 125
No-dig gardening
    background of, 3–4
    creating beds, 5
    preparing for Skyscraper Garden, 49, **49**

O

Obelisks, 47, **47**, **189**
Okra (gumbo, lady's fingers), 163, 163
Okra, Chinese (Chinese loofah gourd,
        sponge gourd, angled gourd), 157
Onions, 163–64, 164
Orchid cactus ("queen of the night")
        (*Epiphyllum oxypetalum*), 320–21,
        321

P

Pandorea jasminoides (bower plant), 290,
        290
Pansies, **189**
Parasitic wasps, 106
Parthenocissus quinquefolia (Virginia
        creeper), **211**, **226**, 336–37, 337, **337**
    climbing mechanism of, 32, **32**
Parthenocissus tricuspidata (Boston
        ivy), **213**, **214**, 311–12, 312
Passiflora caerulea (blue passion vine),
        321–22, 322
Passiflora coccinea (red passion vine),
        322–23, 323
Passion vine (*Passiflora*)
    blue (*P. caerulea*), 321–22, 322
    red (*P. coccinea*), 322–23, 323
Peaches, espaliered, **204**, 257
Pears, espaliered, **205**, **256**, 257
Peas (edible). *See also* Sweet peas
        (ornamental) (*Lathyrus*)
    asparagus (winged), 137–38, **201**
    climbing mechanism of, 32, **32**
    English, 164–66, 166, **187**
        'Blue Podded', 165
        'Golden Sweet', 165–66
    homemade trellis for, 29
    pregerminating, 84
    purple-podded (blue peas), **203**
    seedlings, **87**, **194**
    sugar, **198**
    sugar snap, **12**, **39**
        height of plant supports for, 45
        mulch and, 125

Peat
    black, **183**
    as mulch, 125
Pelargonium (geranium), **iv**, **159**, **192**
    Botrytis blight of, **196**
Pelargonium peltatum (ivy-leaf
        geranium), **186**, **193**, **208**, **213**,
        266–67, 267
Peppers, 166–67, 167
Pepper sprays, 109
Pergolas, 35, **184**, **222**, **226**
Perlite, **183**
Persicaria aubertii (silver fleece vine,
        mile-a-minute), 130–31, 286, 331–33,
        332, 333
Petrea volubilis (queen's wreath), 325–26,
        326
Petunia (*Petunia*), **191**, **192**
    climbing (*Petunia integrifolia*), 277–78,
        277, 278
    'Million Bells', **210**
Philodendron, **228**
Phyllostachys aureosulcata (yellow-
        groove bamboo), 29, **185**
Phyllostachys nuda (green bamboo), 29
Pine needles, as mulch, 126
Plant diseases and conditions. *See* Diseases
Planters, **5**. *See also* Containers
    compost bins as, **70**
    hanging, **xi**, **192**, **193**
    planter boxes, 10, **10**
    plastic bags and pouches, 42–44, **189**
        upside-down (Topsy Turvey), 43–44
    tower pots and systems (*See* Tower pots
        and systems)
    Versailles boxes, 68–69, 69, **191**
    window boxes, 69, **190**, **193**, **208**
Plant selection
    for containers
        cascading plants, 63
        foundation plants, 69
        skyscraper plants (erect vines), 64, 64
        trailing plants, 64, 65
        for urns, 68
        for Versailles planters, 69
        weeping plants, 68
    purchasing, 100–101
Plant stands, tiered, **36**, 55–56, **56**, **187**, **188**
Plastic, as mulch, 126
Plectranthus australis (Swedish ivy),
        272–73, 273

T